EMOTION, IDENTITY AND DEATH

Emotion, Identity and Death
Mortality Across Disciplines

Edited by

DOUGLAS J. DAVIES
Durham University, UK

CHANG-WON PARK
Durham University, UK and Sogang University, South Korea

ASHGATE

Published by
Ashgate Publishing Limited
Wey Court East
Union Road
Farnham
Surrey, GU9 7PT
England

Ashgate Publishing Company
Suite 420
101 Cherry Street
Burlington
VT 05401-4405
USA

www.ashgate.com

British Library Cataloguing in Publication Data
Emotion, identity and death : mortality across disciplines.
  1. Death--Psychological aspects. 2. Funeral rites and
  ceremonies.
  I. Davies, Douglas James. II. Park, Chang-Won, Dr.
  155.9'37-dc23

Library of Congress Cataloging-in-Publication Data
Emotion, identity, and death : mortality across disciplines / edited by
Douglas J. Davies and Chang-Won Park.
    p. cm.
  Includes bibliographical references and index.
  ISBN 978-1-4094-2414-7 (hardcover) – ISBN 978-1-4094-2415-4 (ebook) 1. Death–
Social aspects. 2. Death–Psycholgical aspects. 3.
Death–Religious aspects. 4. Emotions. 5. Identity (Psychology)
I. Davies, Douglas James. II. Park, Chang-Won.
  GT3150.E496 2012
  306.9–dc23

2011033888

ISBN 9781409424147 (hbk)
ISBN 9781409424154 (ebk)

Printed and bound in Great Britain by the
MPG Books Group, UK.

Contents

List of Figures and Tables

Figures

Tables

List of Contributors

Editors

Douglas J. Davies is Professor in the Study of Religion in the Department of Theology and Religion and Director of the Centre for Death and Life Studies at Durham University. His recent works in the area of death studies include *Encyclopedia of Cremation* (Ashgate 2005), *A Brief History of Death* (Blackwell 2005) and *The Theology of Death* (Continuum 2008), and on emotion, *Emotion, Identity and Religion* (Oxford University Press 2011). He holds the Oxford higher Doctorate of Letters, an Honorary Dr. Theol. of Uppsala University, and is an Academician of the Academy of Social Sciences.

Chang-Won Park holds his PhD from Durham University (2009). He is currently Honorary Research Associate of the Centre for Death and Life Studies at Durham University and Research Fellow at the Institute for the Study of Religion at Sogang University, South Korea. His recent works include *Cultural Blending in Korean Death Rites: New Interpretive Approaches* (Continuum 2010). His current research projects include an AHRC funded network project on emotion, identity and religious communities (2008–10), as well as the 'distinctive nature of Korean cremation' funded by the South Korean Government (2010–11).

Contributors

Arnar Árnason is a lecturer in social anthropology at Aberdeen University. He has carried out fieldwork in the UK, Japan and Iceland. His research interests are in the anthropology of death, emotion and subjectivity. His work has mostly focused on the politics of grief work. He has published widely on this topic, for example in *Mortality*, *Journal of the Royal Anthropological Institution* and the *British Journal of Sociology*.

Tim Bullamore has written for the *Daily Telegraph*, *The Times*, *Independent*, *Guardian* and *British Medical Journal*. In 2008 he was joint winner of an international award from the Society of Professional Obituary Writers for his work in the *Daily Telegraph,* to which he contributes frequently. His first book was *Fifty Festivals* (1999), a history of the Bath International Music Festival. He has given several academic papers on the art of obituary writing and is now engaged on a doctoral study of the craft at Cardiff University.

Jacque Lynn Foltyn, PhD, is Professor of Sociology in the Department of Social Sciences, National University, La Jolla, California. A social theorist, her research focuses on dying and death, fashion, beauty and the erotic, and media representations of the human body. As a scholarly expert, she has appeared on CBS National News/48 Hours and the BBC, and in the *New York Times* and fashion/ lifestyle magazines. She guest edited a special issue of *Mortality*, The Corpse in Contemporary Culture (2008, 13.2), and is editor of/contributor to *Fashions: Exploring Fashion through Culture* (The Inter-Disciplinary Press 2010).

Christina Marsden Gillis (PhD, English Literature) is founding Associate Director of the Townsend Center for the Humanities at the University of California, Berkeley, and has organized, over a period of 16 years, numerous innovative programs on aging, death and dying. She has published in journals such as *Death Studies*, *Journal of Medical Humanities*, *Bellevue Literary Review* and *Raritan*. She edited *Seeing the Difference: Conversations on Death and Dying* in 2001; now retired from the university, her most recent book, published in 2008, is *Writing on Stone*, a meditation on loss and place.

Eva Jeppsson Grassman holds a chair as professor at NISAL (National Institute for the Study of Ageing and Later Life) at Linköping University. Her research spans diverse life course and aging issues, not least in connection with chronic illness and disability. Furthermore, she has conducted research in the area of care, notably spiritual care in the end of life phase, with focus on the role of the Church of Sweden. Some recent publications: E. Jeppsson Grassman and A. Whitaker (2007) 'End of life and dimensions of civil society. The Church of Sweden in a new geography of death', *Mortality* 12(3): 261–80; E. Jeppsson Grassman (ed.) (2008) *Att åldras med funktionshinder* [*Ageing with a Disability*]. Lund: Studentlitteratur.

Peter Groote works as a cultural geographer at the Faculty of Spatial Sciences of University of Groningen, the Netherlands. His main research interests are the meanings of places of death, disabilities and well-being, and cultural heritage. Major publications: Mirjam Klaassens, Peter Groote and Paulus Huigen, 'Roadside memorials from a geographical perspective', *Mortality* 14(2): 187–201 and Peter Groote and Tialda Haartsen, 'The communication of heritage: creating place identities', in Brian Graham and Peter Howard (eds), *Ashgate Research Companion to Heritage and Identity* (Ashgate 2008), 181–94.

Meike Heessels studied Cultural Anthropology, and is a PhD researcher within the NWO-research project 'Refiguring Death Rites' in the Faculty of Religious Studies at Radboud University Nijmegen, the Netherlands, focusing on post-funerary rituals such as secondary burial and ritualized behaviour with cremated remains. She published an article in *Mortality* (2009) entitled 'Secondary burial in the Netherlands: rights, rites and motivations'. A second article on rituals after cremation was published in *The Body and Food in Ritual* (2010), entitled 'From commercial goods to cherished ash objects: mediating contact with the dead through the body'.

Tim Hutchings completed his doctoral research in January 2010, conducted at Durham University, on five examples of 'online Christian churches' with attention to leadership, worship, community and the relationship between digital and everyday life. This research was funded by a Durham University Doctoral Fellowship and by the Arts and Humanities Research Council. Major publications: 'Theology and the online church', *The Epworth Review* 35(1) (2008); 'Creating church online: a case-study approach to religious experience', *Studies in World Christianity* 13(3) (2008).

Hyun-Ah Kim is a Fellow at the Centre for Reformation and Renaissance Studies and an Adjunct Professor at Trinity College in the University of Toronto. Dr Kim's research focuses on theology of music, music and rhetoric, and music and death in world religions. Her recent publications include *Humanism and the Reform of Sacred Music in Early Modern England* (Ashgate 2008), and 'Erasmus on Sacred Music', *Reformation and Renaissance Review* 8(3) (2006).

Mirjam Klaassens is a PhD student at the Department of Cultural Geography, Faculty of Spatial Sciences, University of Groningen, the Netherlands. Her research concentrates on final places and analyses the cultural meanings that people attach to different types of places of death and/or remembrance: crematoria, natural burial places, roadside memorials and virtual places of remembrance. Publications: M. Klaassens, P. Groote and P.P.P. Huigen (2009) 'Roadside memorials from a geographical perspective', *Mortality* 14(2): 187–201; M. Klaassens and P. Groote (2009) 'Post-modern crematorium Haarlem: a place to remember', in: M. Rotar, V.T. Rosu and H. Frisby, eds, *Proceedings of the Dying and Death in 18th–21st Centuries Europe*, International Conference. Alba Iulja: Editura Accent, 9–26.

Tamara Kohn is Senior Lecturer in Anthropology at the University of Melbourne. Field research in Scotland, Nepal, California and Japan are linked by common interest in migration, identity, creativity and trans-national communities of embodied practice. Recent publications include *The Discipline of Leisure* (Berghahn 2007, ed. Coleman and Kohn), 'Waiting on death row' (in *Waiting*, University of Melbourne 2009, ed. Hage), and 'The role of serendipity and memory in experiencing fields' (in *The Ethnographic Self as Resource*, Berghahn 2010, ed. Collins and Gallinat).

Wolfgang Marx is Senior Lecturer at the School of Music, University College Dublin. His research interests include the representation of death in music, György Ligeti and the theory of musical genres. He has established the research strand 'Death, Burial and the Afterlife' at UCD. Among his major publications is *Klassifikation und Gattungsbegriff in der Musikwissenschaft* (*Classification* *and the Concept of Genre in Musicology*), Hildesheim 2004. He has co-edited a volume with Louise Duchesneau entitled *New Perspectives on Ligeti* (2011) and is preparing a monograph on requiem compositions in the long nineteenth century.

Thomas Quartier is Assistant Professor for Ritual Studies at the Faculty of Religious Studies at Radboud University Nijmegen (the Netherlands). His research interests are deathbed rituals, funeral rituals and mourning rituals in contemporary society. Next, he has conducted research on rituals in subcultures and new ritualizations in public life in the Netherlands. Among his publications are: *Bridging the Gaps. An Empirical Study of Catholic Funeral Rites*, Münster: LIT (2007); 'Personal symbols in Roman Catholic funerals', *Mortality* 14(2) (2009): 133–46; 'Rituelle Pendelbewegungen. Neue Trauerrituale im Niederländischen Kontext', *Yearbook for Liturgy-Research* 25 (2009): 185–205.

Eva Reimers is Professor in Pedagogic Practices, and Associate Professor in Communication Studies at the Department of Social and Welfare Studies, University of Linköping, Sweden. The common theme for her research is how people communicate and construct notions about norms, identity and society. In her research she explores communicative perspectives on death, loss, bereavement and grief. She has studied funeral practices, norms about grief and mourning, and official Swedish media representations of media events of disaster and death.

John Troyer is the Deputy Director and RCUK Research Fellow in the Centre for Death and Society at the University of Bath. He received his doctorate from the University of Minnesota in Comparative Studies in Discourse and Society in May 2006. From 2007 to 2008 he was Visiting Assistant Professor in the Department of Comparative Studies at The Ohio State University teaching the cultural studies of science and technology. Within the field of death studies, John focuses on delineating and defining the concept of the dead human subject. He is a co-founder of the Death Reference Desk website, and his first book, *Technologies of the Human Corpse* (University of North Carolina Press) will appear in 2012.

Eric Venbrux is Professor of Anthropology and Director of the Centre for Thanatology at Radboud University Nijmegen, the Netherlands. He is the author of *A Death in the Tiwi Islands: Conflict, Ritual and Social Life in an Australian Aboriginal Community* (Cambridge University Press 1995/2009), and co-editor of *Exploring World Art* (Waveland Press 2006) and *Ritual, Conflict and Media* (Oxford University Press 2011). Currently, he directs the research project 'Refiguring Death Rites: Post-Secular Material Religion in The Netherlands', funded by the Netherlands Organisation for Scientific Research (NWO).

Introduction

Emotion, Identity and Death

Douglas J. Davies and Chang-Won Park

The year 2009 witnessed the ninth biennial Death, Dying and Disposal (DDD) Conference. This hallmark DDD Conference had originated amongst a small group of British scholars who had also helped create the journal *Mortality*. That group grew consistently over the years with over 200 delegates now being hosted in Durham by Professor Douglas Davies of Durham University's Department of Theology and Religion and Director of its Centre for Death and Life Studies, greatly assisted by Dr Chang-Won Park and Ms Gwynned de Looijer, and supported by the University's Institute for Advanced Studies and Faculty of Arts and Humanities. Some 40 per cent of these interdisciplinary scholars came from beyond the UK. During this Conference a notable event occurred in Durham Castle with the launch of the new Association for the Study of Death and Society (ASDS), with its first President being Prof. Jenny Hockey of Sheffield University. ASDS would, in the future, be closely aligned both with the Editorial Board of *Mortality* and with fostering the organization of future DDD Conferences, as with the 2011 Conference hosted by Professor Eric Venbrux of Radbout University's Centre for Thanatology in the Netherlands. Following the publication of a *Book of Abstracts* of every paper given at the 2009 Conference,[1] this present volume reflects a small and highly selective group of papers invited from established scholars and from postgraduate and recent doctoral students to reflect the focused theme of emotions, identity and death exemplified in a variety of disciplinary perspectives.

The year 2009 was noted, amongst other things, as a Charles Darwin year, marking the anniversary of *The Origin of Species* published in 1859 and of his birth in 1809. One of his other works that did not, understandably perhaps, receive much recognition was *The Expression of the Emotions in Man and Animals*, first published in 1872 though actually formulated decades before.[2] Partly to rectify that omission, and partly because 'emotions' had now begun to make an impact as a theoretical field in numerous disciplines, it was decided that the indicative emphasis of the DDD Conference for 2009 should be that of emotions in relation to identity and death. One reason for inviting scholars to appreciate Darwin's role of emotions in association with human bereavement lies in his outstanding capacity

---

[1]   Douglas J. Davies and James Jirtles (eds) 'Book of Abstracts', *Mortality* Vol. 14. Supplement, September 2009.

[2]   Charles Darwin ([1872] 1998) *The Expression of the Emotions in Man and Animals*. Introduction by Paul Ekman. Chicago: Chicago University Press.

to observe the world around him, not least the human world of his own family. This capacity of observation not only needs to be stressed in the social sciences, but also to be fostered through practice, since it often takes a considerable period of time before we come to 'see' aspects of the things we study. While his own experience of grief remains a tale to be told at length, here we simply note the way he was able to develop his own interpretative descriptions with the observations and research of others. His observations on grief included a potential sense of guilt in a bereaved person such that that he or she might feel they could have prevented a death, an attitude he associated with an excited-depressed theory of emotion in which, for example, such guilt might pass rapidly into a depressed condition of 'despair or deep sorrow' in which 'the sufferer sits motionless, or gently rocks to and fro', and so on: he also depicts facial expressions and the brief use of what he called the 'grief muscles'.[3] Indeed, one of the conference plenary lecturers, the well-known Dr Colin Murray Parkes, referred to this facial factor in his account of 'Love and Loss: the Roots of Grief and its Complications'. His work is so familiar to many that it has not been reproduced in this volume.

Darwin's lifetime (1809–1882) was rooted in the period of 1800–1850 which Thomas Dixon, for example, described as the one during which the very 'category of the emotions' developed as a 'recent invention' and as distinct from the preceding mode of discourse that privileged 'the passions', 'sentiments' and 'affections', not least 'of the soul'.[4] The later nineteenth and early twentieth centuries would, of course, witness rapid growth in psychology as a discrete discipline with all that would involve, for example Freud's treatment of grief and subsequent theories of attachment and loss. The rise of social learning theories during the mid and later twentieth centuries would, to a degree, shape the discussion of human sentiments in terms of social values and identity, not least in terms of 'continuing bonds' motifs of narrative theories of self. The decades bridging the twentieth and twenty-first centuries would, increasingly, offer the possibility of developing and refocusing studies of the human condition not only through a bio-cultural grasp of emotions that had already been influential in anthropology, but also in the light of new insights derived from cognitive science and evolutionary biology: but much remains to be done in that direction.[5]

As for this volume, it reflects the Conference's welcome address from Professor Ash Amin, then Director of Durham's Institute of Advanced Studies and now at Cambridge, who spoke of the 'trans-disciplinary' nature of the DDD9 Conference. So it is that some of the following chapters are more explicit and

[3]   Charles Darwin ([1872] 1998: 84–5). See also pp. 176–94 on 'Low Spirits, Anxiety, Grief, Dejection, Despair'.

[4]   Thomas Dixon (2003) *From Passions to Emotions: The Creation of a Secular Psychological Category*. Cambridge: Cambridge University Press, p. 3.

[5]   Pascal Boyer (2001) *Religion Explained*. London: William Heinemann, pp. 233–61. Boyer presents crucial questions rooted in the response of complex human cognitive systems when confronted by death.

some more implicit on the influence of emotions on human identity in relation to death, dying and the disposal of human remains. As Amin indicated, this volume could be approached from many different theoretical perspectives and through numerous kinds of research data, to this can be added the strong cross-cultural material pervading conference papers. At the very outset, for example, we can contrast Tim Bullamore's account of British obituaries, whose public world deals with the identity of the dead still treated with a respect that does not always allow the 'darker' side of their lives to emerge, with Eva Jeppsson Grassman's Swedish work showing how chronic illness and an awareness of death shape people's view of their own identity. Her life-course perspective offers a foundational theoretical frame for issues of identity and of how identity may change over time and through the impact of experience and of one's peers in a narrower and almost domestic sphere. Eva Reimers, by contrast, lies closer to Bullamore's public domain, and takes us into a dramatic, televised and publicly stage funerary-memorial rite for a young woman whose 'farewell ceremony', following an 'honour killing' amidst Sweden's strong social welfare sense of society, prompted a major, almost state-like, funeral in a high profile church context. Here national identity is advanced in a reflexive and highly charged yet controlled ecclesial environment, exemplifying formal religion in one of its roles as a managing of emotion whilst intensifying social values. An even wider social world, albeit of a more virtual kind, is documented by Tim Hutchings who shows how electronic spaces have come to serve as a medium for communication of grief. His chapter is important for highlighting just how the study of death online may, itself, become a significant field for interdisciplinary research.

Just who the individual is whose identity may echo within bereavement and memorializing behaviour, whether online or not, becomes an issue in Arnar Árnason's theoretical account of identity as he questions, for example, the very recent notion of continuing bonds through a critique of the dominance of the 'western individual'. His is an important reminder of the need for critical reflection upon cultural presuppositions underlying some aspects of death studies and the 'individuals' and 'relationships' portrayed there. He also introduces the notion of 'presence' as a valuable part of his analysis, and it is with some such notion of 'presence' in mind that we might also ponder Tamara Kohn's exploration of the lives of some prisoners on Death Row in a US prison context. Her deeply humane consideration allows privileged access to the way individual men work to create a meaningful and worthwhile sense of self-identity for themselves before they are brought to death. Equally moving, and as a deeply humane depiction of someone making sense of death, is Jacque Lynn Foltyn's narrative of her personal involvement with a former partner now stricken by illness. Her recollections of a time when, as a 'death studies' scholar, she was rapidly encompassed by illness in a friend and of one who was more than a friend, offers its own example of emotional dynamics impacting upon pre-held theories. Complementing the dynamics of interpersonal emotion in both Kohn and Foltyn is Christina Marsden Gillis' account of the importance of place, somewhere created in and through family events in the United States, and which helped her family come to 'see things differently' in the process of grief for a son killed in an accident. Here emotion and identity are both familial and rooted in a familiar location where memory and the power of imagination underlie the sense of consolation following bereavement.

A group of chapters derived from the Netherlands then takes us from ritualized deathbed scenes, through funerary buildings to sites of celebratory remembrance, each raising issues of emotion, ritual and identity whether in terms of organizing relationships, ritual space or ritual action. Thomas Quartier's chapter highlights the nature of ritual-symbolism in end-of-life care as he asks how appropriate forms of spirituality may be furnished by professionally trained personnel. He emphasizes the enduring challenge of death in human relationships, especially when involving parting and saying goodbye, not least as secular attitudes lie alongside traditionally religious values in the constitution of identity and fields of emotion. Meike Heessels then takes us a step further to consider those who help manage funerary rites in Holland and she reveals the dialectical dynamics between a professional's desire for some idealized and perfect ritual event on the one hand and the wishes of the bereaved on the other whose knowledge of the deceased sometimes leads them to subvert the proffered rites through 'disruptive practices'. With Mirjam Klaassens and Peter Groote we then discover how the architectural framing of emotional experiences surrounds crematorium funeral activities. They argue the case for setting Modernist assumptions involving a certain negation of the impact of death upon the living against a Postmodern shift to individuals who wish their own sense of choice to foster 'emotional reflections' on the very identity of their dead. Then, Eric Venbrux presents valuable details on the invention of secular tradition of memorializing the dead in collective, artistically creative, gatherings framed by the All Souls period of traditional Christianity. Though traditional eschatological beliefs are vague there remains a sense of bridging the living with the dead through newly devised rites.

From the Netherlands with its deathbeds, funerary architecture and ritual innovation we move to highlight the role of music in many of those contexts, fully aware that human emotions surrounding death often engage with music's pervasive effect upon our identity. Accordingly, we first meet Hyun-Ah Kim's scholarly musicological analysis of Mahler. Here we not only listen in on one man's 'life-long struggle to come to terms with death', but also see this European's creative engagement with some Eastern symbolism. This is then complemented by Wolfgang Marx who gives an illustrated account of nineteenth-century Requiem Masses, including those by Fauré and Dvořak. In less familiar but illuminating ways, he demonstrates how a Requiem engages emotion and intellect when responding to death in analysing the different influences of church and concert hall contexts as arenas of receptive experience.

Finally, in a fashion that bears relevance for many of the chapters covered above, John Troyer's study of death and the dead bodies of contemporary American soldiers raises crucial issues of the politics of death and identity where a national level of concern links with the grief of individuals and families. Here we find echoes, albeit in different forms, of the public recognition of the murdered women in Reimers' chapter on Sweden, as well as the politics of Bullamore's obituaries, and the power of place in Gillis' family grief. Repatriation, a most powerful aspect of identity conferral, carries a resonance in all these cases.

In conclusion we can, of course, note that if death often appears as a strange thing to people so also does the slightly more abstract notion of mortality, and so too the developing field of 'death studies'. Despite possessing journals carrying such names as *Death Studies* and *Mortality* this area, represented in this volume as an interdisciplinary field, carries with it great promise as well as some potential pitfalls. The promises, some of which sparkle within later chapters, lie in different methods and perspectives that can be shared across societies within the context of conferences and journals whose boundaries are not fixed and policed by normative theories. The pitfalls, by contrast, lie precisely in theories that may easily become rigid and regarded as the sole domain of their immediate practitioners. There is much to be gained from pondering each topic area and 'ethic of knowledge', as Jeremy Carrette has put it in relation to 'religious experience in the knowledge economy', always with an eye to a sense of 'humility' within our modes of thinking.[6] And this often seems to be the case in scholars engaged in death studies at large with several of the following chapters highlighting ways in which our own encounters with death and grief contextualize our life-ventures. Together, all the chapters offer insights, data, and a perspective that fosters freedom from excessive constraints of habit and encourages a desire for shared creativity.

References

Boyer, P. (2001) *Religion Explained.* London: William Heinemann

Carrette, J. (2007) *Religion and Critical Psychology.* London: Routledge.

Darwin, C. ([1872] 1998) *The Expression of the Emotions in Man and Animals.* Introduction by Paul Ekman. Chicago: Chicago University Press.

Davies, D.J. and Jirtles, J. (eds) 'Book of Abstracts', *Mortality*, 14. Supplement, September 2009.

Dixon, T. (2003) *From Passions to Emotions: The Creation of a Secular Psychological Category.* Cambridge: Cambridge University Press.

---

[6]   Jeremy Carrette (2007) *Religion and Critical Psychology.* London: Routledge.

Chapter 1

The Postmodern Obituary:
Why Honesty Matters

Tim Bullamore

The lessons of history play an important role in helping to construct both our collective memory and our identity as individuals, with obituaries providing one way in which we learn who we are and where we are from. While, for many years, the principle of *de mortuis nil nisi bonum* (of the dead speak only good) was widely held to apply to obituaries, since the mid-1980s the British press has changed this approach by introducing some wit, humour and accounts of misdemeanours to obituaries to produce what I have termed the 'postmodern obituary'. Nevertheless, this chapter argues that the transformation is incomplete for, to an unfortunate degree, newspapers continue to omit, make light of, or play down, the darker side of these life studies. In so doing, newspaper obituaries continue to portray an unrealistic ideal of how a life has been lived, thus potentially causing a confusion in identity among readers who cannot hope to live up to the virtues of those of whom they read. The chapter suggests that it is possible for the obituary pages to dispatch the deceased with what Nigel Starck (2006. 89) calls a 'tincture of charity' while still giving an honest account of the downsides of life that beset us all.

The study of the obituary as a 'distinctive genre in literary journalism' (Bytheway and Johnson, 1996) is a relatively recent phenomenon. Some have argued that it is the obituary pages 'that save British journalism from the banalisation of mediocrity' (Kirkup, 2002) and that they are 'an essential contribution to history' (Hattersley, in Howard and Heaton, 1993). Others claim that obituaries combine 'the reporter's craft with the scholar's judicious sense of perspective' (Stewart, 2005) and that 'their formal characteristics and place in newspapers have led them to be included in the genre taxonomies of journalistic practice' (Corona, 2006). Some have gone farther and eulogised that '(y)ou could look elsewhere in newspapers for many weeks and fail to find anything so close to poetry' (Ferguson, 2002), while others suggest that 'on the British obituary page harsh value judgment gives the sense of listening to one family member talk about another, with the reader presumed to be part of the family' (Ledbetter, 2002). According to one of the art's practitioners, '(t)he best reaction an obituary can create … is for the reader – having perhaps embarked on a piece about someone unknown to him, and from a field in which he has no real interest – to conclude that he wished he had heard of this fascinating figure before' (McKie, 2003). However, too many newspaper obituaries paint an unrealistic portrait of a life, suggesting that the life in question has followed a perfect – even predestined – course or trajectory. Take for example:

> Everyone knew that Muriel [Bradbrook] was destined for great things ... (*Guardian*, 19 June 1993)

> [Juliette Huxley] found herself engaged to Julian Huxley, an untested biologist ten years her senior at the time, but obviously destined for great things. (*Times*, 3 October 1994)

> Given such a home environment [Raphael Pati] was predestined for academic achievement. (*Independent*, 7 August 1996)

> [Sir Guy] Fison was given a traditional education at Eton [*sic*], where he excelled at sports. (*Times*, 30 October 2008)

This had, in fact, been the way of obituaries since newspapers first appeared in Britain. The death of an Establishment figure was reported as news, with a narrative that reinforced his position – and it usually was 'his' – as a faultless individual. If a newspaper felt obliged to record the death of someone outside the Establishment, it would generally do so in a mean-spirited manner, such as the *Times*' account of the death of Oscar Wilde:

> The verdict that a jury passed upon his conduct at the Old Bailey in May 1895 destroyed for ever his reputation, and condemned him to ignoble obscurity for the remainder of his days ... Death has soon ended what must have been a life of wretchedness and unavailing regret. (*Times*, 1 December 1900)

The Daily Telegraph was even less forthcoming. When it did record a death, it treated the obituary art with disdain. Starck notes that from the 1950s, for some 30 years or so, the paper published 'a daily main obituary of seven or eight short paragraphs (about 10-12 column centimetres) followed by a collection of one-paragraph death reports. It was colourless stuff' (2004: 99). By 1979, particularly on Mondays, there was in *The Daily Telegraph* just one 'obituary' – if it could be called that – of half a dozen lines or so (2004: 104). What little did appear – even in the *Times*, which at least ran lengthy pieces – was dry, dull and almost exclusively about a member of the Establishment, i.e. those whom Pierre Bourdieu has described as 'dominants'.

Today, fortunately, these are not the only types of obituary that appear in the British newspapers. In recent years some obituaries have contained greater candour, humour and honesty, while others poke fun gently at the eccentricities of otherwise blameless individuals, recalling anecdotes or sexual proclivities that, while not necessarily pertinent to their public career or persona, nevertheless give a more rounded appreciation and understanding of the character in question. Take for example:

> The 3rd Lord Moynihan, who has died in Manila, aged 55, provided, through his character and career, ample ammunition for critics of the hereditary principle. His chief occupations were bongo-drummer, confidence trickster, brothel-keeper, drug-smuggler and police informer … (*Telegraph*, 26 November 1991)

> Despite his outrageous antics and boorish behaviour, many of [Gerald] Kingsland's former companions, wives and mistresses retained a soft spot for him. (*Times*, 16 May 2000)

> Knighted in 1953 (the same year in which he was fined £10 for importuning in Chelsea), [Sir John Gielgud] was appointed Companion of Honour in 1977. The Order of Merit followed in 1996. (*Times*, 23 May 2000)

> [David Tomlinson] steered well clear of anything devoid of laughter – 'Personally I wouldn't go near *Hamlet*. Far too serious' – and spurned all but occasional small-screen roles. 'Television is all so rushed,' he explained. 'It's run by civil servants, you see – and all they know about the business is one line that goes "It'll be all right on the night". They've no idea how to deal with nervous actors like me.' (*Times*, 26 June 2000)

> [Fritz Spiegl] had several fallings out with successive editors of the *Liverpool Daily Post* over the content of his column, but such was his following among the paper's readership that he was invariably brought back into the fold. (*Telegraph*, 25 March 2003)

> In the early 1970s [Noel] Mander [an organ builder] took to using lineage advertisements in *The Times* to alert potential purchasers to instruments he had acquired … [One] claimed, rather startlingly, 'Progressive synagogues need organs'; it was sandwiched between notices for 'Unisex Massage' and 'Chelsea Girl Escorts for all occasions'. (*Telegraph*, 27 September 2005)

Academics, such as Nigel Starck at the University of South Australia, and enlightened practitioners, such as James Fergusson, obituaries editor of the *Independent* from its founding in 1986 until 2007, suggest that this change in the obituary, to include greater honesty and – at times – more humour, can be traced to changes in the structure of the newspaper industry around 1986, including de-unionisation, computerisation, the exodus from Fleet Street and a collapse in the price of newsprint. Starck (2006: 67) records that Hugh Massingberd, obituaries editor of *The Daily Telegraph*, Fergusson (*Independent*) and John Grigg (*Times*), working independently of each other, brought about these changes.

Grigg, although not the author of the *Times* piece in question, was obituaries editor and allowed to be published an extraordinarily direct account of the choreographer Robert Helpmann: 'His appearance was strange, haunting and rather frightening. There were, moreover, streaks in his character that made his impact upon a company dangerous as well as stimulating. A homosexual of the proselytising kind, he could turn young men on the borderline his way' (*Times*, 20 September 1986). At *The Daily Telegraph*, the newly-appointed Massingberd – whether aware of Grigg's indiscretion or not – had been inspired by *Brief Lives*, Roy Dotrice's one-man show about the seventeenth-century antiquarian John Aubrey: 'Picking up a work of reference, he read out an ineffably dull biographical entry about a barrister: Recorder of this, Bencher of that, and so on. He then snapped shut the volume with a "Tchah", or it may have been a "Pshaw", and pronounced: "He got more by his prick than his practice."' This, wrote Massingberd, was his 'blinding light'; he would dedicate himself to 'the chronicling of what people were really like through informal anecdote, description and character sketch rather than merely trot out the bald curriculum vitae'. Massingberd was always quick to point out that his new-look obituaries began to appear in September 1986 – the same month as the *Times'* infamous Helpmann obituary. From then on, according to Starck (2004: 136) 'the *Telegraph*'s subject selection was to be driven by the quality of the life story, rather than by the rank of the individual'. The *Independent*'s first edition appeared on 7 October 1986, with an obituary page edited by Fergusson. According to Starck (ibid.), it was the pictorial treatment – in a manner that, until then, had been reserved for magazine features – that set the *Independent*'s obituaries apart, as well as the inclusion of an author's by-line (which is still omitted from obituaries in the *Times* and *Telegraph*).

Representatives of all three papers have claimed to be first with transforming the obituary, although many commentators concede that Massingberd was the driving force. In his introduction to *The Guardian Book of Obituaries*, the editor Phil Osborne directly acknowledges Massingberd's work at *The Daily Telegraph*: 'All obituaries editors, in one way or another, are indebted to Massingberd for paving the way for much more rounded insights into people's achievements – and their failures' (2003: 1). Anthony Howard, obituaries editor of the *Times* from 1993 to 1999, has declared Massingberd to be 'the founding father of the modern craft' (Howard, 1999). Fergusson (1999: 154) states that, when planning the obituary page for his new paper in the spring of 1986, he decided that the *Independent* should 'do something different: it should seek a new audience, write a new agenda. There should be transparency'. He adds: 'Where the *Independent* sought to open up and demystify the obituary … the *Telegraph*, under Massingberd, set out to subvert the traditional obituary from within' (1999: 155).

Clearly we can demonstrate with some degree of accuracy that, from the autumn of 1986, the more humorous, more direct and more indiscreet obituaries – as well as more personal recollections of a life that has ended – began to appear in the British broadsheet newspapers. Thus, with the collapse of traditional boundaries within the art of obituary writing, the postmodern obituary was born.

However, to understand obituaries through the prism of postmodernism one first needs to appreciate 'modern' obituary writing with its dry, factual account of lives, that listed individuals' achievements without providing much colour or assessment of their character. This was the case with the *Times*, as published throughout the twentieth century, and regarded as leading the way in its obituary coverage. Few commentators are comfortable defining postmodernism; but, inasmuch as it represents a change from the order that dominated culture and writing in the bulk of the twentieth century, the examples given above of humorous, irreverent or directly honest obituaries can be said to be postmodern. Indeed, Frederic Jameson stresses that postmodernism is 'not just another word for the description of a particular style', but is a 'periodising concept' (Roberts, 2000: 122). The 'depthlessness' (2000: 126) that is defined by postmodernism is represented in contemporary obituaries with the inclusion in newspapers of obituaries for non-Establishment figures, celebrities, bit players and even criminals. Similarly, the 'warts and all' approach to obituary writing exemplified by Massingberd and his successors – even of traditional or Establishment figures, or dominants – is a further example of how the art of obituary writing has evolved into its postmodern state.

Key to the success of many postmodern obituaries is 'the code', a mechanism developed to its full potential by Massingberd and which, argues Starck, allows the dead to be dispatched with a 'tincture of charity' (2006: 89). 'Tireless raconteur' therefore meant that the subject was a crashing bore; 'gave colourful accounts of his exploits' translated as 'liar'; 'an uncompromisingly direct ladies' man' had in life been a flasher (ibid.). Discussing the code, Marilyn Johnson explains how 'the *Telegraph* never uses the words "pederast" or "disastrous failure" or "raving mad exhibitionist". It doesn't have to. The newspaper employs understatement and mock-delicacy, not to avoid saying something baldly, but to set up the joke' (2006: 163). However it does have its limitations. As Massingberd conceded: '"He was unmarried" could mean anything from, well, he was unmarried to a lifetime spent cruising the public lavatories of the free world' (ibid.).

The life course includes education and the passage of adult years, often through employment; unsurprisingly the dominants will often have been educated at elite universities. However, the absence of negative actions (failed exams, dismissal from jobs, driving offences, reasons behind a collapsed marriage) from the narrative of the dominants' lives – with occasional exceptions such as Lord Moynihan, above, where the obituary writer made a virtue of his subject's misdemeanours – creates an unrealistic impression of life's trajectory. A similar problem arises with military subjects who, according to Howard, 'still receive kid-glove treatment, if only because the pieces about them are nearly all written by products of their own loyalty culture' (Howard, 1999). This, it can be argued, has the potential to cause a confusion in identity among readers, many of whom experience some form of difficulty in their lives but do not read of similar upheavals in the lives that we choose to remember.

Bridget Fowler (2004), who discusses at great length the social value that we place on some lives as opposed to others and the role of the dominants, divides the obituary genre into four categories: traditional-positive, negative, ironic and tragic. While traits of one of these categories dominate in many obituaries, I find this to be an unsatisfactory classification not least because the boundaries – particularly between negative, ironic and tragic – are blurred. Instead, I would argue that most lives contain an element of all these and therefore that an honest obituary – a truly postmodern obituary – should reference good and bad, as well as irony and tragedy, in the life it is recalling. Yet, despite the rise of the postmodern obituary, the traditional obituary – which often reads more like a hagiography – continues to dominate the pages of the British broadsheet newspapers, creating this confusion in identity. Furthermore two papers, the *Independent* and *Guardian*, now encourage family-written 'mini' obituaries, which appear on the obituary pages and, unsurprisingly, lack any semblance of objectivity, let alone any postmodern trait.

Even for the professional practitioner there are pressures – of space, of economy, of sparing the feelings of the bereaved, of perpetuating an image of a type of person or member of a social class – that can leave him or her writing an account that fails to meet the (admittedly ill-defined) criteria of a postmodern obituary. Indeed, in an industry that is experiencing the credit crunch to a greater degree than many others, anecdotal evidence suggests that, at the end of the first decade of the twenty-first century, the postmodern obituary is in retreat, with newspapers increasingly accepting obituaries – often without the need to pay – supplied by friends, colleagues and even family members of the deceased, who will have every interest in painting a eulogised picture of their loved one.

This should not be read as a call to disparage the dead unnecessarily. Indeed Starck, as mentioned earlier, says that the 'code' allows the deceased to be dispatched with a 'tincture of charity' (2006: 89). However, there is no reason why honesty – however coded, however postmodern – should not prevail.[1]

References

Bytheway, B. and Johnson, J. (1996) 'Valuing Lives? Obituaries and the Life Course', *Mortality*, 1, 219–34.

Corona, I. (2006) 'Coming out of the Closet "Six Feet Under"', *Revista Alicantina des Estudios Ingleses*, 19, 67–82.

Ferguson, E. (2002) 'Death is the New Black', *The Observer Review* (28 April, p. 6).

Fergusson, J. (1999) 'Death and the Press', in *Secrets of the Press*, ed. S. Glover, pp. 148–60. London: Allen Lane.

---

[1] My thanks to Dr Nigel Starck (University of South Australia) and Professor Bob Franklin (University of Cardiff) for their comments on an early draft of this chapter.

Fowler, B. (2004) 'Mapping the Obituary: Notes towards a Bourdieusian Interpretation', *The Sociological Review*, 52 (2), 148–71.

Howard, A. (1999) 'One Thing Never Failed to Surprise Me – the Number of People Who Sent in Their Own Obituaries', *The New Statesman* (12 February).

Howard, A. and Heaton, D. (1993) *The Times Lives Remembered: Obituaries from 1993*. Blewbury: Blewbury Press.

Johnson, M. (2006) *The Dead Beat: Lost Souls, Lucky Stiffs and the Perverse Pleasure of Obituaries*. New York: HarperCollins.

Kirkup, J. (2002) 'The Grateful Dead', *The Author, Journal of the Society of Authors*, pp. 182–3.

Ledbetter, J. (2002) 'Deadline Journalism', available at: www.slate.com/id/2065827 (accessed 9 September 2009).

McKie, A. (2003) 'When the Obituarists went West', *The Daily Telegraph* (13 June, p. 21).

Osborne, P. (ed.) (2003) *The Guardian Book of Obituaries*. London: Grove Atlantic.

Roberts, A. (2000) 'Postmodernism, or the Cultural Logic of Late Capitalism', in *Frederic Jameson*, pp. 111–33. London: Routledge.

Starck, N. (2004) *Writes of Passage: A Comparative Study of Newspaper Obituary Practice in Australia, Britain and the United States*. PhD thesis, Flinders University, Australia.

Starck, N. (2006) *Life after Death: The Art of the Obituary*. Melbourne: Melbourne University Press.

Stewart, G. (2005) 'Instant Post-mortem Verdicts', *The Spectator* (5 November, pp. 69–70).

Chapter 2

Chronic Illness, Awareness of Death, and the Ambiguity of Peer Identification

Eva Jeppsson Grassman

Introduction

In this chapter, patterns of death awareness in chronically ill people are discussed from a life course perspective and *with a focus on the impact of peer relations and peer identification* for this awareness. The discussion is based on results from a longitudinal study where 14 chronically ill and visually impaired adults were repeatedly interviewed over 25 years. The experience of peer relations in life transitions are often described in positive terms: they may facilitate life adaptation by offering support and encouragement. A crucial element here is the potential for identification. However, peer relations with people who are in the worst part of their illness trajectory may also entail greater anticipation of the prospects ahead, an intensified notion of the shortness of life, and arouse death awareness. This ambiguity of peer relations and identification was unravelled in this 25-year analysis, which uncovered patterns of connectedness between peer relations and awareness of death that changed over time.

The role and meaning of peer relations in different situations, not least stressful ones, and for various outcomes, have been explored in earlier research. There is, however, with some exceptions, a void in our knowledge concerning the connection between peer relations and death awareness (cf. Young et al. 1998, 1999). In fact, there are a number of situations in which the impact of death awareness is yet to be studied, and which have to do with peer contexts. With a more precise bearing on this chapter, there is a lack of literature concerning death awareness and the role of comparison and identification in long-term peer relations among chronically ill people. This chapter will discuss this particular theme.

The concept of a 'peer' has been associated with a vast number of interpretations and meanings. It may simply denote a friend but also, more precisely, someone with whom one shares a specific experience, for instance, of chronic illness or disability. Literature taking its point of departure from the peer concept is extensive, not least in the area of illness, rehabilitation and peer support (Dibb and Yardley 2006; Gallant 2003; Pescosolido 2001; Schwartz and Sendor 1999). The experience and role of peer relations in life transitions are often described in positive terms, perhaps in facilitating adaptation in stressful situations. The idea is that people who have faced and endured illness or disability can offer useful support, hope and encouragement to others now facing similar problems (Borkman 1999). The crucial element here is the potential and power of identification: this has to do with *proving sameness* and in this process *comparison* is a key concept (Dibb and Yardley 2006). Peer identification may take place in all sorts of non-organised "spontaneous" situations. Peer relationships of a more organised kind are particularly considered to provide positive role models, which may facilitate and encourage the individual to recognise their ability to cope with losses, illness, disability, etc. (Bülow and Hydén 2003; Karlsson et al. 2002). The picture conveyed by an extensive review of the literature in this field, while not unambiguous, remained mainly positive when it comes to functions and outcomes of peer relations and support. The literature is more limited over possible negative or more ambiguous aspects and outcomes of peer relations and peer support, notably in severe life transitions. Some exceptions are Campbell et al. (2004) and Uccelli et al. (2004). Little is known about the function and meaning of peer relations – positive or negative – in the lives of chronically ill people *over time* and from a life course perspective, and this also goes for their function and meaning in connection with *death awareness.*

Death Awareness

Awareness of the finitude of life and of our mortality is part of the human existential condition. We are constantly reminded of death, yet the day of our own death is uncertain. This fundamental situation has been addressed with different interpretations. The concept of death awareness is not unambiguous since it is used to denote different situations – from the very general, societal level to the very personal. The use of it also seems to mirror a continuum – from the individual awareness of one's mortality, in different social contexts and phases of the life course, to the awareness that a dying person may have concerning terminal illness and his or her own impending death (cf. Little and Sayers 2004). We seem to be witnessing a revival of awareness of death in many contemporary societies with questions pertaining to the social situation of dying patients, end-of-life care issues, spirituality, and bereavement never having been as intensively discussed as today (see Bryant et al. 2003; Jeppsson Grassman and Whitaker 2007; Walter 1994). However, this societal awareness does not necessarily reflect increased death awareness in the personal life of the individual. Death awareness has been extensively studied as the awareness of people who are actually facing imminent death and who are in the terminal stage of an illness. The focus has more often been on cancer patients in palliative care contexts than on, for instance, older dying people (cf. NBHW 2004). The classical work by Glaser and Strauss (1965) about awareness contexts pointed to the highly relational aspects of dying. The reciprocal aspects of death awareness involving the interactions between the dying person and his/her knowledge of impending death and the awareness that this may trigger in family members have been studied, as has the issue of disclosure from staff. However, less attention has been given to the death awareness that may be aroused in friends and workmates, namely, peers, in relation to the death of a person close to them or to the dynamics of such a process (Kirk et al. 2004; Young et al. 1998, 1999).

In life course research, with its focus on norms about the phases and ages of life, it has been argued that the theme of death awareness is typically associated with certain phases of life (Hayslip and Hansson 2003). The right "timing" for certain events, what is normal "for age", etc. are notions that are assumed to be constructed relative to age norms. Along this reasoning, there are also norms about the "right time for death", which is usually regarded as being old age (Howarth 1998), and timing becomes an important challenge in the face of the unpredictability of death (Kellehear 2007). Such norms are assumed to guide not only decisions in everyday life but also deliberations about the future (Fortner and Neimeyer 1999). Death awareness through life is likely to be a process of meaning that is constructed and reconstructed by the individual on the basis not only of various norms but also on very personal experience and specific social situations, such as situations enabling informal comparisons relative to various groups of reference. These situations stand out as under-researched. However, certain situations in which individuals are confronted with their mortality have more often been explored. Losses, such as the loss of a close relative, are one such situation (Davis and Nolen-Hoeksema 2001). The onset of illness and severe disability are other such situations (de Vries et al. 1993).

Some groups are at risk of having to face several illness transitions through life, as with those who live for many years with serious, chronic illness. These people live with an ever-present serious health condition, often with a progressive illness trajectory that implies multiple losses and an uncertain future (and timing of death) (Jeppsson Grassman 2008; Locker 2003). However, little is actually known about how awareness of death and dying is contextualised in the illness process through the lives of these people and what types of situations they have to face. In fact, there is a lack of literature on death and dying issues in connection with chronic illness on the whole, in spite of the fact that most deaths in developed Western societies occur as a result of long-term illness (Field 1996). To capture fully the intertwined process of chronic illness and death awareness a longitudinal life course approach would be desirable yet, here, the literature is even scarcer.

Method and Material

The discussion in this chapter is based on results from a prospective study of chronically ill, visually impaired people, followed through repeated interviews over 25 years. Its overall purpose is to understand the lives and life changes of people who live for many years with chronic illness and severe disability, and to consider the situations that are or have been of formative importance for the biographies of the studied group. Data collection has been carried out through qualitative, semi-structured interviews, repeated five times, with the first round of interviews completed in 1981. Further interviews were conducted in 1985, 1988/9, 1999 and 2006. The population consisted of 14 people (at baseline), aged 30–45 at the time of the first interview. All of them had acquired severe visual impairment due to chronic illness; in 11 of the cases, this was juvenile diabetes. At the beginning of the 1980s diabetes was the major cause of acquired visual impairment and blindness among younger adults in many Western countries. The first interview took place 1–2 years after the onset of visual impairment at which time eight of the people interviewed were already totally blind. When the last round of interviews was conducted in 2006, 10 out of the 14 people at baseline were still alive. Those for whom the primary cause of visual impairment was diabetes had all had various complications to the primary chronic illness, which had affected them over the years. The analysis of data was mainly carried out as qualitative, comparative content analysis with a focus on present conditions, retrospective comparisons and reflections about the future. In this way, life-course-related patterns of change could be identified (cf. Giele and Elder 1998; Saldăna 2003).

Results

A study that encompasses data collected over 25 years offers unique possibilities not only to identify central themes but also to explore how their meaning changes over time. The duration of disability, age and the unfolding of the illness trajectory were such themes. The life course approach also makes it possible to establish *when* in the longitudinal process a new theme appears. In this study, death awareness was such a theme, being absent in the first round of interviews but making an appearance in the narratives of the second interview. The importance of this theme lay in its discovery, in the sense that I had not asked about it. Instead, the theme was spontaneously brought up by the interviewees. Another such theme was that of peers and patterns of change in the meaning of this concept.

Furthermore, there seemed to be multi-faceted links between peer relations, identification and death awareness that changed over the years. The ambiguity in this connectedness was unravelled in the 25-year analysis. Death awareness and identification with peers followed patterns whose meaning could be understood in categories, each grounded in the narratives of the interviews of the different years of data collection.

1981: Peers as Positive Role Models

The narratives of the first round of interviews with the group were dominated by accounts of the totally overwhelming life transition caused by the onset of severe visual impairment about one to two years earlier. Selection criteria for inclusion in the study were that the visual impairment was acquired in adulthood and that the person in question was employed at that time. It was clear, however, that all areas of life were more or less affected by the loss of eyesight. Narratives were marked by expressions of considerable motivation, in most cases, and of some belief in the future. "Getting back" was a recurring expression. *Peers* seemed to play a crucial role in this attitude and constituted another central theme in these accounts. At that time in Sweden, rehabilitation for severely disabled people who wished to return to work was organised in the form of full-week programmes running from six months to more than a year within the premises of boarding school facilities that you "went away to". Without exception, all of those interviewed who had gone through such a programme highlighted that the most important thing during that time had not been the attainment of new skills but the social and emotional impact of the experience. *This was the first time they met peers.* In their accounts the positive power of shared experience was a dominating theme. Several of the people interviewed were eager to stress how important it had been to realise "that you were not alone ... others were in the same boat". The shared experience and the mutual support gave them strength to venture into new situations. Certain peers became important role models – those who had been at rehabilitation longer and were "ahead of you in terms of skills" could give guidance and they were living evidence of the fact that it was possible "to get a functioning life" again. Upon returning home most of those interviewed joined a local organisation for the visually disabled and spoke about this in positive terms. Despite all their uncertain and transitional features, the lives of those interviewed were, at the time of the first interview, focused on the future and on how to cope with visual impairment. Getting back to work was the most important goal.

1985: Peers as Door-openers

The second round of interviews was conducted four years later. It was an upsetting experience in certain ways. Three themes seemed to dominate the narratives now: the trajectory of the chronic illness, a new awareness about the uncertainty of the future and about the shortness of life, and, in connection with this, new, ambiguous feelings towards visually impaired peers. For some of the 11 people suffering from diabetes, the focus was by now less on the visual impairment and its consequences and more on the chronic illness that had caused it. It was clear that visual impairment was just one of several complications that the primary illness could cause. Some of the interviewees that were suffering from diabetes had not only experienced continued loss of eyesight but now also had additional complications. The unpredictability of this chronic illness was now mentioned by several as very stressful to live with and something that influenced how they planned their lives. It was not that they had not previously understood the risks of their illness. Rather, it had now become much more difficult to avoid thinking about these risks. A recurring theme was the *new awareness* that these illness-complications seemed to have conveyed. This awareness was not an anticipation of imminent death but rather an insight into the prospect that the illness would probably shorten their lifespan and that death could happen any time, depending on the onset and seriousness of the complications. As expressed by one man:

> The complications … not knowing how fast they will proceed … how many years I have left. Each time I have a new health problem I wonder: how much longer …?

This awareness was ever-present for some of the individuals, while others said "they knew but tried not to think about it too much". An expression that appeared frequently in the interviews at this time was "time left" and the image of "a short life". There was the likelihood that life would be short. The painful meaning of this insight was explained by one of the interviewees:

> A short life … I think quite a bit about that … that I shall have a short life. I have such desire to live that it is hard to accept it … A short life is a much more distinct thing for me today than six years ago … Then, I did not have that experience.

What new experience was that? It was the experience of one's own failing body but also, as it turned out, the experience of *the failing bodies of peers*. Friends and fellow participants in rehabilitation who four years earlier had been described as "being ahead of you" in terms of new skills were now, in some cases, people ahead of you in a downward illness trajectory and who, in a particular way, now acted as "guides" and "door-openers" into a world of decay and premature death. "It is like a door that has been opened. You can never forget what is behind that opened door once you have seen it", concluded one interviewee. Comparisons and identification with the difficult lives of "fellow sufferers" seemed inevitable in certain situations: Daniel (49) felt that he was constantly reminded of his situation since he had a friend "who had all the complications a person suffering from diabetes can possibly have". Nevertheless, some interviewees continued to stress the importance of close relationships to visually impaired peers, for instance, new friends in the local association for visually disabled or old friends from the time of rehabilitation. However, these friendships now tended to be associated with loss: "Some of the people I kept contact with after we finished rehabilitation are already dead", said one woman overwhelmed by sorrow. "How can anyone expect me not to think about that?"

It was also clear that this new awareness of the heightened risk of death and the anticipation of a short life impacted on choices and priorities concerning different aspects of life. Several of the interviewees said that they would not make long-term plans for their professional life anymore. Still, the patterns varied.

1988/9: Peers as Constant Reminders of Future Prospects

The third round of interviews was conducted after another four years. The long-term perspective enabled by the eight years of study clearly demonstrated the ongoing transitional character of the chronic illness and its disabling conditions that were the fate of the interviewed individuals. It was clear by now that it had been difficult for many of them to find any stable adaptive solutions to certain everyday situations, such as compensatory measures in the workplace. Some of the interviewees had left working life partly because of these problems. They were "still young, but retired". It was rather common by now for them to have suffered not one "biographical disruption" (Bury 1982) but several, owing to kidney failure, heart failure, various symptoms of neuropathy, etc. One interviewee had died since the last interview and a couple of those still alive were very ill. The coping-with-loss perspective that seemed to be relevant when describing the lives of several of the interviewees could be complemented by the reverse perspective, which was equally relevant: trying to live as ordinary a life as possible *between* losses and disruptions, until the next complication occurred. At no point throughout the study did the feeling of being different seem stronger among those interviewed than now, namely, different from non-disabled friends and colleagues, and of being out-of-sync with common age norms. In addition, at no point throughout the study did the interviewees spend more time speaking with me about their anticipation of death. The theme was usually brought up in connection with life planning: how should one plan life now that it is so obvious that life is provisional and could end at any time? The state of their bodies impacted on the meaning of that perspective for whether death was apprehended as an imminent risk or as more of a threatening prospect. One man, multi-disabled by now and very ill, expressed his views in the following way:

> I view my existence differently now. Maybe I will not wake up tomorrow … My
> life is like waiting for death now. One wakes up and feels happy about that extra
> day … one does not want to throw it away but really live it to the full.

For others who were in better condition the situation meant either "take each day at a time", "live as intensively as possible *now*", or just "live on as before" as if severe illness complications would not happen, *at least not now*.

The severe health condition or the death of peers became a sort of marker of the life course: "I lost my girlfriend last year. She also had diabetes. After her death, I gave up all plans of a family life", one man said. It was also clear that disabled peers continued to play the role of *constant reminders of future prospects*: "At the rehabilitation centre we numbered 32. About 1/3 of them are dead now … none of them lived to be 50", one man said. "I live on overtime." With the length of life of dead peers as a measure, the expression "life on overtime" was now frequently used by several of the interviewees, with the undertone that he or she "ought to" be dead too. This expression would also be used in the rounds of interviews to come, with somewhat changing meanings.

The positive power of shared experience still made friendship with disabled peers valuable but it was also clear that some of the interviewees had developed avoidance strategies in order to handle the dilemma of being reminded of prospects ahead by keeping more distance from what they called "the visually impaired world". Friends in the "seeing world" were more important and trying to reconnect to them became an important goal, but one not always easy to fulfil.

1999: Surviving your Peers

The fourth round of interviews was conducted 10 years later. By then, I had followed the group for 18 years. Two more people had died owing to severe complications. The theme of "a short life" was once more brought up. Through analysis of the narratives from this round of interviews and comparison with the patterns in earlier interviews, an interesting discovery was made, namely, that the experiences of "a short life" and "time left" were not static, but had changed over time. For some of the interviewees these notions were still connected with very strong feelings that coloured their deliberations about their remaining time. For others, and these seemed to be in the majority by this point, the notion of "time left" seemed to have changed: the future had expanded and the horizon of possible planning had been extended. Some of those who had had a very strong feeling of time running out when we last met had actually survived another 10 years. They felt more confident. An overall impression was one of cautious optimism. They had actually survived many of their disabled peers. "Back there, I never thought I would make it", one man said, "so many died". The group seemed less overwhelmed when comparing themselves to disabled peers. A couple of the interviewees pointed out that it was wrong to see them all as *one* group with the same trajectory. Their trajectories might differ. Through the illness the ageing process accelerated, some felt. However, how fast the ageing process progressed could differ from person to person:

> I think that one's body ages more rapidly with this illness. But different people
> with the same illness can age at different speeds. (Krister, 48)

Even if the interviewees, in terms of their outlook on the future, took a point of departure in their personal illness trajectory, the fact that they had survived another 10 years seemed to reassure them about the possibility of living a longer life than expected: "Who knows, I might live to be 65", one woman exclaimed. "Living on overtime" seemed to imply that you could be an exception to the rule that was set not only by the state of a close group of peers but also by some kind of general "survival norm" discovered by the interviewees. It had to do with how old you could get with severe diabetes, after certain complications etc. and it was based on general knowledge about the illness acquired through the illness process, and with peers as points of reference.

However, at this point some of the interviewees spoke less about disabled peers. They referred more to non-disabled people of their own age. Ten years back, some of them had had strong feelings of being deviant relative to age norms: being 45 and already retired – that had been deviant; so young and already in considerable need of care and assistance – that was also deviant. Now, some appeared more synchronised and identified with their non-disabled friends. In the aftermath of the economic crisis at the beginning of the 1990s "pals have lost their jobs too, so in that respect the difference is not that great", said one of the interviewees. Friends retired too. The interviewees seemed less "off time" according to age norms and, in some respect, had become closer to "the seeing world". There seemed to be a connection, not easy to validate, between this identification and the fact that death awareness was mentioned less.

2006: Generalised Peers as a Norm for the Limits of Life

At the time of the last interview, which took place about seven years later and some 25 years after the first interview, 10 people were still alive, seven of whom had diabetes. Complications related to the primary illness had continued to afflict them to various degrees: kidney failure, cardiac problems, neuropathy, etc. Some of the interviewees now lived strikingly secluded lives. One reason for this was their extensive disabilities, which hindered participation in various activities. Another reason concerned losses: in one case, the spouse had died, in another the partner had left. A couple of the interviewees had always lived alone. With one or two exceptions, the interviewees no longer had any contact with visually impaired peers. This was often a conscious choice. A very important reason for this was also, however, that the disabled friends had died. This also meant that there were no longer close peers there to *remind one* of the possible risks of a short future.

The group was now 25 years older, and so was I, the researcher. This last round of interviews became more than usually retrospective in character. This was a conscious approach to some extent, with some focus on memories of events 15–20 years back that we had discussed then and which I wanted to bring up again. However, it was to some extent more a question of a "spontaneous looking back" that can happen when people who have known each other for a long time meet. When I brought up the theme of "a short life" that had been so frequently mentioned in some of the previous interviews, several people stressed how important peers had been for that heightened death awareness: "At that time, you know, in 1985", one man said, "when I was active in the disability movement, people just died all around me … Now there is no one left to remind me". In a way, this was a relief, he said. His own illness "provided enough reminders". Another man expressed this instead in terms of loneliness: "They are all dead now, all my pals from the time at the rehabilitation centre, Sofia, Peter, Magnus … Tom … *I am the only one left*". It was lonely.

Several highlighted how the life span of their peers had functioned *as a norm or measure* for estimating the span of their own life: one woman, now 65, was reminded by me about how she had used to say that she did not think she would live to be 50. She had compared herself, she said:

> not only to people around me that I had met at rehabilitation. There were even
> people way back in my village that I remembered. They had diabetes. They did
> not live to be 40.

The 25-year perspective that the data allowed for clearly revealed that the theme of "a short life" and "a limited future" varied in intensity over time but also between individuals. One or two of those who had expressed this awareness most intensively were now dead. On the other hand, some of those who in 1988 had expressed very strong death awareness had actually managed to survive these many years. Some of the interviewees maintained that "things had worked out better than the odds suggested". "The odds" had to do with the state of their body, but also referred to what they knew about the long-term prognosis of their illness. Instead of referring to disabled friends, older diabetic people on the whole – *generalised peers* – were now used as a norm for the oldest age that you could possibly attain. Some were surprised "to have survived the twentieth century", and that they had lived to be much older than they had expected. One man even maintained that he was older "than he ought to have become", according to the general prognosis of "people with his illness".

At the same time, it seemed much less appropriate to refer to "a short life", particularly for those who were now around 65. This old age was viewed as proof of the possibility of a rather *long life* and of the possibility of even having a future. However, the contrary reasoning could also be true, according to some: this "old" age was an indicator of the fact that life would very soon be over. One could not possibly live much older with this illness: "*No one* among people I knew who had this illness ever did that", one woman said.

One strategy was, as it had been throughout the process, to *ignore the future*: "I know things can happen to me … but I try not to think very far ahead … otherwise I would not have the strength to go on", one woman (65) said. Another strategy was to live with "double agendas": adopting a short- and a long-term planning perspective at the same time. "Who knows, I might be an exception to the rule", one man exclaimed. Being an exception relative to peers meant escaping death for some additional time.

Concluding Remarks

The 25-year analysis presented in this chapter validates the relational character of death awareness. Just as awareness of imminent death has been described as a social process (Young et al. 1999), the awareness that life is likely to be short

– shorter than that for most people – also needs to be understood as a social, relational, process. The focus here has been on the impact of peer relations for chronically ill people. The temporal dimensions of the studied process were more complex than it has been possible to disclose in the presented chronology: time with disability, age, the bodily time of the illness trajectory, "time left" *and* relational time – all these dimensions are interwoven in complex ways that need further exploration. However, the life course approach uncovered multi-faceted patterns of connectedness between peer relations, awareness of death, and of changes in their expressions and meanings over time. Peer identification, which was supportive at the beginning of the process, entailed anticipation of "prospects ahead" and aroused death awareness at a later stage. However, as even more time went by, the role of peers and that of comparison took on further meanings. For those interviewed who were still alive after 25 years, friends had died and the theme of "a short life" was now more connected to comparisons with long-term sufferers of diabetes in general. These people functioned as a norm or measure for estimating the possible span of the lives of those interviewed. Normative reflections about longevity were now on the whole more common and death awareness seemed less intrusive. This ambiguity in the meaning of peer relations and identification was unravelled in this 25-year analysis. Those interviewed who were still alive in the last phases of the study were *survivors* who had lived for a long time and aged with illness and disability. The results presented in this chapter may be also interpreted within the framework of that experience. People who live long lives in spite of severe illness and disability represent growing groups in the Western world. The results, with their focus on peer relations and death awareness, will hopefully contribute to expanding the knowledge within this field.

References

Borkman, T. (1999) *Understanding Self-help/Mutual Aid – Experiential Learning in the Commons*. New Brunswick: Rutgers University Press.

Bryant, C.D., Edgley, C., Leming, M.R., Peck, D.L. and Sandstrom, K.L. (2003) "Death in the future. Prospects and prognosis", in Bryant, C.D. (ed.) *Handbook of Death and Dying II*. Thousand Oaks: Sage, pp. 1027–39.

Bülow, P. and Hydén, L.-Ch. (2003) "Patient school as a way of creating meaning in contested illness: the case of CFS", *Health: An Interdisciplinary Journal for the Study of Health, Illness and Medicine*, 7 (2): 227–49.

Bury, M. (1982) "Chronic illness as biographical disruption", *Sociology of Health and Illness*, 4 (2): 167–82.

Campbell, H.S., Phaneuf, M.R. and Deane, K. (2004) "Cancer support programs – do they work?", *Patient Education and Counseling*, 55 (1): 3–15.

Davis, C.G. and Nolen-Hoeksema, S. (2001) "Loss and meaning. How do people make sense of loss?", *American Behavioural Scientist*, 44: 726–41.

Dibb, B. and Yardley, L. (2006) "How does social comparison within a self-help group influence adjustment to chronic illness? A longitudinal study", *Social Science & Medicine*, 63 (6): 1602–1613.

Field, D. (1996) "Awareness and modern dying", *Mortality*, 1 (3): 255–65.

Fortner, B.V. and Neimeyer, R.A. (1999) "Death anxiety in older adults: a quantitative review", *Death Studies*, 23: 387–411.

Gallant, M. (2003) "The influence of social support on chronic illness self-management: a review and directions for research", *Health Education and Behavior*, 30 (2): 170–95.

Giele, J.Z. and Elder Jr., G.H. (eds) (1998) *Methods of Life Course Research*. Thousand Oaks: Sage.

Glaser, B. and Strauss, A. (1965) *Awareness of Dying*. Cambridge: Cambridge University Press.

Hayslip Jr., B. and Hansson, R.O. (2003) "Death awareness across the life span", in Bryant, C.D. (ed.) *Handbook of Death and Dying*. Thousand Oaks: Sage, Volume 1. pp. 437-448.

Howarth, G. (1998) "Just live for today. Living, caring, ageing and dying", *Ageing and Society*, 18: 679–89.

Jeppsson Grassman, E. (ed.) (2008) *Att åldras med funktionshinder* [Ageing with Disability]. Lund: Studentlitteratur.

Jeppsson Grassman, E. and Whitaker, A. (2007) "End of life and dimensions of civil society: the Church of Sweden in a new geography of death", *Mortality*, 12 (3): 261–79.

Karlsson, M., Jeppsson Grassman, E. and Hansson, J.-H. (2002) "Self-help groups in the welfare state: treatment program or voluntary action?", *Nonprofit Management and Leadership*, 13 (2): 155–67.

Kellehear, A. (2007) *A Social History of Dying*. Cambridge: Cambridge University Press.

Kirk, P., Kirk, I. and Kristjanson, L.J. (2004) "What do patients receiving palliative care for cancer and their families want to be told? A Canadian and Australian qualitative study", *British Medical Journal*, 328: 1343–9.

Little, M. and Sayers E.-J. (2004) "The skull beneath the skin: cancer survival and awareness of death", *Psycho-Oncology*, 13: 190–8.

Locker, D. (2003) "Living with chronic illness", in Scambler, G. (ed.) *Sociology of Applied Medicine*. London: Saunders, pp. 83–97.

NBHW (2004) *God vård i livets slut. En kunskapsöversikt om vård och omsorg om äldre* [Good End-of-Life Care]. Stockholm: National Board of Health and Welfare.

Pescosolido, B.A. (2001) "The role of social networks in the lives of persons with disabilities", in Albrecht, G.L., Seelman, K.D. and Bury, L.M. (eds) *Handbook of Disability Studies*. Thousand Oaks: Sage, pp. 468–89.

Saldãna, J. (2003) *Longitudinal Qualitative Research: Analyzing Change through Time*. Walnut Creek: Alta Mira Press.

Schwartz, C. and Sendor, M. (1999) "Helping others helps oneself: response shift effects in peer support", *Social Science and Medicine*, 48 (11): 1563–75.

Uccelli, M.M., Mohr, L.M., Battaglia, M.A., Zagami, P. and Mohr, D.C. (2004) "Peer support groups in multiple sclerosis: current effectivenss and future directions", *Multiple Sclerosis*, 10 (1): 80–4.

Walter, T. (1994) *The Revival of Death*. London: Routledge.

de Vries, B., Bluck, S. and Birren, J.E. (1993) "Understanding death and dying from a life span perspective", *The Gerontologist*, 33: 366–72.

Young, E., Seale, C. and Bury, M. (1998) "It's not like family going is it? Negotiating friendship boundaries towards end of life", *Mortality*, 3 (1): 27–42.

Young, E., Bury, B. and Elston, M.-A. (1999) "Live and/or let die: modes of social dying among women and their friends", *Mortality*, 4 (3): 269–289.

Chapter 3
Nationalization and Mediatized Ritualization: The Broadcast Farewell of Fadime Sahindal

Eva Reimers

On 4 February 2002 the Swedish television network TV4 broadcast live a farewell ceremony for a female student of social work; Fadime Sahindal (TV4 2002). Although the deceased held no official position in Swedish society the ceremony was held in the major cathedral of the Church of Sweden and, close to the coffin, were representatives from the royal family, the government, county and municipality. Why did the death of this woman result in what was close to a state funeral? How were sentiments and notions of nationality and death made meaningful in the broadcast? These are some of the queries in this chapter which takes Fadime's Farewell ceremony as the basis for discussing death and memorialization in relation to constructions of nationality.

Official Mediatized Death Rituals and Collective Identity

As argued by for example Peter Berger and Thomas Luckmann (1966: 118–21), Zygmunt Baumann (1992) and Douglas Davies (1997: 11), death and the awareness of everybody's mortality pose existential threats not only for individuals, but for society at large. Death threatens individuals, collectives and cultures with annihilation. Nations, groups and power positions are all threatened by obliteration as an awareness of everybody's and everything's temporal existence makes it easy to conclude that there is no meaning to those social structures and communities that constitute the social fabric. This means that death can seriously undermine solidarity towards social institutions and conceptions of a coherent and durable "nation". Death threatens the social construct of societies and nations not only by the fact that, not far ahead, all who now constitute the nation will be gone, but also because deaths of significant individuals, accidents and catastrophes endanger the conception of the nation as a stable entity.

Elizabeth Hallam and Jenny Hockey (2001) claim that different forms of memorialization can be understood as a means of safeguard against threats of annihilation and meaninglessness. Practices of memorialization makes the transient, if not everlasting, at least a little more durable, and this is also true for the notion of nationalities or nations. As Benedict Anderson (1991) argues the imaginations of nations are constituted by the presumption of a shared history and common norms and values (see also Cillia et al. 1999). Death evinces the transient and contingent nature of these imaginations.

The analysis in this chapter is conducted in the tradition of some of the classic functionalists in ritual studies, such as Emile Durkheim (1915/1965), Mary Douglas (1966) and Victor Turner (1969). They maintain that rituals are enacted in situations of crisis, with the function of establishing order in the face of imminent chaos. This is accomplished because rituals draw on pre-existing authoritative actions and emotions, and situate individuals and groups within a common and shared history (Bird 1980). This is, not least, apparent in death rituals that bridge the gap between past, present and future and thereby diminish the threat that death poses for the notion of the persistence of individual and collective identity. In and through death rituals the deceased and the bereaved become anchored in a specific common culture, in a specific value system and worldview which is expected to persist, regardless of the demise of its singular constituents. Besides serving as means to show respect for the deceased and providing support for the bereaved, death rituals can also be regarded as tools for the construction of individual and collective identity, as this chapter will demonstrate. For the ritual discussed in this chapter is a *mediatized ritual* (Cottle 2006), and is so in two ways: it is a ritual mediated through public media, and it displays the traits that according to Simon Cottle characterize mediatized rituals:

> Mediatized rituals are those exceptional and performative media phenomena that serve to sustain and/or mobilize collective sentiments and solidarities on the basis of symbolization and subjunctive orientation to what should or ought to be. (2006: 415)

The citation points to mass media as a site for the performance of rituals that create and sustain collective solidarity. A similar idea is expressed by Mervi Pantti and Johanna Sumiala (2009) who state that mourning rituals on television function as integrative events that contribute to enforcing a conception of consensus regarding certain values. An aspect of this that I believe is not sufficiently stressed either by Cottle or Pantti and Sumiala is that collective solidarity is always constructed and made meaningful in relation to its "constitutive outside", i.e. to those who are considered Other and who delineate the borders for the community in question. The imagination of a coherent nation and nationality requires the notion of people and values that do not belong to the nation (cf. Anderson 1991). And this, I believe, is crucial for understanding the relation between nationalization and memorialization.

Rituals as Performative Practices

The overarching questions for this chapter are shaped by these issues and focus both on the way the broadcast ceremony constructs and communicates notions of nationality, and on how significant traits of history and values are articulated. The analytical perspective driving this analysis, not least the topic of memorialization, is theoretically informed and inspired by discourse theory (Laclau and Mouffe 1985; Smith 1998), especially by the notion of "articulation" or "articulatory practices". This concept stresses that discourses, norms and values only exist and have effects if they are articulated; in words, in artefacts, in legalization, policies and so forth. By being articulated, they temporary stabilize, or make a specific version of reality appear stable and self-evident. It is important to note, however, that each articulation slightly changes and destabilizes the hegemonic discourse, because it is never completely identical with previous articulations.

This poststructuralist theoretical perspective is in line with several notions in ritual studies as with Victor Turner's (1969) emphasis on the performative aspect of rituals and Judith Butler's stress on the performative aspect of enactments and articulatory practices (Butler 1990, 1993). A common trait for rituals and articulatory practices is that, primarily, they are not about different events, norms and ideologies, but that they actually bring about, make, or construct, events, norms and ideologies (Driver 1991: 93), a point central to my present argument.

The Broadcast Farewell Ceremony of Fadime Sahindal

The Preceding Story of an Honour Killing

On 22 January 2002 Fadime Sahindal was shot to death by her father as she was about to leave the home of one of her sisters. She had, already, broken with the family and moved to study at a college in the middle of Sweden because of a conflict with her father and brother over her choice of boyfriend and way of life. She had also reported to the police certain threats and harassments from her father and brother who were both arrested and brought to court. Her father was sentenced to fines and her brother to a short imprisonment. Moreover, Fadime Sahindal had informed the media about the conflict with her male family members. This resulted in a televised documentary, a long article in Sweden's leading tabloid, and an invitation to a hearing in the parliament concerning the situation of immigrant girls. Despite these events and social action Fadime was killed with the subsequent representation of the killing being framed in the media as a culture conflict between "them" and "us" (Reimers 2007).

The Killing as an Atrocity and the Praise of the Swedish Nation

The broadcast repeated, in different ways, the story of a beautiful young Kurdish woman killed by her father because he considered her choice of fiancé and way of life as a threat to the honour of the family. The broadcast begins with a photo of a young woman with long dark hair seen in profile. The background is dark and the text carries the programme title – "Farewell Ceremony for Fadime" – in white letters. Significantly, the name of the deceased is given by her first name "Fadime", and not her full name. To use someone's first name is to signal familiarity and closeness. Indeed, by the time of the farewell ceremony Fadime Sahindal had become so well known that the media mostly used only her first name.

The actual footage begins with viewers being presented with the background for the service, its official character, and reasons for its general interest, all described by the commentator, a man with a deep voice, and accompanied by displayed footage. The first shows a bird's-eye view of the town of Uppsala: at the bottom of the screen is the text "Uppsala 4 February 2002". After a few seconds the commentator speaks slowly:

> Uppsala today. It is gray, cold, and with a tormenting wind, and a cold rain. [Pause] In Uppsala cathedral we will today bid farewell to Fadime Sahindal. She should have turned 27 years on the second of April. [Pause] Two weeks ago she was murdered by her father. [Pause].[1]

While he talks the camera gradually turns to focus on the cathedral. Its two towers come into view from a ground-level perspective. The next shot shows a photo of the face of the deceased woman against a dark background. She wears a red blouse, and the text reads: "Fadime Sahindal 1975–2002". The commentator recommences:

> Fadime Sahindal became a symbol for the right of all human beings to live the life they want to live.

Once more the cathedral appears. The camera focuses upon its closed doors, then on two flag poles in front of the cathedral bearing partly hoisted Swedish flags. Numerous people are gathered outside.

In this introduction, the history of the murder of Fadime Sahindal as an honour killing is articulated in several ways. The commentator states the background, both in terms of how she died – "murdered by her father" – and by delineating the significance of her death as "a symbol of independence and freedom". Two photos of Fadime Sahindal depict a woman with dark hair who, together with her name, does not fit the stereotype of a young Swedish woman. Regardless of whether the murder had previously been constructed as an honour killing in public accounts,

---

[1]   All translations from Swedish to English are made by the author.

the information in this broadcast introduction achieves that goal. By telling the viewers that she was killed by her father and by designating her as a symbol of independence, the commentator signals the presumption that the deceased is a victim of an honour killing.

The opening sequences of the broadcast are not dominated by articulation of the Swedish nation and its history, nor by articulations about the Other. Views of Uppsala, and in particular of its cathedral, set the Church of Sweden – a Lutheran Church that was a state Church until 2000 – as the ritual frame for the ceremony. The place of the ritual performance is central. As stated by Tom Driver (1991), for example, such ritual spaces are places set apart, they are out of the ordinary and also, in a way, outside time. Uppsala Cathedral is a sacred place carrying high symbolic value of the Swedish nation, of its endurance and long history. It is a building that has stood firm for a long time and will continue to stand long after those who now visit it are dead. This is of course significant in relation to death. But it is also a symbol of power. It is a building constructed with the aim of making people feel small and humble. It is a prestigious place, the centre of the Church of Sweden, where archbishops are inaugurated and where funerals are held for important persons. It is a sacred symbol of an enduring Swedish nation.

A State Funeral

There are several traits of the ensuing ritual that point to the national importance of Fadime Sahindal's death. One is the abundance of flowers in the cathedral. The commentator informs the viewers that there are 10,000 white carnations. In Sweden flowers are visual signs of the importance of the deceased and, in the week before the ceremony, people had been encouraged by the newspapers to contribute a specified amount of money for their purchase. Such a contribution became a means of constructing oneself as a mourner, and of constructing the deceased, and her death, as important for the community at large. The same can be said for the high attendance. The cathedral is jammed, with a couple of hundred people also gathered outside and with the broadcast giving everybody the opportunity to participate. Hereby the ceremony is constructed as a concern for the whole nation.

On the floor in front of the coffin is a photo of the familiar face of Fadime Sahindal. After zooming in on a plaque on the coffin bearing her name, year of birth and death, the camera makes a sweep over the front pews where people are dressed in black; some wipe tears from their eyes as the commentator identifies them.

> The crown princess, the press secretary of the royal family Elisabeth Tarras Wahlberg, speaker Birgitta Dahl, Mona Sahlin, the county governor Ann-Catrin Haglund, the head of the city council Jan-Erik Tun. Fellow students from the Middle College. There are many who are saying farewell to Fadime.

The image and the information from the commentator are crucial in making the event a state funeral. The official representatives are the first participants in view.

Their presence at the ceremony communicates the national importance of the death of Fadime Sahindal. The next of kin, those that are usually considered as the bereaved, are placed further away from the coffin and come into view last and are not identified by the commentator. The official representatives on the front pews embrace all levels of public society, from the royal family to the town of Uppsala. Their presence, together with the broadcast itself, makes the ceremony a state funeral.

A Funeral Service according to the Liturgy of the Church of Sweden

The articulation of the death of Fadime Sahindal as a significant event for Sweden is enforced by the way the ceremony – although it is presented as "a farewell ceremony" and not as a funeral – complies with the ritual of funeral services in the Church of Sweden. The officiating priest wears the liturgical gown usually worn at funerals, and the different elements in the ritual, such as music, welcome address, scripture reading, funeral speech, hymn and blessing, all follow the pattern of the Church of Sweden's liturgy.

As the initial organ music fades a female priest in liturgical gown, introduced by the commentator as the dean of the cathedral, positions herself behind the coffin and gives a welcome address to the congregation (and the viewers). The priest maintains that the focus should be on "Fadime" and what she has "given us all". This is a conspicuous formulation because most people present in the cathedral, or in front of their television set, never knew Fadime Sahindal. What she had given "us all" must have to do with her significance beyond herself, rather than her personal actions. The address furthermore indicates that the next of kin are not the primary objects for the ritual. The priest speaks for the family of Fadime Sahindal, rather than to them and concludes her address by saying "welcome" in halting Kurdish. This is one of the few occasions where the cultural background of the deceased and the family members is made explicit.

This welcome is followed by choral music without lyrics sung by a choir dressed in red gowns. According to the commentator the piece is titled "In memory" and can, consequently, be understood as funeral music. During the song the footage continues to shift between candles, chandeliers, flowers, the photo of Fadime Sahindal, the coffin and the choir. The music is followed by scripture reading from Psalm 139: 1–12 by a male priest, introduced by the commentator as chaplain of the cathedral. This, in turn, is followed by a female soloist singing Eric Clapton's "Tears in Heaven" with Swedish lyrics, a song now common at Swedish funerals, especially if the deceased is a young person. During the song the image shifts between the singer, the coffin, candles, and the abundance of carnations. Although the deceased was not a member of the Church of Sweden, the ceremony follows the pattern of most Swedish funerals. Activities, actors, the liturgical space, symbols, and music together making the liturgy of the Church of Sweden a liturgical frame for the ceremony.

Inserting the Deceased into the National History

The funeral sermon can in many ways be understood as a tool that, discursively and ritually, inserts Fadime Sahindal into a narrative about the Swedish nation. The priest begins by saying:

> Dear friends, Fadime loved her hometown Uppsala. Her wish was to both get married and be buried here in the cathedral. This building has stood here for over 700 years. There is room for a lot of tears and despair under these vaults. This has always been the case. The prayers of our forefathers and foremothers remain in these walls. For generations people have found their way here.

By naming Uppsala "her hometown" the priest positions Fadime Sahindal in Uppsala. This is enforced by the footage which zooms in on the photo in front of the coffin. The priest claims that the wish of the deceased was to be married and buried in this highly symbolic building, i.e. that the deceased considered the cathedral to be a sanctuary with which she identified herself. This makes Fadime Sahindal a link in the chain of people who have been married and buried in the cathedral. It is noteworthy that the priest does not mention baptism, only marriage and burials. Fadime Sahindal was never baptized. According to what the commentator says later, her family were non-practising Muslims. In the sermon, however, this is not made explicit; instead she is talked of as if she had the life trajectory of a person who was born and raised within the Church of Sweden. The funeral sermon can be seen as a performative articulation which inserts the deceased into the history of the people of Uppsala, not the Kurdish people. It hereby becomes essential for how this mediatized ritual contributes in constructing Fadime as Swedish, as one of "us". This is further reinforced by the wording "our forefathers and foremothers", and the expression "for generations". Besides incorporating the deceased into a Swedish history these formulations disclose the imagined audience as those who identify with ancestors that belonged to the Church of Sweden. Viewers who have a different cultural, religious or ethnic affiliation are hereby made into the Other. In the next section of the speech the priest speaks of Fadime Sahindal as a martyr:

> In here it has been easy to get close to God. The cathedral is situated towards the east, that's where the light comes from. The shape of the building is the cross, a cross that is like open arms. The cross has for many become a sign for death. According to the faith that this church rests upon, the cross is a witness of suffering love. Suffering love does not seek its own, is not puffed up, the suffering love that forgives is the strongest force in life, and that, despite all, conquers in the end.

In this citation, as already indicated, the ritual place is not only articulated as the point of departure for the speech, but as a materialization of the message. The building is in the shape of a cross, which, according to the priest, makes it a witness of him who died on the cross, of him who personalized "the suffering love". In the ceremony the participants bid farewell to a woman who also died because of love, and who therefore can be made sense of as an additional personification of suffering love. The priest hereby constructs an analogy between Fadime Sahindal and Jesus, and between those two and the cathedral. Together with her explicit statement that Fadime was a martyr, the different allusions and the ritual space affirm the construction of Fadime Sahindal as a martyr of love, and as a martyr of independence. During the sermon words and images of the cathedral enforce each other and the ensuing articulation of the deceased as a Swedish martyr.

While the broadcast shows the photo of Fadime Sahindal in front of the coffin, the priest describes the deceased:

> The concern, the commitment that she felt for her fellow human beings have left traces behind, her joy and positive attitude towards life, has also left traces, in the heart. The power of death cannot reach there. Fadime still lives there. I have said it before, that Fadime, to me, is one of the martyrs of our time. This is something I also want to say here by her coffin. You Fadime have, through your lack of fear, and your strength, through your love of life, given me, and many, many others courage and strength. I and all of us want to thank God for you. May you rest in peace and may the eternal light of God shine for you, Fadime. Amen.

One aim of funerary rituals is to defeat the threat of death. When a young person is killed by somebody she was supposed to be able to rely on, death becomes a most imminent threat, not only to life in general but also to the notion that the nuclear family is a safe place, and that parents always love their children. What, according to the sermon, made Fadime Sahindal into a martyr was "lack of fear", "strength", "love of life". Like the commentator in the introduction of the broadcast, the priest is unspecific. In order to understand what she refers to one has to be familiar with the media event of Fadime, i.e. one has to know the story. Her lack of fear was lack of fear of her father and brother and her strength lay in insisting on her choice of fiancé. The story adheres to what Fadime Sahindal and the media considered Swedish norms and values. Because this apparently entailed a conflict and a breach with her family the Sahindal family is constructed as the Other, those that are incompatible with "the Swedish" factor. By constructing the parent that the deceased obviously could not rely on as the Other, the break between child and parent is legitimized. The ritual hereby mitigates the threat to the notion of the nuclear family as a valuable institution.

In the broadcast the viewers are informed that although the deceased broke with her family, she found a new belonging. The commentator introduces a group of young adults who gather around the coffin by saying: "The fellow students who became her new family when she left her old, or was forced away." The word "family" is significant, both because it serves as a repetition of the opposition between the imagined "Swedish" and the imagined "Kurdish" identity, and because it points to the possibility of a chosen family as an alternative to a nuclear family based on blood-ties. The friends of Fadime Sahindal hold hands while the song "One" by U2 is played on the speakers.

Judging by how people in the cathedral express their sentiments this is the most moving part of the ceremony. Maybe this is because it is the only part where the deceased is represented and mourned as the individual Fadime Sahindal rather than as the symbol Fadime. The image of her friends, and a song that is liked by young people, makes their loss apparent. Together with the story of her life that all viewers are so familiar with, it becomes real that a young woman has died, and that it is a factual loss for friends and family. However, by showing the crying priest, the crying crown-princess and minister, the loss also becomes one for society at large. Showing these official representatives crying in national television makes the loss a national loss, and makes Fadime Sahindal a national figure. While most elements in the ceremony contribute to an articulation of the deceased as "Swedish" there is one musical piece that refers to her Kurdish heritage and thereby makes salient her relation with the Other. It is a musical piece on clarinet presented by the commentator as "Kurdish music, a lamenting song from southern Kurdistan, a song entitled Fadime".

Order is Restored

At the end of the ceremony the priest leads the congregation in prayer and closes with a benediction. The benediction itself ends with the words "In the name of God the compassionate and merciful". The commentator observes this as something of "a different ending of the benediction". What he is referring to, and later explains, is that this is the way Muslims address God. The ending of the benediction can be seen either as a construction of the bereaved, and the deceased, as Other, or as a formulation that encompasses both Christians and Muslims and thereby somewhat subverts both the hegemony of the Church and the notion of who and what belongs to the imagined Swedish factor. This potential subversion is however swiftly restored by the final hymn, which is the most common Swedish funeral hymn "Härlig är jorden" [Wonderful is the Earth]. This gives the ceremony a very traditional Swedish conclusion.

The hymn concludes the actual liturgy, and is followed by the carrying out of the coffin, an action that was heavily commented on in the media because all the bearers were women (Reimers 2007). While one sees funeral wreaths being handed over to family and friends who will carry them to the hearse in order to place them at the gravesite, the commentator informs the viewers that Fadime will be buried at a graveyard in the centre of the town and next to her former boyfriend – "her beloved Patrik" – who had died in a car accident a couple of years before. As the commentator speaks six young women position themselves around the coffin in order to carry it to the hearse. The choice of using only women as bearers is presented by the commentator as a breach of both Swedish and Kurdish funeral traditions. By giving this task solely to women Fadime Sahindal's female gender, and the notion that she was killed because of how she wanted to perform her gender, is placed at the forefront and affirmed as something good.

The end of the broadcast signals that the ritual has succeeded in restoring the order disturbed by the killing. The image shifts once more to the bird's-eye perspective outside the cathedral. The church bells are ringing, and the coffin is placed in the hearse. The commentator evaluates the ceremony: "A beautiful, dignified, warm farewell ceremony." He also sums up the legacy of Fadime in these words:

> The courage, stand for what you believe in, and the fact that nothing, no culture, no religion, no traditions, no ideology, may deprive a human being from the right to live her own life.

As the hearse slowly drives away the perspective in the footage is once again the cathedral towers from a ground perspective. This is also the concluding image. The cathedral is standing firm. Sweden, at least in the media, was shaken for two weeks, but order is, at least partially, restored.

Discussion

Televised broadcasts of funerals are rare in Sweden. Between 1961 and 2008 there have been 19 broadcast memorial services (Davidsson-Bremborg 2009). Except for the farewell ceremony of Fadime Sahindal and a broadcasted funeral in 2008 of a brutally raped and murdered nine-year-old girl, all the deceased in the broadcast funerals were official persons, such as politicians, actors or authors. This shows that the decision to broadcast a funeral is usually motivated by the life of the deceased. It is the significant achievement and importance of a deceased individual that is commemorated. A pillar of society is gone, so the construction of the nation is in need of repair.

Fadime Sahindal was not an official person. The decision to broadcast the ceremony seems therefore to have been motivated by how she died rather than who she was or what she had accomplished. But in what way did her death threaten the notion of the Swedish nation and Swedish values? The broadcast suggests that the value(s) that were brought forward as threatened were connected to views about women. Fadime Sahindal was celebrated as a woman. Her gender was crucial. The female, or the liberated, free and self-sufficient female, was in the ceremony constructed as a signifier of Swedish identity, as the decisive difference between "them" and "us". Almost all of the representatives of the official image of Sweden in the cathedral were women. The royal family was not represented by the king but by the crown-princess. The government was not represented by its male prime minister but by the female minister of integration. The officiating priest was a woman. The majority of family and friends were women, and the bearers were all women. This indicates that the values at stake were values connected to women.

Representations of Fadime Sahindal through words such as a "symbol for the right of all human beings to live the life they want to live", "a symbol of independence and freedom", "lack of fear", "strength", "love of life", "martyr of our time", not only constructed the deceased in line with what is believed to signify Sweden and Swedish women – thereby enforcing that construction – but also, simultaneously, constructed its opposite, i.e. practices and notions about women that were made foreign and alien to those of Sweden. The constitutive outside of what is understood as Swedish is consequently depicted as women who are constrained, who cannot live as they want, and who are afraid and weak. I argue that the enactment, presence and effects of these norms was the (or one of the) threat(s) that was addressed – and ritually overcome – in the ceremony.

But why Fadime Sahindal? She was not the first or the only victim of honour killing in Sweden. Why was she commemorated in a state funeral? The answer to this question was not made salient in the ceremony, but one clue might lie in the fact that Fadime Sahindal had turned to the Swedish authorities, media, and even the legal system in order to find support, help and refuge. The threats she was subjected to were well known yet the protection she received did not prevent her father from killing her. So maybe this event was not a farewell ceremony aimed at expressing sentiments following the loss of a prominent individual but, rather, a ritual that aimed to redress a defeat. The official Swedish society, which she was claimed to have chosen, was not able to protect her. In killing his daughter her father "triumphed" over "the Swedish" way through his lethal values. The so-called Swedish values, and the society that asserts these values to be superior, were defeated, or at least severely challenged by the killing. I believe it is here that we can find the reason why it became a public concern to mitigate the threat that the killing posed to the notion of a superior nation that shows concern about women's rights and security. It was not only the death of Fadime that was in need of correction. It was also vital to reassert the value of adhering to what is considered Swedish as something good and valuable.

By incorporating the fate of Fadime Sahindal into the narrative of the Swedish nation the killing was reconstructed. Instead of being seen as a defeat for Sweden as a nation and the role of its women, it was made into a victory. The mediatized ritual can be seen as a symbolic adoption of Fadime Sahindal by the Swedish nation from her Kurdish family. This was enforced by the commentator who repeatedly called her by her first name, a practice that signals closeness and familiarity. By granting Fadime Sahindal the position of a martyr, a person of great significance, a role model and somebody who will always be remembered, and in that sense live forever, death was defeated. Instead of silencing her forever, the killing gave her a position as the foremost representative of women who were willing to suffer and die for adherence to the imagined nation instead of its opponents. Her voice and her opposition would never die. In that sense, the threat from the Other was defeated. By being memorialized Fadime Sahindal lives on. Her father did not manage to kill her.

The "Farewell Ceremony of Fadime" is a case where a troubling death is met by memorialization through nationalization. The fate of the deceased is made into a national concern and incorporated into the story of the nation as a significant event. The connection between death, memorialization and nationalization shows how memorialization by nationalization can not only serve to overcome death as a defeat and end to life, but also to redress the threat to the imagination of the nation the specific death entailed. Memorialization in the form of nationalization mitigates the threat of death at the same time as it stabilizes conceptions of the nation and its constitutive outside, i.e. the Other.

References

Anderson, Benedict (1991) *Imagined Communities: Reflections on the Origins and Spread of Nationalism*. London: Verso.

Baumann, Zygmunt (1992) *Mortality, Immortality, and other Life Strategies*. Cambridge: Polity Press.

Berger, Peter and Luckmann, Thomas (1966) *The Social Construction of Reality: A Treatise on the Sociology of Knowledge*. New York: Anchor Books.

Bird, Frederick (1980) "The contemporary ritual milieu", in R. Browne (ed.) *Rituals and Ceremonies in Popular Culture*. Bowling Green: Bowling Green University Popular Press, 19–35.

Butler, Judith (1990) *Gender Trouble. Feminism and the Subversion of Identity*. New York: Routledge.

Butler, Judith (1993) *Bodies that Matter*. New York: Routledge.

Cillia, Rudolf de, Reisigl, Martin, and Wodak, Ruth (1999) "The discursive construction of national identities", *Discourse & Society*, 10 (2): 149–73.

Cottle, Simon (2006) "Mediatized rituals: beyond manufacturing consent", *Media, Culture and Society*, 28 (3): 411–32.

Davidsson-Bremborg, Anna (2009) "Begravningar n rutan. Tre tv-sända begravningar", in A. Davidsson-Bremborg, G. Gustafsson and G. Karlsson Hallonsten (eds) *Religionssociologi i brytningstider*. Lund: CTS, Lunds universitet, 170–190.

Davies, Douglas J. (1997) *Death, Ritual and Belief*. London: Cassel.

Douglas, Mary (1966) *Purity and Danger. An Analysis of Concepts of Pollution and Taboo*. London: Routledge.

Driver, Tom F. (1991) *The Magic of Rituals. Our Need for Liberating Rites that Transform Our Lives and Our Communities*. New York: Harper San Francisco.

Durkheim, Emile (1915/1965) *The Elementary Forms of the Religious Life*. New York: The Free Press.

Hallam, Elizabeth and Hockey, Jenny (2001) *Death, Memory and Material Culture*. Oxford: Berg.

Laclau, Ernesto and Mouffe, Chantal (1985) *Hegemony and Socialist Strategy*. London: Verso.

Pantti, Mervi and Sumiala, Johanna (2009) "Till death do us join: media, mourning rituals and the sacred centre of the society", *Media, Culture and Society*, 31 (1): 119–135.

Reimers, Eva (2007) "Representations of an honor killing", *Feminist Media Studies*, 7 (3): 239–55.

Smith, Anna Marie (1998) *Laclau and Mouffe. The Radical Democratic Imaginary*. London: Routledge.

Turner, Victor (1969) *The Ritual Process. Structure and Anti-Structure*. New York: Cornell University Press.

TV4 (4 February 2002) *Avskedshögtid för Fadime* [Farewell Ceremony for Fadime].

Chapter 4
Wiring Death: Dying, Grieving and Remembering on the Internet

Tim Hutchings

Introduction

Online networks and digital media have been integrated into contemporary processes of dying, grieving and memorialisation, changing the social context in which dying takes place and establishing new electronic spaces for the communication of grief. This chapter argues that the study of death online should be cultivated as a valuable interdisciplinary research field, with particular attention to three themes: using death and mourning to improve our understanding of digital media, using online communication as a source of insight into experiences of dying and grieving, and examining the changes in the experience and practice of dying and mourning that are being brought about by the integration of digital media into everyday life. These themes are explored here through a number of case studies, including the death of Michael Jackson, the rise of online memorials, the role of social network sites in mourning, and responses to death in online religious and gaming communities.

The Internet supports new opportunities for accessing resources, contacting others and constructing a presentation of the self. Digital media have become the foundation of the 'network society',[1] central to contemporary processes of information retrieval, relationship maintenance, self-expression and entertainment. Death, too, is no exception to this all-pervasive influence of the digital for, as this chapter will demonstrate, online networks and digital media have been integrated into contemporary processes of dying, grieving, memorial-making, changing the social context in which dying takes place, and establishing new electronic spaces for the communication of grief. Online, dying individuals can access information and share their story, their family and friends may, later, gather around digital archives of photographs, video and writing, to share memories and condolences, and complete strangers can exchange accounts of celebrity deaths and global disasters. The social media platforms used to communicate between friends can become, after the death of a participant, spaces for direct 'communication' to the deceased through the same channels that individual had used while alive – moving the memorial site from a distant graveyard into the midst of life. Online

---

[1]   Manuel Castells, *The Rise of the Network Society* (Oxford: Blackwell, 1996).

communities can commemorate their dead through online funerals, memorial services and tributes.

Given such factors, this chapter argues that the study of death online should be cultivated not only as a valuable research field in its own right but also as a key part of any exploration of contemporary dying and the search for insight into patterns of online interaction. Three key research areas deserve particular attention. First, the consideration of dying and grief has long been included in studies of online communities, where the death of a participant can act as a catalyst for expressions of personal relationship and commitment to the group among survivors and so offer an opportunity to explore associated values and tensions. These are issues to which death-studies scholars could add considerable sophistication. Second, the Internet can be used as a resource for understanding the processes of dying and grieving through the stories shared on blogs, forums and social network sites. Third, the appropriation of digital media is actually changing the way society experiences and discusses the end of life: how news of a death spreads, what kinds of memorials and tributes are created, whose voices are heard in those tributes, and how the continuing social existence of the dead person is controlled and managed.

Given that these themes of exploring digital activity, understanding death, and changing the process of dying and grieving are highly complex, this chapter will seek only to illustrate their importance through an overview of online activity. I begin with a discussion of the intense online communication that followed the death of Michael Jackson, before moving on to address three key areas: online memorials, social network sites and online communities.

Case Study: The King of Pop

On 25 June 2009, Michael Jackson died. What made this particular death unique was not the significance of the individual or the manner of his death, though both of course added fascination and intrigue to the unfolding story, but the manner of its reporting. The news was first broken by a Hollywood-based gossip blog called *TMZ*[2] and later confirmed by the *LA Times*,[3] before being spread around the world through independent and professional news websites, all long before television stations or print media picked up the story. Ordinary people outside the news industry were able to discover the story and share it directly with their friends using social media accessed through computers and mobile phones.

Within hours, Jackson's death achieved what media analyst Garry Whannel refers to as 'vortextuality', an unpredictable and short-lived state 'whereby major news stories have the power to dominate the news media to such an extent that

---

[2]   *TMZ* staff, 'Michael Jackson Dies', *TMZ* (25 June 2009).

[3]   Andrew Blankstein and Phil Willon, 'Michael Jackson is Dead', *L.A. Now* (25 June 2009).

all attention appears, temporarily, to be directed towards them'.[4] Feedback loops between different platforms and media recycle and repeat the story, which suddenly becomes the focus of editorials, cartoons, phone-ins and further headlines as the intensity of the news vortex 'grows with bewildering speed'.[5] Whannel's article focuses on the narrower range of professional media involved with reporting the verdict of Jackson's trial in 2005, but the ongoing rise of blogs and social media since that time ensured an even more complex web of references and reports by the time of Jackson's death in 2010. 'The news of Jackson's death produced a vortextual storm, briefly pulling the media and audience alike inwards.'[6]

Jackson's death showed that vortextuality can indeed occur online, drawing the attention of every aspect of social media towards the discussion of a single topic. The story was covered extensively on blogs and websites, and eagerness to access news coverage caused an unprecedented spike in levels of Internet use through mobile phones. Conflicting rumours created an editing battle on Wikipedia, with 500 alterations to Jackson's entry over a 24-hour period as different authors sought to establish the credibility of different sources of information.[7] Direct communication between individuals through digital media exploded, with AOL's instant messenger service reporting crashes; further crashes and slow-downs occurred as Facebook and Twitter were used intensively by posters trying to inform their friends and followers and share their personal responses. The following day, CNN's Technology Blog ran the headline, 'Jackson Dies, Almost Takes Internet With Him'.

The role of Twitter in information and response sharing received particular attention in subsequent coverage of the event. Twitter is a microblogging service that permits individuals to send messages of 140 characters or less to all their registered 'followers', and can operate as a powerful tool for breaking news: 'Any action in the real world usually receives a near instant reaction or feedback in terms of tweets expressing opinions or reactions to the action.'[8] In this case, the first tweet was posted only 20 minutes after the first 911 call. Messages can be copied or 'retweeted', spreading from one social network to another, and this initial rumour was quickly shared around the world.

A second surge of online activity accompanied Jackson's subsequent memorial service on 7 July, again using Twitter to report on the event and share responses. According to an online report for Forbes.com:

---

[4]   Garry Whannel, 'News, Celebrity and Vortextuality: A Study of the Media Coverage of the Michael Jackson Verdict', *Cultural Politics* 6(1) (2010) p. 66.

[5]   Ibid., p. 81.

[6]   Ibid., p. 82.

[7]   Linnie Rawlinson and Nick Hunt, 'Jackson Dies, Almost Takes Internet With Him', *CNN.com/technology* (26 June 2009).

[8]   Jagan Sankaranarayanan et al., 'TwitterStand: News in Tweets', in D. Agarwal et al. (eds), *Proceedings of the 17th ACM SIGSPATIAL International Conference on Advances in Geographic Information Systems* (Seattle 2009) p. 43.

More than 17,000 lucky fans were allowed inside the Staples Center on Tuesday to commemorate Michael Jackson. But for the millions of fans who didn't have a ticket, Twitter served as their backstage pass to the Los Angeles memorial service for the King of Pop.

People from across the world united on Twitter to both pay tribute to the legend and aggregate news circulating the Internet about the day's events. 'MJ's service is on the big screen in Times Square. Tourists are plopped on lawn chairs watching it. Kinda cool/living room-esque,' rippleintime17 tweeted.[9]

Facebook and Twitter remained key media for the sharing of emotional responses, memories and thoughts over the following days. Cha et al. report that well over 600,000 users posted over 1.4 million messages to a total audience of some 23.5 million readers,[10] while Jackson's Facebook page grew from 80,000 to just over 10 million fans, with 20 new members joining every second at the peak of public interest.[11]

As with other celebrity deaths, the passing of Michael Jackson led to a striking reappraisal of his life and work, which suddenly returned to popularity and critical approval, and found new audiences after many years of social unacceptability:

Following Michael Jackson's tragic and untimely death on 25 June 2009, I began to listen and watch again … millions of others … were suddenly buying up his records in vast quantities, putting him on top of the charts for the first time in years.[12]

This reappraisal can be seen at work through the positive, neutral and negative messages posted and reposted online. Selections were repeated in news coverage, including the Forbes report quoted above:

This is an unbelievable moment … we are creating HIStory. Theres such a high level of emotion here.[13]

I am somewhat horrified by the spectacle of the Jackson memorial and the 'debut' of his children on stage. What happened to being private?

---

[9] Emily Cohn, 'Michael Jackson Twitter Mania', *Forbes.com* (7 July 2009).

[10] Meeyoung Cha et al., 'Measuring User Influence in Twitter: The Million Follower Fallacy', *Proceedings of the Fourth International AAAI Conference on Weblogs and Social Media* (2010) p. 14.

[11] Stephanie Busari, 'Michael Jackson Memorial Draws Crowds Online', *CNN.com* (8 July 2009).

[12] Susan Fast, 'Difference that Exceeded Understanding: Remembering Michael Jackson (1958–2009)', *Popular Music and Society* 33(2) (2010) p. 259.

[13] Cohn, 'Twitter Mania'.

MTV aired a special show, encouraging viewers to use Facebook and Twitter to share their responses, and published a selection on their blog:

> I'll never forget Michael. He was like, God in my eyes. Its so sad to see him leave us. But he is in a better place now:/[14]

> 1st time I heard Jackson 5 was when I was riding my bike w/ a transistor radio hanging from the handlebars. ABC easy as 123.

We clearly see here all three of the themes introduced at the start of this chapter: insights into online activity, access to responses to death, and indications that digital media have actually changed the experience of grief.

First, this event has been examined repeatedly by researchers hoping to gain better understanding of new media. Cha et al., for example, analyse Twitter archives to investigate the influence users exert over one another[15] while Sankaranarayanan et al. try to develop a news processing system using Twitter to catch the latest breaking news.[16]

Second, these are public spaces in which thoughts and feelings are freely shared and can offer access to people's responses without the need for surveys and interviews. Journalists have embraced Twitter as an instant source of pithy quotes, publishing tweets from celebrities and other users to add colour to articles on a wide range of topics. Researchers can do the same, treating online media as sources for the study of death, mourning and celebrity culture. As with any research methodology, this approach suffers from a number of weaknesses and limitations and these require rigorous attention. It may, for example, be difficult to establish the context of the author and the intended and actual audience of the message, and ethical issues of consent and privacy are also not clear-cut, but still these qualifications should not disguise the potential research value of social media.

Third, we see here one particularly clear example of the role of online media in actually changing the way death is experienced and shared. Twitter and Facebook were key to the vortextual storm of feedback loops and mutual references, at first pre-empting traditional media, then repeating stories, reporting on television coverage and eventually offering material for journalists to discuss. There are shifts here not only in how people hear news of a death, but in which member of a social network is first to the news and passes that information to friends and family. The form in which news is shared changes, from house visits or telephone calls to brief 140-character updates. New opportunities to share feelings, adopt a public voice, and become part of the story both reflect and contribute to the

---

[14] Tamar Anitai, 'Remembering Michael Jackson: Memories on Twitter and Facebook', *MTV Buzzworthy Blog* (26 June 2009).

[15] Cha et al., 'Measuring User Influence'.

[16] Sankaranarayanan et al., 'TwitterStand'.

shaping of celebrity culture. There are numerous unanswered questions here, but the potential significance of these changes is considerable.

Death Online: A Brief Survey

So far, this discussion has recorded some of the wide range of online practices appropriated in times of mourning, particularly the use of digital media to share information and responses. In the following sections we will outline three other areas of particular interest: online memorials, social networks and online communities, while engaging with recent scholarship and discussing methodological questions where appropriate, all as part of demonstrating the relevance of these areas to the three research dimensions identified above.

Online Memorials

I use the broad category of 'online memorials' to refer to all online platforms established to create a long-term focus for tributes and expressions of mourning, moving beyond the instant communication of Twitter or Facebook status updates to construct a site to which the designer, wider community or general public can return time and again. These may be focused on a particular event, or dedicated to specific celebrities or private individuals.

Online memorial websites have existed since at least 1995, when The World Wide Cemetery (www.cemetery.org) was founded in Canada[17] and Web Healing (www.webhealing.org) in the United States.[18] Over time, these online spaces have appropriated new media and communication possibilities to develop much more elaborate memorial platforms. Mourners can create their own sites or occupy a page in a larger virtual cemetery, sometimes paying a one-off fee or ongoing rent. Typical features include libraries of favourite texts, poems and reflections, photo albums, videos, audio recordings, music and opportunities for visitors to add their own tributes to an archive or guest book.

Pamela Roberts has been writing about online cemeteries since the mid-1990s, and reports that almost all the memorial creators she has surveyed have told other people about their website.[19] This can operate as an indirect channel for demonstrating emotion to other survivors, as well as an effort to help those other readers with their own mourning and to preserve the memory of the deceased. Most had visited the website with another person, sitting together at their computer. The sites studied by Roberts also reached other audiences, however, including

---

[17]   Cypress Chang and Carla Sofka, 'Coping with Loss in Chinese and North American "Cyberspace" Communities: E-Temples and Virtual Cemeteries', *The Forum* 32(4) (2006).

[18]   Tom Golden, 'Healing and the Internet', *The Forum* 32(4) (2006).

[19]   Pamela Roberts, 'From My Space to Our Space: The Functions of Web Memorials in Bereavement', *The Forum* 32(4) (2006).

many people entirely unconnected to the deceased: almost half of the comments on these cemetery guest books were written by strangers, using the memorial to connect with and offer support to other people enduring similar kinds of loss. In some cases, these unknown visitors may be invited to the site through links and webrings connecting online memorials into networks of shared grief.

According to Tom Golden, founder of Web Healing, his site was intended to offer a 'safe space' for visitors to post their stories of grief, generating networks of actual and imagined connections between readers around the world. Golden quotes one author's description of the experience of reading their own story:

> It was a very special feeling. I felt as if I was entering a sanctuary. I've read the other stories before, often bursting into tears, feeling their grief and loss reflected in my own. Now reading about my experience with my own words, I feel affinity to a group of people scattered all over the world, linked by the common human experience of the loss of someone related to them with bonds stronger than death.[20]

Researchers have reported similar kinds of communities of shared grief emerging online around memorials for major disasters. According to Paul Arthur,

> storytelling in the online environment opens up remarkable new opportunities for people who would otherwise have been isolated in their grief to share their memories and emotions with a community of willing listeners, whose lives were suddenly changed by the events of that same moment in history.[21]

In addition to this sense of common experience, a wide range of other benefits can also be gained from online memorialisation. An online memorial space can be accessed globally at any time, offering a focus for mourning if the grave itself is distant or unknown. Sites may be erected very quickly, offering fixed content or inviting visitors to add their own comments, memories, images and tributes, and can serve at first to offer help and publicise arrangements. The easy addition, storage and access of multimedia resources makes it possible to combine images, artworks, sound recordings and video to create detailed, complex and flexible tributes that each individual can navigate according to their personal interests. Online memorials are also immune to the dangers of physical decay, although their permanence is subject to other considerations – 'the maintenance of a domain registration and a server, regular backups on evolving storage media, and occasional migration between platforms'.[22]

---

[20]   Golden, 'Healing and the Internet'.

[21]   Paul Arthur, 'Pixelated Memory: Online Commemoration of Trauma and Crisis', *Interactive Media* 4 (2008) p. 9.

[22]   Kirsten Foot, Barbara Warnick and Steven M. Schneider, 'Web-based Memorializing After September 11: Toward a Conceptual Framework', *Journal of Computer-Mediated*

The inclusion of guest books in many online memorials seems to intensify a kind of communication commonly identified as part of offline mourning practice. Friends and family members use online communication to post messages intended for the deceased, just as they might leave written messages at a gravesite. Kylie Veale describes online and offline memorials as 'surrogates' for the deceased, enabling survivors to maintain relationships that enable them to articulate and eventually recover from their grief. Communication is one part of these ongoing relationships: 'the living speak to the dead as if they were still alive, as the memorials become a "living" social presence for the deceased.'[23] This theme is further explored in the next section, in connection with social network sites.

Veale identifies physical proximity as a crucial factor in the effectiveness of offline memorials and graves, acting to invoke memory of the deceased. The Internet's lack of physicality therefore poses a problem, which is overcome by detail, imagery and sound:

> Similar to photo albums depicting the life of the deceased at funerals, I find online memorials mitigating their lack of proximity to the deceased by providing a vast array of textual and visual remembrances. A montage of photos, sounds, and video reflects the personal values of the deceased, and hence bring into play perhaps more remembrance than a static physical memorial.

Foot et al. examine a series of online memorials to the 9/11 terrorist attacks, and identify both similarities and differences between these online spaces and more traditional forms of public memorialising:

> Webbased public memorials often display the same characteristics seen in offline public commemorative sites—imposed uniformity of expression, limitations on what can be said, and the sort of fixity that accompanies officially planned memorials.[24]

These features are not universal, however, and Foot also identifies important shifts. Online sites can blur the categories of public memorialising, 'controlled, official, carefully planned forms of expression' which emerged in the late nineteenth and early twentieth centuries, and vernacular memorialising, 'often manifested more immediately after the loss ... unplanned in its inception'.[25] In offline memorials these categories can engage and co-opt one another, so that 'institutionally-sponsored memorials ... become sites for individual, personal memorializing'. The Internet greatly facilitates this merging of categories, and both the institutional

---

Communication 11 (2006) p. 79.

[23] Kylie Veale, 'Online Memorialisation: The Web as a Collective Memorial Landscape for Remembering the Dead', *Fibreculture* 3 (2004).

[24] Foot et al., 'Web-based Memorializing', p. 78.

[25] Ibid., p. 75.

and individual-created websites examined by Foot combined customary 'public' themes, including the emphasis of impersonal values and ideals, with a more 'vernacular' interest in recording the details of specific individual lives.

In some cases, online memorials are being integrated into the official services offered by funeral directors,[26] a development criticised by Roberts who argues that official packages are stilted, rushed and highly controlled.[27] Funerals can be broadcast live online or recorded for subsequent download, to allow those unable to attend to participate in some way in the event. In some cases, kiosks can be erected in cemeteries to allow visitors to access archives of images, videos, recordings, tributes and poems.

Social Network Sites

The online memorials discussed above are dedicated pages, created within virtual cemeteries or as stand-alone websites. There are clear parallels here with the role of the physical cemetery, which relocates the deceased to a place which is accessible but separate from the spaces usually occupied by the living. This is only one option, however, because if the deceased and their social circle were active online it is likely that the key communication spaces, systems and mediated networks through which those relationships were maintained in life will continue to exist after their death. Instead of creating a new memorial website, friends and family members can choose to treat the still-existing online presence of the deceased as a site for tributes and continued conversation, integrating their mourning practices directly into their ongoing social relationships.

Facebook, to pick the best-known example, is an enormously popular social network site that permits users to create their own profile page, upload photographs and connect with friends. One-line 'status updates' posted by one user are received by all that user's Facebook friends, and this constant stream of status messages is aggregated into a 'news feed' keeping each user constantly updated with the communications of all their social contacts. Users can also create and join groups or pages, generating smaller networks with their own dedicated communication spaces. When a user dies, friends and family have several options: they can continue to post messages straight to that user's profile page as if he or she were still alive, contact Facebook management and ask to have that page 'memorialised' to remove certain communication options and delete now-sensitive contact information, or create a group in memory of the deceased.

The popularity of memorial pages and groups has attracted considerable attention from journalists, who now routinely turn to social network sites to gather quotes to illustrate stories about the accidental or violent deaths of teenagers. Scholarly attention has been much more limited, restricted in part by the delicate ethical problems raised by research in this field. Access to a profile page or

---

[26] Veale, 'Online Memorialisation'.

[27] Roberts, 'From My Space to Our Space', p. 4.

group usually requires the consent of the owner, and requesting such consent in the immediate aftermath of a traumatic death could be enormously insensitive. One response to this challenge is to seek out volunteers to interview, identifying bereaved individuals who have and asking them to describe their use of digital media. This approach has been adopted by Odom et al., who posted adverts to online forums, email lists and through a bereavement counsellor and reported a wide range of findings:

> One emergent theme can be characterized as participants' continued use of communication systems in order to communicate with loved ones, despite their passing. Our participants described a range of activities, such as sending private messages to a departed loved one's email account ... posting messages on social networking website pages dedicated to the departed ... and continuing to call and text their loved one's mobile phone.[28]

Jocelyn deGroot's 2009 PhD thesis[29] took a different approach, focusing on Facebook memorial groups that were open to public access, giving no indication of her presence as a researcher, and then recruiting a handful of interviewees through recommendations from acquaintances. Almost every message posted to these memorial groups was addressed to the deceased, rather than other readers, just as in the memorial guest books discussed above. 'Some of these people would write weekly, or even daily, to tell the deceased person about their day or just to say hello',[30] a practice deGroot interprets as an attempt to maintain their relationship with the deceased while making sense of life without them. In some cases, this was apparently interpreted literally – 'group members referred to their deceased friend checking his or her Facebook from heaven'[31] – but living readers were also important, acting as a secondary, often unacknowledged audience for postings. Messages to the deceased could also operate to give comfort to the living, demonstrate grief and emotion, compete with other mourners for pre-eminence, and marginalise contributors perceived to have no genuine relationship with the deceased.

This last comment points to another important issue in which the use of social network sites as spaces for mourning can be seen to differ from the creation of memorial websites in the crucial respect of the demographics of users, and therefore of the kinds of relationships operating between mourner and deceased.

---

[28]   William Odom et al., 'Passing On and Putting to Rest: Understanding Bereavement in the Context of Interactive Technologies', *Proceedings of Computer-Human Interaction 2010: Death and Fear* (2010).

[29]   Jocelyn deGroot, 'Reconnecting with the Dead via Facebook: Examining Transcorporeal Communication as a Way to Maintain Relationships' (PhD thesis, Ohio University, 2009).

[30]   Ibid., p. 99.

[31]   Ibid., p. 86.

Classmates are still somewhat more likely to use Facebook than parents, and this kind of digital mourning can in some cases redefine who leads the mourning group, who can comment, what kind of relationships are displayed, what activities are referred to, and what language is used. Traditional chief mourners, like parents, may find themselves dismayed and wrong-footed by this unwanted contest over the memory of the deceased.

Online Communities

So far, this chapter has discussed a range of online responses to death and mourning, including the sharing of information, the construction of online cemeteries, and the conversion of social network sites designed for communication among the living into spaces for communication with the dead. In each case, digital media are used to share mourning practices with family, friends and strangers, reflecting both the integration of digital media into everyday life and the potential to find new audiences and connections online. These online audiences can be transient, forming loose, short-lived networks around a particular event, but in some cases new connections created online can develop into enduring 'online communities'. Such groups use digital media as their primary and often their only form of communication, and can be found in email lists, web forums, chatrooms, virtual worlds and online games. When participants die, the response of their online friends can be quite different from those identified above.

My own research over the past five years has focused on 'online churches', Christian groups using digital media to share worship, prayer, theological debate and mutual support in online environments. Participants often try to attract new believers online, but the great majority also attend a local church and regard their online activity as a helpful addition to more traditional forms of religious practice rather than any kind of replacement. These groups emphasise friendship, honesty, openness and supportiveness in their online communication, and these themes are displayed with particular intensity during periods of mourning.

One church, St Pixels, has been discussed in print by a group member, Mark Howe, who chooses to demonstrate the reality and significance of online relationships and online belonging through a story of death:

> T was a regular participant in St Pixels … Then, suddenly, T stopped logging in. One of our members managed to piece together the story from local newspaper reports. T had been injured in an accident and died of complications a few weeks later. His funeral had been conducted by a minister he had never met. Another member contacted the family, who were unaware of T's involvement in St Pixels, and asked if they would be happy for the community to hold a virtual memorial service. The family agreed, and registered on the website in order to

attend. One Saturday evening, T's virtual friends gathered in the sanctuary to share their stories about T and to pay their last respects.[32]

This 'sanctuary' is one part of the community chatroom, allowing all participants to communicate through type while the service leader posts texts, images and audio recordings. According to Howe, this online service – at which people who cared about T were able to gather from several continents in a space he had enjoyed, under the leadership of a minister he had known personally – was arguably superior to the physical funeral. T's online friends chose to puncture the social barrier T had maintained between his family and his online activity, but this is not always necessary. The death of another community member, 'S', was communicated to St Pixels by family members, and again these family members chose to join the site to take part in the memorial service.

Both T and S were commemorated through tribute threads in the St Pixels forums. The majority of messages posted to these threads are framed as direct communications to the deceased, some including reassurance that the deceased will be reading those messages from the afterlife. Other themes include support (particularly prayers for the family), memories of the deceased (preserving a particular image of their character and habits and demonstrating a close relationship with the author), and celebration of particular practices (S posted a daily hymn verse, and group members posted their own contributions to continue that tradition).

These examples reflect one kind of online community death practice – the intensification and celebration of group bonds through shared mourning. A completely different kind of event occurred in 2006 in the online game *World of Warcraft* (*WoW*), when a player with the username 'Fayejin' suffered a stroke and died. Her associates in the game decided to organise a memorial event within the virtual world, and posted the following message to a popular *WoW* forum:

> On Tuesday of February 28th Illidan lost not only a good mage, but a good person. [...] I'm making this post basically to inform everyone that might have knew her. Also tomorrow, at 5:30 server time March, 4th. We will have an in game memorial for her so that her friends can pay their respects. We will be having it at the Frostfire Hot Springs in Winterspring, because she loved to fish in the game (she liked the sound of the water, it was calming for her) and she loved snow.[33]

This event parallels some aspects of St Pixels' memorial services, particularly the decision to host a dedicated gathering within the online environment, but in

---

[32]   Mark Howe, *Online Church? First Steps Towards Virtual Incarnation* (Cambridge: Grove Pastoral, 2007).

[33]   'Memorial to Fayejin', forums.illidrama.com/showthread.php?1826-Memorial-to-Fayejin.

this case the environment was selected from a wide range of possible spaces to reflect the personality and taste of the deceased. Video footage shows a long line of mourners queuing up to spend a few moments with Fayejin's character, resurrected for the occasion by another player with access to her game account.

Unsurprisingly, subsequent posts to this forum thread show significant cultural differences between the supportive Christian church and the combat-oriented computer game. Organisers are quickly forced to clarify the nature of the event – would there be a fishing contest? Would there be a fight? – and plead with readers not to 'mess things up'. Alas, these messages had already been seen by members of a rival guild, 'Serenity Now', who organised a mass raid on the funeral party, slaughtered the mourners – including the character of Fayejin – and posted a video to YouTube.[34] That video became an online phenomenon, reposted and discussed across the Internet, and attracted over 4.5 million views and 38,600 comments on YouTube alone by the beginning of July 2010.

These online discussions swiftly polarised into two points of view, each marked by considerable mutual animosity. According to one camp, the emotional significance of the death of Fayejin elevated her funeral out of game-space and created a different set of social norms, which demanded respect from other *WoW* players. According to their opponents, this was nonsense: *WoW* is a game built on contest and battle, including battle between players, and the idea of a sacrosanct funeral event showed a complete misunderstanding of the rules and spirit of the game. As Monica Evans has argued, this is not a simple debate:

> both groups hold an entirely valid way of looking at the gamespace, and conflict only arose when the two ethical belief systems came into close proximity. Both the mourners and the funeral raiders are clearly invested in the gamespace, but for very different reasons, and the mourners consider the funeral event to be much more 'real' and meaningful than the raiders.[35]

Each of these two cases demonstrates the power of death and mourning to illuminate values, tensions and competing priorities within online groups. In St Pixels, online responses to the death of T illustrate some of the complexities of the relationship between online and everyday life. Participants can integrate online and offline activity, like S, or keep them separate, like T, and may derive a range of different benefits from those decisions. The story of Fayejin's funeral reflects different concerns, including conflicting understandings of 'appropriate' behaviour and – one may speculate – different goals. Hosting a funeral celebrates and strengthens relational bonds, while destroying that funeral and posting videos online guarantees instant attention and long-lasting infamy.

---

[34]   'Serenity Now Bombs a World of Warcraft Funeral', www.youtube.com/watch?v=IHJVoIaC8pw.

[35]   Monica Evans, 'Murder, Ransom, Theft and Grief: Understanding Digital Ethics in Games' (2009) p. 6.

Conclusions

This chapter has not attempted to cover every aspect of online death and mourning. A more comprehensive survey would also need to include the use of search engines to find information about illness and death, the use of blogs as spaces to document one's own dying process and learn from the experiences of others, the emergence of online communities dedicated to certain categories of illness or loss and the use of the Internet by teenagers considering suicide, as well as the moral panics raised by journalists in their coverage of those activities. Another dimension might include the regularly-documented appearance online of individuals who pretend to sicken and die in order to attract intense emotional support from the online communities they target. Nonetheless, the four areas discussed reflect some of the most important examples of online mourning practice and serve to demonstrate the importance of the three themes I originally identified.

Scholars trying to learn more about digital media have already made considerable use of case studies of death and grief, and will continue to do so. Anyone interested in the construction of ethical frameworks in computer games, for example, can learn a great deal from reading the endless discussions of Fayejin's funeral; anyone interested in the impact of online media on the news industry can study the relationship between independent blogs, official newspaper websites and Twitter following the death of Michael Jackson. Researchers interested in death can analyse the vast numbers of personal responses posted to different online platforms, or study the impact of a death within an online community where almost every interaction is archived and available to view. The integration of digital media into mourning practice is already changing the experience of death in significant ways, and further attention should be paid to a wide range of issues in both the sociology and the psychology of dying and grief. Such studies could be valuable not only for increasing our understanding of contemporary death – how quickly does news spread and how do people respond? – but also in developing new online platforms to help mourners express and work through their grief. In all three areas, further work is needed, all within what is a highly interdisciplinary field, where scholars of different disciplines can learn much from one another, and future collaborations between scholars of death, students of new media and computer scientists can hope to achieve remarkable results.

References

Anitai, Tamar, 'Remembering Michael Jackson: Memories on Twitter and Facebook', *MTV Buzzworthy Blog* (26 June 2009). Available at: http://buzzworthy.mtv.com/2009/06/26/remebering-michael-jackson-memories-on-twitter-and-facebook/ [*sic*] (accessed 1 August 2009).

Arthur, Paul, 'Pixelated Memory: Online Commemoration of Trauma and Crisis', *IM Interactive Media* 4 (2008). 1-19.

Blankstein, Andrew, and Phil Willon, 'Michael Jackson is Dead', *L.A. Now* (25 June 2009). Available at: http://latimesblogs.latimes.com/lanow/2009/06/pop-star-michael-jackson-was-rushed-to-a-hospital-this-afternoon-by-los-angeles-fire-department-paramedics--capt-steve-ruda.html.

Busari, Stephanie, 'Michael Jackson Memorial Draws Crowds Online', *CNN.com* (8 July 2009). Available at:http://edition.cnn.com/2009/TECH/07/07/michael.jackson.web.traffic/index.html (accessed 1 June 2010).

Castells, Manuel, *The Rise of the Network Society: The Information Age: Economy, Society and Culture*, Vol 1. (Oxford: Blackwell, 1996).

Cha, Meeyoung, Hamed Haddadi, Fabricio Benevenuto and Krishna P. Gummadi, 'Measuring User Influence in Twitter: The Million Follower Fallacy', *Proceedings of the Fourth International AAAI Conference on Weblogs and Social Media* (2010). Available at: http://twitter.mpi-sws.org/ (accessed 1 December 2011).

Chang, Cypress, and Carla Sofka, 'Coping with Loss in Chinese and North American "Cyberspace" Communities: E-Temples and Virtual Cemeteries', *The Forum* 32(4) (2006). 7. Available at: http://www.adec.org/AM/Template.cfm?Section=The_Forum&Template=/CM/ContentDisplay.cfm&ContentID=1554 (accessed 1 December 2011).

Cohn, Emily, 'Michael Jackson Twitter Mania', *Forbes.com* (7 July 2009). Available at: www.forbes.com/2009/07/07/twitter-michael-jackson-technology-internet-twitter.html (accessed 1 June 2010).

deGroot, Jocelyn, 'Reconnecting with the Dead via Facebook: Examining Transcorporeal Communication as a Way to Maintain Relationships' (PhD thesis, Scripps College of Communication, Ohio University, 2009).

Evans, Monica, 'Murder, Ransom, Theft, and Grief: Understanding Digital Ethics in Games (draft)' (unpublished paper, 2009). Available at: www.inter-disciplinary.net/wp-content/uploads/2009/06/Evans-paper.pdf (accessed 1 June 2010).

Fast, Susan, 'Difference that Exceeded Understanding: Remembering Michael Jackson (1958–2009)', *Popular Music and Society* 33(2) (2010), 259-266.

Foot, Kirsten, Barbara Warnick and Steven M. Schneider, 'Web-based Memorializing After September 11: Toward a Conceptual Framework', *Journal of Computer-Mediated Communication* 11 (2006). Available at: http://jcmc.indiana.edu/vol11/issue1/foot.html (accessed 1 December 2011).

Golden, Tom, 'Healing and the Internet', *The Forum* 32(4) (2006). 8. http://www.adec.org/AM/Template.cfm?Section=The_Forum&Template=/CM/ContentDisplay.cfm&ContentID=1554 (accessed 1 December 2011).

Howe, Mark, *Online Church? First Steps Towards Virtual Incarnation* (Cambridge: Grove Pastoral, 2007).

Odom, William, Richard Harper, Abigail Sellen, David Kirks and Richard Banks, 'Passing On and Putting to Rest: Understanding Bereavement in the Context of Interactive Technologies', *Proceedings of Computer-Human Interaction*

2010: Death and Fear (2010). Available at: http://research.microsoft.com/pubs/120862/972-odom.pdf (accessed 1 December 2011).

Rawlinson, Linnie, and Nick Hunt, 'Jackson Dies, Almost Takes Internet With Him', *CNN.com/technology* (26 June 2009). Available at: www.cnn.com/2009/TECH/06/26/michael.jackson.internet (accessed 1 June 2010).

Roberts, Pamela, 'From My Space to Our Space: The Functions of Web Memorials in Bereavement', *The Forum* 32(4) (2006). 1, 3-4. Available at: http://www.adec.org/AM/Template.cfm?Section=The_Forum&Template=/CM/ContentDisplay.cfm&ContentID=1554 (accessed 1 December 2011).

Sankaranarayanan, Jagan, Hanan Samet, Benjamin E. Teitler, Michael D. Lieberman and Jon Sperling, 'TwitterStand: News in Tweets', in *Proceedings of the 17th ACM SIGSPATIAL International Conference on Advances in Geographic Information Systems* (Seattle 2009). 42-51. Available at: http://www.cs.umd.edu/~hjs/pubs/twitter-gis2009.pdf (accessed 1 December 2011).

TMZ staff, 'Michael Jackson Dies', *TMZ* (25 June 2009). Available at: www.tmz.com/2009/06/25/michael-jackson-dies-death-dead-cardiac-arrest.

Veale, Kylie, 'Online Memorialisation: The Web as a Collective Memorial Landscape for Remembering the Dead', *Fibreculture* 3 (2004). Available at: http://www.fibreculture.org/journal/issue3/issue3_veale.html (accessed 1 December 2011).

Whannel, Gary, 'News, Celebrity and Vortextuality: A Study of the Media Coverage of the Michael Jackson Verdict', *Cultural Politics* 6(1) (2010). 65-84.

Chapter 5

Individuals and Relationships: On the Possibilities and Impossibilities of Presence

Arnar Árnason

Introduction

Classic western grief theory and therapy teaches that death is the end of the relationship between the living and the dead. It adds that a key task of grieving for the living is to work through their emotions towards the deceased and readjust their identity. According to the more recent theory of continuing bonds it is both normal and healthy for the living to maintain their relationship with the deceased after death. The task of grieving is to renegotiate a relationship that changes but continues after death. In both theories assumptions are made regarding emotions, identity, relationships or bonds, and the intricate interplay between these. In this chapter I examine these assumptions and will focus in particular on the problematic idea of presence, a fundamental assumption when it comes to emotions, relationships and identity.

As an outsider looking in it appears to me that 1996 marked something of a watershed in applied academic writings on grief. On this the European side of the Atlantic the inaugural issue of *Mortality* opened with Tony Walter's (1996) now influential paper on the 'biographical model of grief'. There Walter argued that bereavement counselling, as practised in the UK at least, emphasises 'emotion work' (see also Hockey 1990), the working through of emotions. He suggested that, in contrast to this, many bereaved people need to talk about the deceased not least with others who knew them. By this the bereaved, Walter added, seek to establish a durable biography of the deceased and find for them a place in their own ongoing lives. Across the waters meanwhile 1996 saw the publication of the seminal work *Continuing Bonds*. The central thesis of continuing bonds is that under the influence of western ideology – or the particular aspect of it that MacPherson (1962) called possessive individualism – classic western psychological theories present disengagement from the deceased as the aim of grief. In their introduction to volume two the editors note that to 'experience a continuing bond with the deceased in the present has been thought of as symptomatic of psychological problems'. They add that a 'continued attachment to the deceased was called unresolved grief' (Silverman and Klass 1996: 4), and has been 'considered symptomatic of pathology' (Silverman and Klass 1996: 5). Against this view Silverman and Klass (1996: 18) 'propose that it is normative for mourners to maintain a presence and connection with the deceased, and that this presence is not static'. Bereavement, they continue, is not an emotional state that comes to an end and from which people recover. It is a cognitive process 'that takes place in the social context of which the deceased is a part'.

There are of course differences of emphasis between Walter's biographical model and the continuing bonds thesis. But both emphasise the importance of ongoing relationships between the bereaved and the deceased and do so in opposition to what they see as dominant theory and practice in grief work. This surely amounted to a watershed. Even so, in what follows I will speak mostly of the continuing bond thesis.

I am a social anthropologist trained in the British tradition of anthropology. This tradition emphasises the fundamental importance of social relationships in human life (see Strathern 2005). I am, as such, extremely sympathetic to the idea of continuing bonds. Indeed my own writings on grief, such as they are, have to date argued for the importance of attending to the ongoing relations between the living and the dead. But, as Strathern (2005) has pointed out, relations are an integral part of western knowledge making practices. Moreover, relationships are important in our knowledge making precisely because we assume the existence of the units (if I can be forgiven being vague for a moment at least) that relationships are understood to link. Thus in the spirit conjured up by Strathern I will seek here to question somewhat the idea of continuing bonds. My questioning will take two seemingly contradictory forms. Drawing on ethnographic and interview material from Japan – examples from there having been important in the development of the idea of continuing bonds – I suggest that for some people the idea of continuing bonds is problematic because it suggests a separation between them and their dead ones. Second, I will investigate the assumption of presence that informs the idea of continuing bonds. I will attempt to demonstrate how it relies upon the western notion of the experiencing subject, a close relative of the individualism to which the continuing bonds thesis objects.

I begin with a closer look at continuing bonds before briefly describing the anthropological engagement with death in Japan and moving to the ethnographic material. Having raised an ethnographic question regarding continuing bonds I will then investigate more closely the idea of presence as central to the continuing bond thesis.

Continuing Bonds

Introducing *Continuing Bonds*, two of the editors, Phyllis Silverman and Dennis Klass, argue that the accepted understanding of grief in twentieth-century western society has been that 'the mourner must disengage from the deceased'. Upon death, that is, the relationship between the bereaved and the deceased has been understood as coming to an end with the consequence that bonds had to be severed, discontinued. Silverman and Klass find this understanding of grief in

Freud and his followers in bereavement work, Bowlby and Parkes. They argue that this insistence on the severing of the bond between the bereaved and the deceased is 'a 20th-century phenomenon. Only in the past 100 years have continuing bonds been denied as a normal part of bereavement behavior' (1996: 5).

Offering a markedly anthropological or sociological argument, Silverman and Klass (1996: 14–16) cite the emphasis upon individual autonomy in western societies as the source for the continued insistence on disengagement. They argue that the 'model of grief that began with Freud is based on a view of the world that stresses how separate people are from each other' (Silverman and Klass 1996: 14). According to Silverman and Klass (1996: 14; following the contribution of Stroebe et al. to their volume) 'there is a consistent basic understanding of the nature of the self and the nature of the self's bonds to others at the heart of the common 20th-century model of grief'. This understanding, Silverman and Klass continue, is characteristic of modern western societies, it 'is not the operant model in human societies in other times and places' (1996: 14). 'A central feature in the modern Western world view', they add, 'is the value placed on autonomy and individuation' (1996: 14). 'Autonomy is the stated goal of human development' (Erikson, 1963; Miller, 1986). Independence, rather than interdependence, is prized. Being dependent is judged as "bad". Relationships with others are viewed instrumentally' (Silverman and Klass 1996: 14–15).

Silverman and Klass (1996: 18) argue 'that it is normative for mourners to maintain a presence and connection with the deceased'. Bereavement, they add, is an ongoing cognitive process rather than an emotional state from which the bereaved recovers. Silverman and Klass emphasise the 'social context of which the deceased is a part'. Bereaved people 'are changed by the experience; they do not get over it, and part of the change is a transformed but continuing relationship with the deceased' (1996: 19). Silverman and Klass borrow the term 'accommodation' from development psychologist Jean Piaget to refer to this process. This, they suggest, captures the experience of bereavement better than such words as recovery, resolution or closure. 'Accommodation', Silverman and Klass (1996: 19) continue, 'does not disregard past relationships, but incorporates them into a larger whole. In this process, people seek to gain not only an understanding of the meaning of death, but a sense of the meaning of this now dead or absent person in their present lives'.

Silverman and Klass then argue that a discontinuing of bonds is kept in place by the western ideology of individualism. As such, discontinuity is not universal but rather a characteristic of modern western societies, although not necessarily uniquely characteristic of these societies. Given that discontinuing bonds is, in other words, a socially constructed and culturally specific notion, it is not surprising that many examples of continuing bonds may be found to exist, with Japan being a particularly important case in the development of the continuing bond thesis. To this I now turn.

The Land of the Dead

The western scholarly enterprise is particularly well served when it comes to death in Japan. Numerous excellent anthropological, sociological and historical studies already exist describing in exquisite detail the intricacies of the extensive and lengthy Japanese mortuary rituals, from the funeral through the daily observances in front of the Buddhist household altar (*butsudan*) to the periodic memorial services that follow, and the annual celebration of *obon*. Anthropologists have pinpointed the enormous variability that exists in what is maybe wrongly termed 'ancestor worship' in Japan (see Smith 1974). They have illuminated the path of the deceased towards ancestorhood (Bachnik 1995; Hamabata 1990), and have spoken of the way in which roles, rights and responsibilities are redistributed at the death of household heads (Bachnik 1995; Hamabata 1990). They have narrated the history of the Buddhist house altar. They have detailed the debated influence of the dead on the world of the living, and the influence of the living on the world of the dead (Hardacre 1997). They have related the often aggressive promotion of Buddhist requiems for aborted foetuses and other dear departed (Hardacre 1997; LaFleur 1992) and the consequences of these, including for aspects of the Japanese economic miracle. They have disclosed the workings of the Japanese funeral industry and have described ideas about the nature, causes and consequences of death (Lock 1980 and 2002; Long 1980 and 1999 Ohnuki-Tierney 1984).

The explanatory frameworks erected to contain these stories tend to be either symbolic where culturally specific ideas make sense because of their links to other ideas, or sociological, where certain activities and ideas seem sensible and necessary because of what they may contribute to safeguarding the social against the threatening chaos of death. The importance and endurance of the *ie* household system and the role of ancestor worship as the religion of the *ie* is a case in point here (Plath 1964).

These studies all speak to and offer evidence of continuing bonds as an integral part of death rituals in Japan. Here, then, the focus is very much on rituals and ideas, on what they mean and on the effect they have on society or social groups. In contrast to this, the seminal work of Yamamoto and colleagues (Yamamoto et al. 1969; see Yamamoto 1970) focuses on the psychological effects of Japanese mourning rituals rather than on their cultural meanings or social functions. According to Yamamoto and colleagues (Yamamoto 1970; Yamamoto et al. 1969) Japanese widows adjust comparatively well to the loss of their husbands. This they attribute to how Japanese mourning rituals require and allow for the continuing relationship between the living and the dead. Japanese widows, for example, frequently find themselves taking care of their deceased husbands in much the same way as they did when they were alive. Here again the focus is on rituals, but on what they do for individuals and their psychological well-being.

This is the line taken by the continuing bond thesis. Dennis Klass (1996), in particular, evokes Japanese mortuary rites in support of continuing bonds. In Japan, as he explains, we find 'an elaborate set of rituals, supported by a sophisticated theory, by which those who are living maintain personal, emotional bonds with those who have died'. Here then the dead are 'available to the living' (Klass 1996: 59) as long as there is a living memory of the deceased. In many households rituals are performed morning and evening in front of the Buddhist household altar, the *butsudan*, which houses the spirits of the deceased members of the household. On these occasions, freshly cooked rice is offered, prayers may be said and news of the family shared with the deceased. The living may also seek the help of deceased and guidance in particular matters, for example how to deal with their children.

Yamamoto and colleagues (Yamamoto 1970; Yamamoto et al. 1969) concluded that Japanese widows adjust better to their loss than British widows because of the continuing bond they retain with the deceased. This is the lead followed by the editors of *Continuing Bonds*. I want to emphasise that I seek, here, not to question the potential psychological benefits of continuing bonds in Japan or elsewhere. Indeed, I find it easy to accept that it may be beneficial to the living that their deceased loved ones are available to them. But I want to examine more closely the idea of bond and of the presence it assumes. And I begin with a Japanese story of grief.

Kokoro no naka ni iru. To You, by Yuki

> You, in grief at the loss of your loved one. You, at a loss for what to do in your life. Still, bravely you became a member of this group. Yet, you hesitate to participate in the meetings. But all the members had to go through this, to travel this road, and you will too. This is the place we finally arrived at as we looked for safety and light.
>
> A drowning man will clutch at straws. For me this group was a straw when I was drowning. My husband left me and our daughter. I had to do everything by myself as the head of the household. Other people's casual remarks whipped my heart [*kokoro*] in sorrow. I felt everyone in this world was my enemy.

Thus did Aoyama Yuki (pseudonym) write in a small newsletter of a self-help bereavement group. When I first met Yuki she knew I was interested in death in Japan and that I had done some work on death and grief in the UK. She approached and introduced herself telling me that she had lost her husband. As we got to know each other I learnt that Yuki constantly felt that she was not coping as well as she should be, that her grief was somehow abnormal, too prolonged. This, Yuki said, was what other people's remarks – the remarks that whipped her heart – made her feel. She asked: how did people in England grieve? For how long? Was her grief normal, or were her 'enemies' right? It was at this time that Yuki told me that she thought that there were two reasons for her grief proving so heavy (*omoi*), both of which relate to the story of her husband's, Haruki's, illness.

It was in January, Yuki told me, that Haruki became ill with a 'cold' (*kaze*). 'Cold', famously (Lock 1980; Ohnuki-Tierney 1984), is a generalised category of often rather unspecific illnesses in Japan, illnesses that can always strike but which are to be expected at times when the weather is either especially hot or cold or particularly changeable. Suffering from a cold can be a legitimate excuse for taking time out from the responsibilities of everyday life in a society were extended holidays are regarded with some suspicion (Lock 1980; Ohnuki-Tierney 1984). Thus the common Japanese farewell 'please don't catch a cold' (*kaze o hikanaide kudasai*) can be seen as a somewhat double-edged concern for the well-being of others with a hint of a reminder of their duties to society.

In the beginning Haruki's illness was little more than a sore throat that would not go away. He continued working, keeping going with vast amounts of the vitamin drinks in small brown bottles so popular in Japan and so aggressively marketed as a bullet-proof cure for tiredness and indeed anything else that may prevent you from working. As is common in Japan the responsibility for monitoring Haruki's health, for making and often attending doctor's appointments and for understanding, translating and communicating doctors' verdicts, fell on the housewife (see Lock 1980). Yuki spent considerable time pouring over German medical terms, common in Japanese medicine since the Meiji era, which the doctor refrained from explaining. Doctors enjoy enormous respect in Japan (see Lock 1980; Ohnuki-Tierney 1984). They are invariably referred to and addressed by a term of respect *sensei* – teacher or master – indicating their authority and knowledge. Yuki did not feel in any position to question or press the doctor.

Haruki's symptoms persisted, indeed they got worse and more extensive examinations followed. Yuki continued to serve as a go-between and so it was that one day, when she was home alone, a telephone call came. The doctor informed Yuki that Haruki was terminally ill with lung cancer. He left it to her to decide the future course of action. Yuki describes the shock as unbearable, the sense of bewilderment as overwhelming, the lack of guidance and assistance as hurtful. At no point had the doctor told Haruki of his condition or impending fate or sat down with the couple to discuss these matters. This is not an uncommon yet by no means universal experience in Japan, where clear directions for doctors regarding what to do in the case of terminal illness did not exist at the time. The decision whether to tell Haruki or not was left with Yuki.

Yuki contacted Haruki's older brothers who told her not to tell Haruki, believing, as is not uncommon in Japan (Ohnuki-Tierney 1984), that knowledge of his imminent death would only harm his spirits. Yuki accepted this 'because they're his older brothers' – she speaks with clear reference to a Japanese hierarchy based on both seniority and gender (see Hendry 2003). Now she bitterly regrets her decision, her lack of power (*chikara ga nakatta*) to resist the authority of others and do things the way she wanted to do them. Because of this lack of power, Yuki says, she had to care for Haruki in his final months without being able to openly acknowledge the reality of his impending death. 'It was such a burden (*omoisa*)', she says, 'to have to keep this a secret (*himitsu*) from him'. Although she is pretty sure Haruki knew what was happening to him, she regrets not being able to discuss properly with him what was going on; to tell him how much she loved him; what he and their life together had meant to her; or, indeed, to hear words to similar effect about her from him. Yuki feels that in this, her lack of power, she failed not only herself but Haruki too. His death would have been a better one if she had had the strength to acknowledge it openly.

When I got to know Yuki, this had become the centre around which her grief revolved. It was a grief, she feared, that had been too prolonged, too heavy. While Yuki blames herself in part for this and wonders about how her coping compares with that of other people, both near and far, she understands too that her grief was made all the heavier, all the more enduring, by particular Japanese structures of authority in which Yuki knows herself to have been caught.

She recognised herself, then, as fuelled by a sense of guilt. Since her husband's death, Yuki has attended to him with exceptional dedication. She bought an expensive and, for the smallish house she has, a relatively big Buddhist altar (*butsudan*). Every Sunday, if she's at home, she goes to Haruki's grave where she washes the stone, replaces flowers, burns incense and offers prayers. Every day Yuki attends the *butsudan*, where, this being a new household, Haruki alone is enshrined. The first thing Yuki does every morning is to open the *butsudan*, arouse the *hotoke-sama* with a ring of the bell, offer him incense and a prayer and present him with newly cooked rice. Newly-cooked rice is also what Haruki is presented with at dinner time whenever it is on offer. The last thing Yuki does before going to bed is to bid her husband good night in his shrine and close the *butsudan*.

Yuki's *butsudan* is invariably decorated with seasonal fruits, different varieties of Japanese *mikan*, fresh flowers and elaborately wrapped Japanese sweets. Beside the photograph of Haruki stands his favourite sake and a bottle of beer. Kirin lager makes way for Asahi black beer, making way for Yebisu all malt, at fairly regular intervals. Every night, after dinner, Yuki brings Haruki a cup of green tea and lights him a cigarette and lets it burn in the incense holder. Yuki does not smoke but her husband liked cigarettes a lot, she explains. He liked them so much, she continues wryly, that they killed him.

Yuki's acts of care-giving are, she says, for her own sake as much as for Haruki's. Yuki describes the result of her attending Haruki as a feeling that is maybe best rendered as 'relief' (*anshin dekita*) in English. Lifting her arms a little she says that it is as if, at least momentarily, a weight is lifted off her shoulders. Yet, Yuki's sense of relief is, she says, inseparable from her care for Haruki and the way in which her actions now may help assuage her guilt for failing him when he was ill. As such Yuki clearly understands herself to benefit from Haruki's availability to her, to paraphrase Klass, from their continuing bond. Yet, tending to Haruki is not entirely unproblematic for Yuki. The problem it causes her speaks to the idea of a bond, a relationship.

One year I spent the August *obon* festival – during which the spirits of deceased family members return for a few days to visit their house – with Yuki and watched her go through all the proper rituals. Having watched the farewell fire that is lit for the departing spirits, and stepped over the dying embers in order to protect ourselves from 'diseases of the nether regions' (*shita no byouki*) we sat down with a cold drink. As I got ready for some wistful reminiscing I was taken aback by Yuki's proclamation. 'I hate *obon*', she said to me unusually forcefully. I was very surprised, to say the least. I thought Yuki of all people would enjoy *obon*. Her everyday dedication to her husband, her careful fulfilling of her ritual duties suggested to me that she would welcome the idea of her husband's return. 'What is it about *obon* you don't like?' I asked. 'I don't like the idea of my husband coming and then going', Yuki explained to me, 'my husband is always with me. He's in my heart (*kokoro no naka ni iru*)'. This, it turned out, was part of a wider concern that was playing on Yuki's mind, a concern not only to do with the *obon* festival. She had gradually come to feel quite strongly that it was unnatural for her to address her husband in the *butsudan* or indeed at the grave (*haka*). 'My husband is in my heart (*kokoro no naka ni iru*)' she says, 'how can I talk to him like he exists outside me?'. What troubled Yuki was the externalisation, even the objectification, of her husband that the ritual practice assumes. This is of course in line with the idea of a bond, or a relationship, more generally. A relationship, by definition, connects at least two otherwise separate entities (Strathern 2005): Yuki and her husband for example. And this, it seems to me, is not how things are for Yuki. She and her husband are not two people joined while at the same time also separated (Strathern 1988 and 2005) by a relationship, even if we understand that relationship as a continuing bond. Rather, for Yuki she and her husband are immersed in one another. He is in her heart while at the same time she is in him. When Yuki visited me later in the UK and went out to explore the city where I was living she always wore her husband's shirt. He became the skin to cover and protect her in an alien if exciting world.

I have suggested above that in some cases, even if it is only a very few cases, it may be misleading to speak of a bond, even a continuing bond, between the living and the dead. It may be misleading because a bond assumes a prior separation that may not be in accordance with how the bereaved understand themselves and their dead ones. While this suggestion is only intended as a minor question mark after the idea of continuing bond it partners another, equally minor question mark, that of 'presence', to which I devote this last main section of the chapter.

Presence

Presence is the surprising key word in the continuing bond thesis. It is the continuing presence of the deceased in the lives of the living that calls for the idea of continuing bonds. It is the experience of the living of that presence which is the crucial point. What are we to make of that presence?

Here I want to draw on the writings of geographer John Wylie (2009), specifically his observation that much of the recent writings on landscape have been informed by phenomenology. The phenomenology of landscape, according to Wylie, 'has sought to define landscape in terms of *presence* in various forms' (Wylie 2009: 9). What is emphasised in these writings is how 'self and world come close together, and touch each other, and then go beyond even that, and become part of each other' (Wylie 2009: 9).

The reader may well be wondering about this excursion into landscape theory in a chapter on grief. The suggestion I'm making is that Wylie's observations about recent landscape theory and certain of its basic assumptions are also applicable to the continuing bond thesis and to much of the literature on grief. Hoping that the reader is willing to entertain this suggestion I highlight Wylie's observation on the influence of the phenomenology of Merleau-Ponty (1968) in recent writings on landscape, especially its assumption of the '*possible-in-principle coincidence* of self with itself, and self with world' (Wylie 2009: 22). The fundamental assumption here is of a direct engagement between self and the world. And here the world for Wylie is landscape but could indeed be deceased loved ones whose presence the bereaved feel.

Now Wylie (2009: 22) evokes Jacques Derrida's critique of Merleau-Ponty's position. Derrida shows that Merleau-Ponty's 'accounts of self-other and self-world relations proceeds by demonstrating that these are founded upon a principle of "auto-affection" – a process in which I seem to coincide with myself, for example by touching myself, by hearing my own voice, or by thinking that I am thinking' (Wylie 2009: 22). Derrida's criticism of 'auto-affection' has to do with how 'Merleau-Ponty attempts to address the issue of my relationships with others, and with the "outside" world by analogising these relationships with my relation to myself' (Wylie 2009: 22). That is, Merleau-Ponty argues 'for the indubitable existence of a shared, common world of seeing and touching, an intersubjective world of intertwining bodies and gazes' (Wylie 2009: 22). Even so 'this shared world can only be posited, in existential phenomenology, from the basis of a primary presencing of me to myself – a givenness of the auto-affective, perceiving subject' (Wylie 2009: 22–3).

For 'Derrida … it is precisely this assumption regarding self coincidence, this "metaphysics of presence", that is the problem. How could I ever coincide with myself, be myself, in any fulsome way?' (Wylie 2009: 23). In a line that would seem to correspond beautifully with the idea of continuing bonds, Derrida (2005: 180; quoted in Wylie 2009: 23) argues that 'the constitution of the body … already presupposes a passage outside and through the other, as well as through absence, death and mourning'. I am haunted from without, constitutively, as Wylie (2009: 23) adds. But that correspondence is only partial, for the starting point of the continuing bond thesis is the experiencing subject who experiences the presence of the deceased. And in this, as I will go on to discuss, the continuing bond thesis retains an integral part of the western individualism it sought to leave behind.

Conclusion

Most studies on death in Japan, as I noted above, focus on extensive mortuary rites, their meanings and social functions. They have not, by and large, considered in detail the impact these rites have on people's psychology. It can thus be suggested that these anthropological and sociological studies appear to share with classic western social theory the assumption that social relations exist between points, or roles, in a structure, or at best *between* the people temporarily occupying these posts. As such the relations are seen to be *external* to the persons that they connect. Here the continuing bond thesis offers a markedly different perspective. It considers also the relations between people but emphasises the impact these relations have upon individual persons. Even so, we need to recognise that focusing on relations, as opposed to individuals, has long been part of western knowledge making practices (Strathern 2005). And we need to recognise too, as Yuki's story indicated, that relations assume separation as much and at the same time as they suggest connection (Strathern 2005).

Furthermore, as I argued above, the continuing bond thesis arrives at relationships from privileging the experiencing subject, a subject inseparable from the western individual (Mansfield 2000) from which the continuing bonds theme hoped to move away. Such a move may indeed require embracing what some call the anti-humanism of structuralism and post-structuralism that have attempted to make sense of cultural and social phenomenon without reference to subjectivity, consciousness (see Mansfield 2000).

The residue of the western individual is also evident in how the continuing bonds theme tends to read mortuary rituals in terms of their potential psychological benefit. In this, it seems to me, continuing or discontinuing bonds risks appearing to become a matter of choice. And in that some very western assumptions again slip in. As anthropologist Adam Reed (1999: 45) has pointed out, 'the juridical subject, [the] rights-bearing individual who acts to create [and I might add "sever"] relations and thereby cement society' is an important ideological figure in the western political imagination. As such the idea of continuing bonds may fit surprisingly well within western therapeutic practices. But if, in grief work, we want to consider ways that question rather than reinforce ideological positions, we may need to look beyond individuals and their relations.

References

Bachnik, J. 1995. 'Orchestrated reciprocity: belief versus practice in Japanese funeral ritual', in *Ceremony and Ritual in Japan: Religious Practices in an Industrialized Society*, edited by J. van Bremen and D.P. Martinez. London: Routledge, pp. 108–45.
Derrida, J. 2005. *On Touching: Jean-Luc Nancy*. Stanford: Stanford University Press.
Erikson, E.H. 1963. *Childhood and Society*. Second edition. New York: W.W. Norton.
Hamabata, M.M. 1990. *Crested Kimono: Power and Love in the Japanese Business Family*. Ithaca: Cornell University Press.

Hardacre, H. 1997. *Marketing the Menacing Fetus in Japan*. Berkeley: University of California Press.

Hendry, J. 2003 [1987]. *Understanding Japanese Society*. London: RoutledgeCurzon.

Hockey, J. 1990. *Experiences of Death: An Anthropological Account*. Edinburgh: Edinburgh University Press.

Klass, D. 1996. 'Grief in an eastern culture: Japanese ancestor worship', in *Continuing Bonds: New Understandings of Grief*, edited by D. Klass, P.R. Silverman and S.L. Nickman. Washington, DC: Taylor & Francis, pp. 59–70.

LaFleur, W.R. 1992. *Liquid Life: Abortion and Buddhism in Japan*. Princeton: Princeton University Press.

Lock, M. 1980. *East Asian Medicine in Urban Japan*. Berkeley: University of California Press.

Lock, M. 2002. *Twice Dead: Organ Transplants and the Reinvention of Death*. Berkeley: University of California Press.

Long, S.O. 1980. 'The ins and outs of doctor-patient relations in Japan', *American Journal of Chinese Medicine* 8 (1): 37–46.

Long, S.O. 1999. '*Shikata ga nai*: resignation, control and self-identity', in *Lives in Motion: Composing Circles of Self and Community in Japan*, edited by S.O. Long. Ithaca: Cornell University Press, pp. 11–25.

MacPherson, C.B. 1962. *The Political Theory of Possessive Individualism: From Hobbes to Locke*. Oxford: Oxford University Press.

Mansfield, N. 2000. *Subjectivity: Theories of the Self from Freud to Haraway*. New York: New York University Press.

Merleau-Ponty, M. 1968. *The Visible and the Invisible*. Evanston: Northwestern University Press.

Miller, J.B. 1986. *The New Psychology of Women*. Boston: Beacon Press.

Ohnuki-Tierney, E. 1984. *Illness and Culture in Contemporary Japan*. Cambridge: Cambridge University Press.

Plath, D.W. 1964. 'Where the family of God is the family: the role of the dead in Japanese households', *American Anthropologist* 66 (2): 300–17.

Reed, A. 1999. 'Anticipating individuals. Modes of vision and their social consequence in a Papua New Guinean prison', *Journal of the Royal Anthropological Institute* 5 (1): 43–56.

Silverman, P.R. and D. Klass 1996. 'Introduction: what's the problem?', in *Continuing Bonds: New Understandings of Grief*, edited by D. Klass, P.R. Silverman and S.L. Nickman. Washington, DC: Taylor & Francis, pp. 3–23.

Smith, R.J. 1974. *Ancestor Worship in Contemporary Japan*. Stanford: Stanford University Press.

Strathern, M. 1988. *The Gender of the Gift. Problems with Women and Problems with Society in Melanesia*. Berkeley: University of California Press.

Strathern, M. 2005. *Kinship, Law and the Unexpected: Relatives are always a Surprise*. Cambridge: Cambridge University Press.

Walter, T. 1996. 'A new model of grief: bereavement and biography', *Mortality* 1 (1): 7–25.

Wylie, J. 2009. 'Landscape, absence and the geographies of love', *Transactions of the Institute of British Geographers*.

Yamamoto, J. 1970. 'Cultural factors in loneliness, death, and separation', *Medical Times* 98: 177–83.

Yamamoto, J., K. Okonogi, T. Iwasaki and S. Yoshimura 1969. 'Mourning in Japan', *American Journal of Psychiatry* 125: 1661–5.

Chapter 6
Crafting Selves on Death Row[1]

Tamara Kohn

In the early 1990s, when visiting my family in California, I asked my sister Jessica (a California State Public Defender) if I could join her to visit San Quentin's Death Row to speak to Manuel (Manny) Babbitt – her client at the time. This first meeting led to a few others as well as to several years of written correspondence. Through Manny, as well as Jessica's colleagues, I also began a long correspondence with another man on the Row, Jay Siripongs.[2] These two men spent some 18 years on Death Row before both being executed by lethal injection by the State of California in 1999.

Nearly a decade after their deaths I unpacked a box full of the numerous handwritten letters, essays, sketches, paintings, poems and other artefacts that Manny and Jay had sent to me over several years, as well as copies of the letters I had sent to them. I also found many other 'texts' in that box that pertained to these men's stories – articles cut out from Californian and other States' newspapers, printouts from Internet pages, legal documentation, eulogies. Reading through them I felt a deep disjuncture between the men's representations of themselves in their private letters and even the most supportive representations of their lives

---

[1] I wish to express my thanks to my sister, Jessica Kohn McGuire, for initially inviting me to visit her client on Death Row and meet other colleagues involved in the California State Public Defender's office. I also wish to thank colleagues at the University of Melbourne who helped me work through initial ideas (see note 4 below), to Sean Williams, Stuart Kirsch, Jens Zinn, Erin Fitz Henry and to Douglas Davies and Chang-Won Park, the editors of this volume. Finally, I am forever grateful to Manny and Jay for teaching me so much.

[2] Note that these are the 'real' names of the protagonists of this story. As an anthropologist I am accustomed to providing pseudonyms for informants in order to comply with personal and institutional ethics. Here, there are no formal ethical constraints imposed as both men are now deceased, and personally I believe that Manny and Jay would have been happy to share their letters. Interestingly, I was hoping I would be able to do some interviewing of other Death Row inmates through my legal contacts, but was told that such qualitative research would be out of their control and thus could possibly interfere with the legal briefs being compiled, and that it would be very hard to find a willing defence team to allow for this while their clients' lives were still in their charge. See Rhodes (2001) for a useful discussion on the restraints imposed on prison research and how these affect our understanding of the role that empirically driven anthropologists can play in 'steering between abstract and fetishized representation' (ibid.: 77).

made by most others for public consumption. The latter seemed to be referring to men I never met personally whose only important, relevant (to others') experiences took place in their younger days. You need only put their names into Internet/ Google searches to find out about these past experiences – you will find out about war, psychological illness such as post-traumatic stress disorder, race, poverty, abuse, crime, family, victims – and also details about the prisoner's final hours and the technology of execution. However, the men represented by the letters in my box will not be very visible there. The experiences that they offer in those letters from Death Row that do not look back at these events are important ones too, however – not because they erase or heal the past, but because they make us understand the potential resilient power of creativity in 'the now' preceding death. This chapter explores this potential as it is expressed through Manny and Jay's prison lives and deaths.

When I rediscovered this box of material and the ideas that the men's private[3] words and creations were revealing to me about their then-present selves and what they felt was worth reporting about their lives at that time, I began reflecting upon different potential qualities of existentially 'being' in waiting for one's own execution.[4] To begin to do this I have had to challenge my own culturally-shaped urge to narrate in linear historical time their lives from their troubled, violent, beginnings. Instead of narrating, I will begin at the end by telling you that in the years leading up to their deaths, these men developed skills and sensitivities that would amaze you. In this chapter I will use their written ghostly voices to suggest, more generally, that prevalent public imaginations (fuelled in part by popular media) that view such prisoners as 'dead men walking' and see the space of Death Row as an entirely dead and deadening space, combined with detailed contested descriptions of the conditions and deeds that lead people to capital convictions, do not do justice to the prisoner as person, even if it serves a purpose in the defence or prosecution of an individual case or in larger debates around the im/morality of capital punishment.

So, in the following sections, I will begin to consider how time near death is variously spent and conceived through Manny and Jay's letters; how this fits (or contrasts) with other written representations of time in captivity; how personal artistry may be developed and quietly expressed deep in the bowels of our saddest institutions and can work in a comforting way towards reorienting and treasuring 'time left'; how living skilfully is a source of dignity; and how phenomenologies

---

[3]   The meaning of 'private' here, of course, is conditioned by the space and surveillance of the prison where no written words or objects pass through the gates without thorough examination.

[4]   My preliminary reflections are published in a volume edited by Ghassan Hage called *Waiting* (Kohn 2009), produced collaboratively with fellow colleagues at the University of Melbourne. Some letters and ideas discussed there are re-presented here and then further developed.

of self, time and transcendence speak to one another through the empirical samples offered here.[5]

Manny

Before I examined the details of his case history, I met Manny several times in the visiting room of San Quentin and I began to correspond with him. My growing appreciation of him as a person was formed out of these interactions that we shared in the moving present and continued until his execution. He sent my young son presents constructed from scraps he could access on the Row. He had a hotplate in his cell and he cooked Cape Verdean dishes for other men on his block. I sent him spice packets that he said one could only get in the UK. Manny taught himself how to read and write in prison by rote memory and he eventually came to write with fluency and style. In one letter he demonstrates a connection drawn between his conscious work on protecting his mind from darkness through activity and his embarkation on a new craft:

> My days are (all) filled with some thing different. I plan them that way. Seldom do I stay in darkness, I'm starting to paint not so good right now. I use my finger more than the brush!

In another he recounts a series of visits from his daughter ...

> I heard a lot from her I never knew, being the father she knew little of she let me do most of the talking. I really couldn't do much talking about Vietnam, my street life or prison life, only what I want to do with the rest of my life. She will read about me as I send her some statements later on. I guess all my life's story is already down on paper, I wont bother to edit any of it, God Knows what the truth is. I figure when I'm gone he will judge me. I know I've been sober and Good for 18 years! So I just wait like we all do.

He waited as we all wait for whatever comes after death, but he didn't do so passively (*'For me it's wait and see; I have things to do and no time to worry about the future'*, 29 October 1998). In a place where most conceivable freedoms are removed, the waiting space can be busily filled – new languages to learn, letters to write, painting to do, food to cook – and the future will take care of itself. And his words suggest that on Judgment Day, his God will know the truth – whatever that

---

[5]   I wish to reiterate that there are countless individuals with totally different characters, reactions, levels of capability and hope that await capital punishment, and these two very sympathetic cases are far from representative, but they were the only men I had written to and their cases, I believe, should be as powerfully illustrative as exceptions as they would be as representative models or rules.

might be from out of the many versions of his dark past that have been recorded by lawyers, judges, witnesses, family. But part of the judgment, he implied, will also be about what he'd done in jail during his last 18 years being 'sober and Good'. His cell was a place where the busy 'I' resided in his letters, and what he achieved there appeared to be neither visible nor newsworthy to people outside of family, close lawyers and loved ones.

It is only after I got to know Manny in the present that I investigated his past. Manny was a black Vietnam veteran convicted by an all-white jury of the first-degree murder of an elderly woman in 1980. The tale that led him to Death Row included a childhood of poverty and violence; active service in Vietnam, including the vicious battle of Khe Sanh; and evidence of acute mental illness (post-traumatic stress disorder, or PTSD) and drug abuse upon his return to the United States. His poor initial legal representation, his unstable mental state, the political environment, the terrible sadness and fury of the victim's family who demanded 'justice' – were repeated in most legal briefs and newspaper articles that I read.

Just a few months before his death, a *San Francisco Chronicle* article began, 'There are two sides to Manny Babbitt – the Vietnam War hero, and the convicted killer of an elderly woman'. As these two identities (hero and killer) relate to events and times long past, the article implied that Manny's notable personhood ended when he was a young man well before his wait on Death Row had even begun.

It is important to remember that those 'two sides' to Manny were not named by Manny – his own sense of self at the time that article came out was anything but stuck in that time warp, but forces larger than his truth determine what is understood as meaningful in his tale. In a contemporary middle-class liberal vision of self-making, we are all free to imagine our 'selves' out of whatever we find available and meaningful in our lives. If we consciously work at hanging on to our past titles and achievements, or, in this case, our horrific experiences and violent actions as a source for our identifications to others, we can. We can also choose to move to a new town or to start again – a new career, new friends, a new set of hobbies, even a changed body. But even without such freedom and mobility, we have the capacity to constantly act on ourselves in the present and judge ourselves there, too, even if we are also accountable for our past deeds.

Shortly before his execution, Manny wrote:

> I think while I'm here at these crossroads it matters little if I look back, nothing there can be changed but I can continue to change with each passing moment 'but into what'? If I were any more driven to do good, people would say look he thinks he's a saint now. And I know some people who would say that!! I'm just a man who through public opinion finds himself in a pickle. I don't hate myself as I once did nor am I in love with what I see … I was never afraid of the unknown, only in suspense of it.

Manny eloquently describes here a relation between time and self-character analysis. He judges himself in the present and recognises that his 'goodness' affects those moving through time with him who can witness or at least imagine some of his present through his actions and words – the friends he fosters inside jail and out. He finds himself 'in a pickle' through 'public opinion' that judges his past and locks his present into cells designed to deprive men of their freedom and hold them for years or even a lifetime of waiting in fear. He doesn't deny his past deeds, but he empowers himself in his private writing by removing the fear from his state of 'suspension' in the wake of death.

Jay

Manny's friend, Jay Siripongs, was a Thai immigrant convicted of assisting with a burglary that ended in the murder of two shopkeepers in 1981. Jay became an accomplished artist during his 17 years on Death Row as well as a qualified Buddhist monk. He sent me a letter to respond to my questions about his training in art. It opens with one sentence that includes his name, age, ethnicity, migration dates from Thailand, his employment in LA and his arrest, trial, sentence and arrival on Death Row. The rest of the long letter is all about himself as an artist. I indulge here in a significant excerpt.

> I recall that I always loved painting and wanted to be an artist, but never felt it would be possible, especially in Thailand. In my early years, I was influenced by traditional Thai murals, Eugene Garin ... Thomas Moran, John Singer Sargent then Robert Bateman ... Any skill I now possess has come from years of trials and errors painting. I prefer to learn by doing rather than devising an intellectual guideline before beginning ... It is important to me to keep evolving and growing as a painter. One good work keeps me alive to do another and another. Painting is something I do for relaxing, I think about doing all the time, and something I can do without thinking ... I'm really not a very sophisticated person, at least not as a painter ... I enjoy the challenge of experimenting with techniques and media to produce a painting which provides an intimate view of its own world. I am inspired by everything which brings about harmony and adds to the 'Quality of life', rather from any material side of existence ... Painting is my lifetime project, but my time is short, so I try to paint as often and as steady as possible. After all, I have 20 something years of catching up to do. It's important for me to keep learning. My final thought on being an artist, is how lucky we artists are, art is something that will not leave or betray us. People say an artist has to suffer before he can accomplish anything worthwhile. I don't agree with that. An artist has all the fun! ... The sheer joy I feel when I am involved in a painting and it is coming out well ... I feel terribly fortunate to have the gift of art in my life. Well, that's my point of view as a painter, and as a person, I used to be very shy, and didn't come out of my shell until 4 years ago ... In a way, I know I was not

stupid, but it has everything to do with self-esteem. That's the key to inner peace. I now feel that I can achieve anything I put my mind to.

Jay knew he could not escape his physical incarceration and looming execution, but in his reflection on his art experiences developed in prison he felt he could, intellectually as well as aesthetically, grow in a way that his previous life circumstances hadn't allowed. He gave away over 600 art pieces to friends over the years – butterflies appear in many that he took to symbolise his transforming self in prison. He meditated and studied Buddhist texts. Six days before his execution (3 February 1999), he sent me a packet filled with copies of three long essays he had written (on 'death', on 'karma and rebirth', on '227 Rules of Discipline'). The one on death ends with: 'All the great masters wish for us one thing: that we become able to identify with the true part of our being – our essence, our inner self, our soul – before we leave our physical body.'

By examining his writing on the self-esteem and peace gained out of his challenging artistic practice together with news reports of his final hours, Jay may well have achieved identification with the 'true part of (his) being'. One of Jay's poems is posted on a website about his case:[6]

> Last night's sleepless mind explained this well,
> But what sounds ease the heart when petals freeze?
>
> Leave treatises and poems, leave ink and brush,
> Leave fall's last flowers. Leave the S.Q.'s walls.
> What I knew of gardens, or old texts,
> lies dead with my ambitions, my lost past.
>
> Ride out past quick-sprung poplars, white-barked pines
> Past farmer's shacks – and past more sallow blooms
>
> Yet no road quits self pity, outruns sorrow.
> Better to stay and taste what's in the heart.

This poem written from Death Row in San Quentin opens with a mournful reflection on lost possibilities but then brings his imaginary flight back to the present – no road outruns sorrow, so stay and savour whatever emotion is in the heart.

Death Watch

Poets and philosophers have long brought us to the idea that the immediate proximity of death brings life vividly to the fore. The German philosopher Martin

---

[6]   See www.firstyearbook.umd.edu/DMW/Templates_CSS/Siripongs.html.

Heidegger, in *Being and Time*, argued that human beings cannot achieve authentic existence, cannot have a meaningful life, without facing their own mortality head on (1953[1927]). To do this, he said, one must acknowledge one's own temporality – one's position in historical time. Ironically, for Jay in the poem above, facing mortality is to get one's consciousness off the temporal road in order to truly 'taste what's in the heart'. Nigel Rapport, in his assessment of Nietzsche's notions of the individual, writes: 'To become "what one is" … is to liberate oneself from resentment; true selfhood calls for self-affirmation not the negation of others. One must also liberate oneself from historical ties, recognising one's potential dominion over time; a true master morality is grounded in a willingness to separate oneself from the past (one's own and that of others)' (Rapport 2003: 124). In elaborating on Nietzsche's philosophy, Rapport effectively speaks to Jay's own Buddhist sensibilities. In that wake of death we have choices to make, pasts to leave behind, things to do.

Countless scholarly writers muse and debate the human condition – we all face our own mortality. But people do face it differently dependent on their socio-culturally and personally derived beliefs about death, on their emotional or physical well-being, on their maturity, on their conditions of life, on their expected conditions of death.

Zygmunt Bauman writes, 'Through its many deputies, death presides over life. Fighting death is meaningless. But fighting the *causes* of dying turns into the meaning of life' (1992). This rings so true, but only up to a point. Think of some terminally ill patients who consciously approach the present-ness of what pleasures in life remain – who find 'meaning of life' in that instead of the fight. We all have probably known some of these people, loved them, consumed their stories and revelations, and empathised with them, accepting their decision to stop struggling against the causes of their dying. We can do this only when we imagine the possibility of our growing, learning selves that may too react in such a way. And yet most publicly consumed representations of people on Death Row, even the most sympathetic, tend to deny this possibility. The 'persons' get pushed aside in the process of preparations for or fights against execution. In the flurry of legal, academic, political, popular media, and religious writing on the history, morality, politics and technology associated with capital punishment, the incarcerated are imagined to be in limbo – they lose their subjectivity. Even the life stories of individual cases with a focus on conditions, events and deeds and the effects on victims and families, still do not manage to allow the prisoner the possibility of self-making in the shadow of their death even when they often provide evidence for their agency in their artistic productions.[7]

Michel Foucault's seminal study of the structure and history of the modern prison demonstrated that prisons were originally designed to be instruments

---

[7]   See Ivan Turgenev's recounting of 'The Execution of Tropman' for a classic humanistic reflection on the problem of the 'person' lost in the process of State killing (published in Lopate 1995).

of transformation (like hospitals) but that they failed bitterly from the start, only producing more delinquency (Foucault 1980: 39–40). This production of delinquency can been seen to emerge from a sub-cultural socialisation (Sykes 2007: 138) or 'prisonisation' process in tandem with the violence of keeper and kept that begets more violence. It is no wonder that prisons are popularly portrayed as human dustbins preparing for final disposals. We, as members of the society that produced the systems of control, also come to accept these representations as natural and inevitable, particularly when they are offered to us as poignant truths in film[8] and other mass mediated representations and in public debate (Sloop 1996: 3; Tylor 2005: 131). So one might suggest that the public gaze on the prison itself (as wasteland) conditions the gaze that is occasionally turned on the individual 'criminal' who passes into it and then out (mostly through death).

On Time, Culture and Transcendence

The proximity to death is a feature of many imprisoning spaces. So, is waiting on Death Row somehow qualitatively different from waiting in a high security jail for one's term to end? I am not qualified to compare the physical conditions in different incarcerating settings, and it is also true that some people wait on Death Row and then their sentence is commuted to life or a shorter term or even freedom, so nothing is totally certain until death knocks. Manny and Jay, however, saw far more people leave San Quentin dead than alive, so the big qualitative difference was that neither Manny nor Jay would see themselves as 'doing time' – they were not anticipating a return to the free world – they were 'doing death watch'. There was an urgency in their attentiveness to the present, while perhaps for those expressive souls 'doing time' before their freedom, the focus of urgency shifts to the outside social world and the place they would occupy in it. Eldridge Cleaver, for example, wrote letters that would be compiled into the book, *Soul on Ice* (1968). It tells a series of powerful tales about the 'colonised' black man, about religion, boxing and love. It is a deeply thoughtful work from one who knows he will be released after a trying period 'on ice' and can work 'on becoming' the man he wishes to be in the future.

What people write about in any context is likely to be shaped by that context. For a person passing through hell and doing time for a number of years, hell will likely be reflected in his or her writing. The person's story, one might suggest, is made most vividly from the immediate environment (Boulanger and Sarat 2005), but then, too, the culture of the prison is produced out of the cultural backgrounds

---

[8] *The Green Mile*, *Monster's Ball* and *Dead Man Walking* are fairly recent examples of films that bring the horror of Death Row to life and raise emotional responses in viewers. Cultural and literary critics have examined how capital punishment and murder are mediated by literature, media, film and other aesthetic forms – both to produce 'sentiment' and 'controversy' as well as to sell their products (Kennedy 2007: 30) and their politics.

of its residents as well as by the demands and values of the carceral society that builds and maintains the prison from 'outside' (Hallinan 2001[9]). Interested commentators and social theorists who tackle the whole brutal process of the death penalty in their writing sometimes observe it as a type of 'communal ritual' (Boulanger and Sarat 2005: 16) or 'ritual sacrifice' (Turnbull 1996), its symbolic and culturally derived meanings being constantly explored and debated by those engulfed within it and attentive to it. For those prisoners and ex-prisoners writing for an outside audience and who have a goal to affect change (for themselves and/ or for 'society'), then cultural realism is critical.[10] A notable example is Stanley Tookie Williams, an ex-gang leader in LA recently executed on California's Death Row who was nominated for the Nobel Peace Prize for publishing several books in his later years on Death Row. He used his time and his life story of redemption to write for future youths in his home community (Williams 2005). Another example is Ernie Lopez who published his personal life story of ill deeds and arrests and time spent on Death Row for a crime he insisted he did not commit (Lopez and Perez-Torres 2005). He was eventually released, and his book passionately exposes the inflicted violence and arbitrary torture of minority prisoners, examples of immense human resilience, as well as showing through his own fought case many clear faults in the American criminal justice system (ibid.). His story echoes George Jackson whose letters, compiled more than 30 years earlier (*Soledad Brother*, 1970), mixed personal testimony with an intelligent sense of rage around the disenfranchised, the war in Vietnam, violence and racial hatred and growing dissent as expressed then in the Black Power movement. He wrote eloquently about the pain of incarceration and how society's most harmful vices are most vividly present in the prison where its convicts are controlled by terror: 'Capture, imprisonment, is the closest to being dead that one is likely to experience in this life' (ibid.: 19–20), and death eventually found him in jail – Jackson was suspiciously shot dead by a guard at the age of 30, allegedly for trying to escape (cf. Sloop 1996: 106).

Williams' writing was used as a tool for achieving community change, while Lopez and Jackson's writings have functioned to provide the inside view of a corrupt institutional system that they believed needed to be exposed. These

---

[9] Hallinan, in his closer observation of a number of American prisons and the political machine that fills them, critiques the potential for 'rehabilitation': 'You couldn't rehabilitate a man if he had never been habilitated in the first place, (having) never had those basic things … essential to developing a decent human being: a loving home, a decent education, a faith of some kind. To expect a man to find these things in prison is, on most days, laughable' (2001: 216). So for our purposes here, this presents a grim vision of inevitability for the person in terms of his relation with the moral, educated, loving 'other' (if 'rehabilitation' is about getting someone fit to live in the world of others). On Death Row, however, change is not about reuniting the convict with the public, it is about uniting the convict with his potential to accept his fate.

[10] See Rossi (2001), Mulvey-Roberts (2007), Arriens (2005) for examples.

writers, and so many more, have appealed for social change through their narratives, and realism has aided their efforts. But surely some work may take one into a remembered or purely creative imaginary zone far from the prison's walls – where butterflies roam, where geese fly over stunning mountains (as a large mural painted by a Death Row convict and artist on the inside wall of the San Quentin visiting room demonstrates). Surely some prisoner writing avoids any contemplation on the prison environment. As Jay wrote at the end of his long letter about his art: 'I don't like to write that much about this place – once you know all the routines, that's about it. I'd rather write when there's something worthwhile to say.' What was worthwhile in his case was to work incessantly on 'being' a productive painter. His concerns were existential at that stage in his life. His time was precious because he had '20 something years of catching up to do', painting for himself before he would be executed. This then is a celebration of an individual who can achieve some degree of transcendence (Carnochan 1995: 428) played out in an active mode of being.

Manny and Jay in their final years demonstrated such transcendence in their productions. Of course, I base this suggestion purely on the evidence of their reported activities, their creative writing and their artwork (words and images that can present genuine as well as imagined or misleading feelings, but which I choose to accept as real and revealing here). When the men were locked alone in their cells painting and writing, they were not fuming warriors like Jackson and Cleaver and many others. They were not fighting a psychic battle that would lead them to an escape from the pains of their prison life and towards a different future after the passage of time. Instead, they were attending to themselves – they were working on making themselves into people they could live with (in the present) and die with (in the immediate future). The relation between past, present and future in prisoner consciousness and activity is *necessarily* affected by one's proximity to a premeditated and nearly certain death in a space where time is running out.

Prisoners' writings from Death Row often consider the problem of such historical time specific to the Row, and these reflections needn't focus on the positive creative potential of that space. In 1994, an inmate on Death Row in Texas wrote the following in a letter:

> Time was once my ally. It was a future, potentially a wonderful one, just waiting. Now time is the enemy. Only part of the problem is that it runs out, or is running out. Mostly it is my enemy because it crushes me … Even for someone 'doing time,' facing a set sentence, the time is only slowed down before it eventually passes on. But 'the Row' is different because there is nowhere for the time to go – it's closed, not open; ended. And something else – when someone dies, their time doesn't just evaporate or go away with them, it stays here as a weight for the rest of us to bear … When time gets compressed like this … (it's) tangled beyond comprehension so that a day or two can't be told from a month or two – or a year or two – ago. (Arriens 2005: 113)

So time can be compressed and suffocating for some of these men. For others it can provide a place of possibility and discovery, as we see eloquently expressed in a stanza from UA Fanthorpe's poem about 'Death Row Poets' who

> Look straight in Time's face, and see
> The unrepeatable marvel of each second.
> (in Mulvey-Roberts 2007: 201)

On 19 Jan 1998, Manny's letter began by reflecting briefly on my recent visit with him in the visiting room of San Quentin's death row and then he leaped straight into his day's creation:

> I just made a meal out of rice, ½ meat log Italian salami rolled in pepper and chives. I steamed it along with pinto beans and Herb and Garlic soup mix with very little water to make a gravy. Yum! I cooked a bowl of white rice with a clove leaf and twig of a sage bush. Such aroma, and rice should always be fluffy. Ha Ha Ha. BOY I'm good! Well, needless to say I did send some to Terry in #25. I'm in #24. He smelled it under his nose like the cartoon finger. When that happened I had to do another rice bowl … Write to Jay about some Thai dishes. I'm sure he will enjoy doing that for you. He's a great artist too.

Of course in the last sentence, Manny most likely meant that Jay was an artist who paints and draws, but in its position against his happy recollections of his own creative cooking on his hotplate, one can also feel he truly enjoyed his own artistic culinary production as much as he savoured the final edible product, as a true craftsman would. It showed he was truly alive in the moment – not filling time but savouring it. I could almost feel his smile and smell the gravy. I'm reading this recipe again now, at a time when culinary mastery is celebrated nightly on prime-time television in the form of *MasterChef* – where young hopefuls dream of fame and fortune in the kitchen and learn to taste and create with innovation and sensitivity. Manny's dish was an enormous achievement that would make those judges gasp to think about the conditions it was created in. There was no prize at the end of the game for him, no future career, and no message for an outside world that was intended when he cooked and reflected on his recipe. He did it all for him*self* (and maybe a little bit for Terry in #25).

Kirsten Hastrup has suggested that the self has no essence, only character, emerging from one's actions (2007: 199), and that 'creativity resides in the ability … to act – without incorporating an anticipated consequence into the perception of the action … (that) creativity belongs outside of historical time' (ibid.: 201). We can understand Manny and Jay's writing, painting, cooking, etc. as a source of such self-production in action outside of historical time – as a refuge from the pressure of time. These men daily lived with death – Manny told me that he can't get *too* close to anyone – just like in Vietnam – because he could be killed tomorrow – but in his attentiveness to the present and to living skilfully he celebrated self-growth and dignity in the ever-present wake of his own death. This expression happens and is terribly important to note regardless of whether or not you feel this was or should have been relevant to the final outcome of his case.

It is essential to consider Death Row in a book on emotion and identity in the context of mortality. Death Row is a frightening and brutal killing machine in many States that has been designed purely for human storage and disposal. In these pages I have argued that, at least for Manny and Jay, to wait as a prisoner on Death Row permits one to become extremely focused on the present when attending to one's sense of self. The self that is attended to is far from dead on the eve of death but works hard to demonstrate to itself its sense of worth and can achieve this through its actions and the things it learns to create with care. Those creations remove one from the crush of historical time into an artistic space that provides some comfort. Manny and Jay's final narrative discourses offer strong evidence of how powerful the human spirit can be as it concocts beautiful stanzas, elegant brush strokes and rich flavours from under death's shadow; it illustrates how an impulse to learn and to craft can refigure a person into a better self that one can die with.

References

Arriens, Jan (ed.) 2005. *Welcome to Hell: Letters and Writings from Death Row*, 2nd edition. Boston: Northeastern University Press.

Bauman, Zygmunt 1992. 'Survival as a Social Construct', *Theory, Culture and Society*, 9: 1–36.

Boulanger, Christian and Austin Sarat 2005. 'Putting Culture into the Picture: Toward a Comparative Analysis of State Killings', in Sarat, A. and C. Boulanger (eds) *The Cultural Lives of Capital Punishment*. Stanford: Stanford University Press, pp. 1–45.

Carnochan, W.B. 1995. 'The Literature of Confinement', in Morris, N. and D.J. Rothman (eds) *The Oxford History of the Prison: The Practice of Punishment in Western Society*. New York and Oxford: Oxford University Press, pp. 381–406.

Cleaver, Eldridge 1968. *Soul on Ice*. New York: McGraw-Hill Book Company.

Foucault, Michel 1980. *Power – Knowledge: Selected Interviews and Other Writings 1972–1977* (ed. Colin Gordon). New York: Pantheon Books.

Hallinan, Joseph T. 2001. *Going up the River: Travels in a Prison Nation*. New York: Random House.

Hastrup, Kirsten 2007. 'Performing the World: Agency, Anticipation and Creativity', in Hallam, E. and T. Ingold (eds) *Creativity and Cultural Improvisation*. Oxford: Berg Publishers, pp. 193–206.

Heidegger, Martin 1953[1927]. *Being and Time*, translated by Joan Stambaugh. Albany: State University of New York Press.

Jackson, George 1970. *Soledad Brother: The Prison Letters of George Jackson* (introduction by Jean Genet). New York: Bantam Books.

Kennedy, Rosanne 2007. 'The Media and the Death Penalty: The Limits of Sentimentality, the Power of Abjection', *Humanities Research*, XIV (2): 29–47.

Kohn, Tamara 2009. 'Waiting on Death Row', in Hage, G. (ed.) *Waiting*. Melbourne: University of Melbourne Press, pp. 218–227.

Lopate, Phillip 1995. *The Art of the Personal Essay*. New York: Anchor Books.

Lopez, Ernie and Rafael Perez-Torres 2005. *To Alcatraz, Death Row, and Back: Memories of an East LA Outlaw*. Austin: University of Texas Press.

Mulvey-Roberts, Marie (ed.) 2007. *Writing For their Lives: Death Row USA*. Chicago: University of Illinois Press.

Rapport, Nigel 2003. *I am Dynamite: An Alternative Anthropology of Power*. London and New York: Routledge.

Rhodes, Lorna A. 2001. 'Toward an Anthropology of Prisons', *Annual Review of Anthropology*, 30: 65–83.

Rossi, Richard M. 2001. *Waiting to Die: Life on Death Row*. London: Vision Paperbacks.

Sloop, John M. 1996. *The Cultural Prison: Discourse, Prisoners and Punishment*. Tuscaloosa and London: The University of Alabama Press.

Sykes, Gresham M. 2007 [1958]. *The Society of Captives: A Study of a Maximum Security Prison*. Princeton: Princeton University Press.

Turnbull, Colin 1996. 'Death by Decree: An Anthropological Approach to Capital Punishment', in Koosed, M. (ed.), *Capital Punishment: Volume 1: The Philosophical, Moral and Penological Debate over Capital Punishment*. New York and London: Garland Publishing, pp. 12–34.

Tylor, Louise 2005. 'The Cultural Life of Capital Punishment in European and American Film', in Sarat, A. and C. Boulanger (eds) *The Cultural Lives of Capital Punishment*. Stanford: Stanford University Press, pp. 129–146.

Williams, Stanley Tookie 2005. *Blue Rage: Black Redemption: A Memoir*. New York: Touchstone.

Chapter 7

Sojourn, Transformative: Emotion and Identity in the Dying, Death, and Disposal of an Ex-Spouse

Jacque Lynn Foltyn

For Matthew

Introduction

While Hurricane Katrina demolished the Gulf Coast, displacing hundreds of thousands of people and killing 1,836 individuals,[1] I was gripped by a different drama. I had spent the last weeks of August and the first part of September at a hospice facility in San Diego, California, where on September 4, 2005, Matthew, my ex-husband, died in my arms of a rare form of cancer. I am writing this chapter at the five-year anniversary that commemorates the landfall of Hurricane Katrina and the death of Matt; for me, the events are connected. In the six-month period between Matt's diagnosis with Stage IV neuroendocrine pancreatic cancer and his death from that disease, I became his part-time caregiver and full-time emotional support. Even though we were divorced, and I was married to another at the time, I found myself acting in "wifely" ways toward Matt. Our journey toward his death proved transformative, causing me to reassess our relationship, re-evaluate my own life, and develop new conceptions and expressions of myself as an individual. Matt's dying changed me, requiring shifts of emotion and identity; I was sensitized to the meanings of death in ways that caused me to rethink aspects of my research.

In this chapter, I discuss these changes, provide an account of Matt's death, and revisit our relationship to establish why I was there when he died. I use myself as a source of data to discuss how social norms governing dying, death, and bereavement for formerly married spouses can be unexpectedly accommodating in a time when the commitments that bind individuals are easily undone and can leave mortally ill individuals on their own.

Matt was a clinical professor of medicine and renowned reconstructive and plastic surgeon. He was co-developer of the artificial skin used to assist with the healing of burn patients and was part of a surgical team that separated co-joined twins. Committed to alleviating the suffering of his patients, he published dozens

---

[1]   Hurricanekatrinarelief.com.

of important papers, gave wound care workshops, and hosted a weekly televised health and public policy program. In the months before he died, we pondered the mysteries of human sufferings, and the beginnings and endings of human relationships and lives. He asked me to write about his transition from the living to the dead, which came unexpectedly and far too soon.

Diagnosis

On March 19, 2005, I received several phone messages from Matt. I was tired, it had been a busy day, and so I delayed returning the call. He had gone through a second divorce in 2003, and I figured that he wanted to apprise me of the latest chapter of that acrimonious drama, whose reverberations would not be quieted. But there was something about the tone of his voice that kept nagging at me, and when the phone rang a short while later, and I saw that it was Matt once again I answered. "Jacque, this is Matt, and I have really bad news. I have cancer and it's a really bad one," he said. Stunned, I expressed anguished disbelief and then I just listened, learning that besides the tumor in his pancreas, Matt had 20 more in his liver, some as large as grapefruit. The lining of his stomach was involved. Almost clinically – he was a physician after all – Matt observed that the cancer had been hidden and misdiagnosed for years, while he was tested for a variety of chest and intestinal complaints that required a colonoscopy, an endoscopy, and an angiogram. The results for those tests were normal.

"It's hopeless," he said, his voice breaking. "I knew something was seriously wrong when I couldn't do my usual 20 mile ride." As he said those words, I had an image in my mind of Matt on his titanium Italian racing bicycle, training for the Iron Man Competition in Hawaii. Instead of serving as the competition surgeon, as he usually did, he was planning to compete in the coming year. "I was tired all of the time," he continued. "I thought I might have picked up hepatitis during surgery so I ran a liver panel and the enzyme levels were all over the place." After he read the results, Matt talked with a surgeon friend; they ordered a CT scan and the catastrophe hiding in his body was revealed. An endocrinologist cancer specialist gave Matt the devastating news that he likely had no more than six months to live and recommended that Matt not undergo treatment, be made comfortable, get his life "in order," and do whatever he had always wanted to do.

Listening to Matt talk about what he was already calling "my cancer," I thought it impossible that our long journey, begun as first-year university students, was coming to an end. I thought back to the day we met as 18 year olds in a calculus class and how we were engaged at 19, married at 20, separated at 30, and divorced at 32, our union a proverbial casualty of having married "too young." The naïve assumption that individuals I love would live to be elderly was shattered. Matt was middle-aged; while his hair was turning a lovely silver shade, his face was unlined and he had a beautiful physique. His career was at an apex; he was in the "prime" of life. He couldn't die, and yet the evidence that he was dying would not be denied. Other than my ancient grandparents who passed away in their late eighties or early nineties and my beloved dogs, who in dog years were centenarians, I had not known death. At least not death of this kind – unforeseen and seemingly unfair. While the deaths of my grandparents and dogs were sad, they were hardly tragic. They had lived long lives; they had not been cut off mid-life, mid-plan.

"We had our whole lives ahead of us," Matt said, quietly, as if he were reading my mind. The way that he used the word "we" caught my attention for there was still a "we." While no longer spouses, we were more than friends, connected by our pasts and present.

Matt was the kind of individual who made five-year plans. He had moved out-of-state during his second marriage and his revised plan was to move "home" to San Diego and open a new practice. Already, he had signed a contract for a medical space and was looking for a beach house, which he planned to decorate in whites and blues. As I listened to Matt speak the unthinkable, on the edge of my thoughts was an image of the Grim Reaper straight from Ingmar Bergman's *The Seventh Seal*, a cloaked icon of death who arrives unexpectedly and thwarts carefully laid plans. Matt's father, who died in 2001 and was a sardonic counterpart to Matt's glowing optimist, would mock his son's stratagems. "Make your plans, Matt, and watch God laugh!"

"I will help you through this. I promise. I will not abandon you." I spoke these words without hesitation and as I did I sensed Matt's slightly crooked smile on the other end of the phone. He believed me. The assurance was important for he had little family left. Family was important for him in an almost mythical way that those who have secure, intact families, don't quite understand. We take for granted that we are loved deeply and without reservations. Matt's parents divorced when he was 16, and they never spoke again. My loving, large family was an attractor for him. He adored the Foltyn family life, and I used to tell him that he fell in love as much with them as with me. It was a family joke that Matt was my parents' sixth child. So strong was their connection that he invited them to his second wedding – and they attended. When that marriage ended, Matt lost not only a second wife but a stepson, whom he had brought up as his son. Since his father had died, his elderly mother was hospitalized with severe depression, his sister and he had been estranged for years, and his brother lived thousands of miles away, Matt seemed a bit lost. Our post-divorce years had been relatively friendly, but since we had no children together, were geographically separated after Matt moved away, and were busy with our careers, our contact became less frequent. But we reconnected after his second divorce, and I became his confidante and source of comfort. This felt natural and right. We had grown up together; I was still fond of him and felt committed to and responsible for him. He was family.

"I can't put you through this," Matt said, softly.

"Don't worry about me, Matt. I can handle it. If I can't handle it, who can? I'm a death researcher," I replied, wryly.

We laughed ruefully for a moment at this bit of black humour, but then caught ourselves. After the conversation ended, I collapsed on the floor and cried.

Dying

The quest to save – or at least extend – Matt's life began. His surgeon mentor performed an ambitious set of procedures that removed a portion of his pancreas and debulked some of the tumors in the liver. Matt "died" on the table during that 11-hour surgery, his body exsanguinated, but he was revived. Time was critical, and Matt had begun a chemotherapy regimen before his surgery, and he resumed it almost immediately after. There was no period of healing, and besides how much could Matt heal with one of the most virulent forms of cancer growing inside him? Accustomed to cutting open the bodies of others and restoring some normality to the disfigured, it was as though Matt's body had turned on him, playing a perverse joke. He struggled to survive. There were hospitalizations for infections that left him clinging to life; there were incidences of bradycardia that required "resetting" of Matt's heart, a procedure that panicked him as that organ was stopped, and he felt himself "die," only to be shocked to life again. I feared that these "small deaths" were the prodroma for what was to come. Watching Matt cling to life while "his" cancer ate him alive, caused me to suffer along with him. When we were together, I would be coolly confident, the proverbial "pillar of strength," but when I came home I would call my mother and whimper like a child.

The negotiation of a new identity somewhere between an ex-wife and a wife commenced. I was one of two individuals on his family hospital visitor list; his brother, who was able to come just four times to visit Matt, was the other. I had unrestricted 24-hour access to his room, was contacted regularly by his attending physicians, had copies of all of Matt's medical records, and accompanied him to medical appointments. Since Matt was far from his own home, when he was not hospitalized, he stayed in guest quarters of a wealthy, generous friend, whose staff bathed and cooked for him, and generally assisted him. For periods of days and weeks, I stayed with him there, helping him as well. I was with Matt every step of the way, holding his hand as medications and chemo were administered, drains and sutures were removed, and test results delivered. I did my best to distract him from his pain, with conversation but also by massaging his shoulders and feet. I walked and fed his beloved Chocolate and Golden Labradors and gently chastised him for allowing those "filthy, muddy but wonderful beasts" to lie on his bed, reminding him of the infection risk. I have photographs of Matt, my Papillon Isabella and Ranger and Scout on the bed with him.

Matt loved to eat but it was now a pleasure for the most part denied him. The cell poison sickened him and tumors compressed his stomach. When well enough to eat, he asked me to bring exotic juice drinks, vanilla ice cream, and Old Fashioned and Bear Claw donuts. I happily indulged him, willing to do anything that might stop the weight loss. But when it became impossible for him to eat more than a few tablespoons of Jell-O, Matt's oncologist ordered intravenous Total Parenteral Nutrition (TPN).

"This means I am dying," Matt said, inconsolable, at first refusing the TPN. "It's just until the chemo kicks in and you can eat again," I told him, not very convincingly. He relented and began the new regimen, which I learned to administer through a port in his chest.

Although his physicians continued to act as if they could cure Matt, I slowly grasped that his life was ending. Although Matt wanted to believe otherwise, he understood this too. I have a memory of Matt lying silently on a sofa, tears in his eyes. We had been discussing areas of San Diego where he wanted to buy that beach house. I was sitting across the room, but when I saw that he was suddenly overwhelmed, I sat on the floor next to him and took his hand in my own. "Is it because you are afraid that you won't make it?" I asked. He shook his head in affirmation, and thanked me for broaching the unspeakable subject. "I'm tired of trying to be 'up' all of the time," he said.

After another hospitalization for yet another infection, a social worker talked with me about having Matt moved to a skilled nursing facility (SNF). There, a physician took me aside, and told me that the chemo was not working and that Matt belonged in a hospice. Later that day, Matt told me to listen carefully to the words he was about to speak. "I have made a decision. If my next test results show no improvement, I'm stopping treatment. I'm in pain all of the time. I am having difficulty breathing. I want to die." I didn't protest, squeezed his hand, and said I understood.

I called the office of the oncologist and demanded that Matt be examined before "another drop of chemo is administered." Informed that Matt's oncologist was on vacation, I insisted that he be seen by another. When we arrived at the chemo center, Matt was so weak that he stumbled and leaned on me as we walked; a nurse brought a wheelchair and he collapsed in it, barely able to hold up his head. After the substitute oncologist examined him and reviewed all of Matt's charts, he told us frankly that the chemo treatments had not made a dent. "There is no hope of recovery," he said forthrightly. The memory of the moment the truth was delivered is tinged with great sadness. I cradled Matt in my arms and wept with him. Understanding that Matt was far from his own home, that kindly oncologist spent hours arranging for Matt to enter an extraordinary inpatient hospice facility. As we sat in a private room waiting for the ambulance to arrive, Matt made new plans and asked me to take notes, as he gave me instructions for the care of his dogs and a list of bequests.

At the hospice, Matt designated me his official "gatekeeper." When I looked at his chart, I saw that I was listed as his wife. I marked "ex" next to that word but doing so was soon beside the point. We settled him into a large private room, with a lovely terrace and view, where Matt signed "do not resuscitate" papers and listened to the physicians explain his pain management regimen and what to expect as his life entered its last stages.

As Matt's hospice gatekeeper, I honored his wishes about who was allowed to visit or call him – and who should not be given access. His brother referred to me as a "tigress" protecting Matt like a cub. The hospice gave my telephone number to sometimes a dozen people a day, who called me at home, seeking information and solace. Matt's father's widow was an overnight guest in my house several times.

I had long talks with his brother, and with his estranged sister and second ex-wife, two people whom Matt did not want to see. I served as courier for legal documents that needed Matt's signature and met with his lawyer. Several days before he died, I received a phone call from a Catholic nun, a hospice chaplain, who told me that Matt had asked for Last Rites. "But he's not Catholic," I exclaimed. She explained that being an official follower of the Church of Rome was not a requirement for what was now called the Sacrament of the Anointing of the Sick and that Matt could have a "baptism" by faith. Matt loved the beauty of the rituals of the Catholic Church and while he knew that I was no longer a practicing member of the faith, he also knew that I still felt an emotional connection to the religion. Because of me, Matt felt more connection to Catholicism than he did to his Congregational Protestant background. He wanted to be linked to something bigger than he was and believed that the ritual would provide a transition to a peaceful death. So it was that I stood by Matt's hospice bed as a Mexican-American priest anointed him with oil and sang to him in his gorgeous baritone voice in this ancient ritual of atonement and release.

In the final days of his life, Matt's visitor list collapsed to one name, mine. "You know me better than anyone does," he told me, noting that my presence was soothing rather than a burden, unlike that of some well-meaning visitors. "I'm the one that is dying and I'm the one comforting him," he confided. "I can be myself with you." A couple of Matt's friends, including one physician, attempted to convince Matt that he should check himself out of the hospice and not "give up hope." They, like so many members of our culture, could not face the reality that people they care for die and apparently viewed Matt's dying as a "failure of a cure," as Philippe Ariès so elegantly put it.[2] Matt banished them.

Death

After Last Rites were administered, Matt began his inexorable decline. Day-by-day he grew weaker but more peaceful. The last four days of his life were marked by sleeping and a gradual retreat from life. Whereas before he had been avidly watching the news about Hurricane Katrina, the television was now off. Two days before he died, he called me at home and with a small voice left a message on my answer machine, telling me that I didn't need to come in that night, that I needed to rest myself. "I love you. Thank you for taking care of me."

On the morning of the day he died, Matt had difficulty speaking; it sounded as if he was talking underwater and I could see panic in his eyes. He was on oxygen, and I did my best to soothe him as he slipped into a coma. The hospice nurse coached me about how to be there for him and warned me to be careful about what I said, because he very likely could still hear me. In the next hours I moistened his mouth with a sponge; read him poetry, humorous essays, and psalms; played

---

[2]   See Ariès, *Western Attitudes toward Death*, 1974.

his favorite music; and told him how much I loved him, over and over again. "It's okay for you to let go, Matt. It's okay for you to leave me, to leave this life," I said. When I was apprised that his brain was shutting down and that he no longer needed the oxygen feed, I gave permission for the tubes to be taken away. The responsibility of that decision created some panic as I realized that his death was near, and the nurse, registering my fear, suggested that I call my parents and ask them to come in.

"But it is my mother's seventy-third birthday," I explained. "They have dinner plans. I can't ruin her special day."

"Call them. They will come," she replied. They arrived in 20 minutes. Because they did, Matt's former in-laws were there when he died. I climbed onto the bed next to my former husband, held him, and felt his last heartbeat and breath against my chest.

Disposal

Twenty minutes after Matt died, my sister Christine, his former sister-in-law, arrived. We arranged his body in a position of peaceful repose and gathered his belongings to take them home. With his gray-blue skin, hollow cheeks, and emaciated body, Matt's cadaver reminded me of an El Greco Christ, beautiful and horrible at the same time. Tenderly, I pulled up his pyjama top and touched the upside down half moon crescent incision scar that stretched across his abdomen. "Look what he's been through. He was so brave." I tried to close his mouth and eyes, but they kept popping open. "It's not like you see in the movies," the nurse told me, informing me that it was futile to keep trying to make them shut.

There was no fixing the corpse that Matt had become. While the hospice staff told us we could delay removal of the body for a while, I found myself, unexpectedly, ready to leave. Before Matt died, I believed I would have enormous difficulty surrendering his body to the mortuary workers, but as I looked at his ravaged remains, I understood that he was "gone." The life force that made for Matt's unique presence had disappeared, and I was left with this statue-like being that really looked "dead." The body I gazed upon was and was not Matt. Suddenly I comprehended the origins of the mind/body, soul/body divisions, and conceptions of an afterlife. Matt had "left" his body, and I wanted to leave before what remained of his earthly presence was placed in a body bag. That was not the last visual memory I wanted to have of the body of the man I had loved for so long. I kissed him on the forehead, folded his hands across his chest, and left, knowing that his corpse would be handled respectfully.

In the days before Matt died, I had worked with hospice staff and his brother to arrange for his cremation. Ten days after Matt's demise, I picked up his cremains. I wept as I drove him home, and kept glancing at the passenger seat where the box of what remained of him rested, remembering the last time he sat in the seat, on the way to the cancer clinic. The only solace I had was that the unwelcome disease that had taken up residence in Matt's body had died along with him. I was relieved that he had chosen cremation. Matt had requested that I keep his ashes until a time when his brother, his stepmother, and I could meet to scatter them along the spectacular coast of Big Sur, California, where his father's cremains had also been dispersed.

In the weeks and months that followed, I was one of three speakers at a large memorial service for Matt, attended also by his adored dogs. I was listed as one of his survivors in obituaries. The hospice sent me notifications of monetary gifts made in Matt's name, treating me as if I were his widow. My opinion was sought by school of medicine trustees who wished to rename a major medical scholarship in Matt's honour, and I wrote the biography that was distributed to the board for consideration. There is now a scholarship awarded annually to a medical student in Matt's name.

The dispersal of Matt's property was the next emotional challenge. An unexpected aspect of this disposal process was that the couple who bought Matt's house wanted to buy it fairly intact, i.e., with all of his furniture, linens, cookware, and china, and even paintings. A decision was made to sell them what "we," the family, did not want. I wonder what Matt would have thought about these individuals (people he knew) moving into his house and living with so many of his belongings, while relinquishing their own.

Before the house was turned over to that couple, I, along with Matt's brother and his father's widow, sorted through his belongings. I watched sadly as objects loaded with meanings important to Matt were distributed to designated survivors, donated to charities, or tossed in a huge dumpster. I moved through layers of artifacts like an archaeologist, sometimes jumping into the dumpster to retrieve an object that I knew Matt would not want discarded or that had meanings for both of us (e.g., antique scrimshaw purchased on our Hawaii honeymoon). His most treasured items, his photographs, writings, myriad medical degrees and awards, certain paintings and sculptures, and the miscellaneous memorabilia accumulated in a lifetime were left to me. I was touched by the things he had saved – golf score cards from his boyhood, a broken hockey stick, a ticket and boutonnière from a high school winter ball, Boy Scout badges, and every scrap of paper on which I had ever written a note to him. I could not toss them and they reside in boxes under my piano. One day I will give Matt's possessions a second sort, but I find it difficult to "edit" his life and discard items that were precious to him.

To mark the one-year anniversary of Matt's death, Christine and I drove his cremains 400 miles to Big Sur. The incongruous confluence of dates that had figured in Matt's death continued, as our niece Natalie was born as we drove up the coast. With my Catholic sense of ritual that Matt appreciated so well, I took out several photographs of him and placed them on a large rock in the surf next to a box that housed his cremains, and led his brother and two stepmothers in a ritual ceremony commemorating his life. We each took handfuls of "Matt" and released him into the sea.

Aftermath

After Matt's death, I went through a period of profound sadness. There were sleepless nights, a sense that he was "still there," survivor's guilt, disbelief, and other symptoms of bereavement commonly discussed in the literature about grief. I had the expected epiphanies about the preciousness of life, registering Matt's words to me, "you have your health; you have everything." Most distressing were the nightmares in which Matt was alive and whole again, his witty, robust self. In other dreams, I would see Matt as he was at 18, a strapping, confident, athletic boy who would kiss me goodnight each night at the dorm room door. Other times, my dreams would take a dark turn and I would relive his dying all over again.

During part of this period, his cremains sat in a box on my dining room table. Soon his mother's cremains joined those of her son, for I was a dutiful ex-daughter-in-law as well as ex-wife and picked up her ashes from the crematorium; she had died several days after Matt did. I was troubled by the sense that there were more dead than living people in my home (my husband was in Sweden), and my mother insisted that I take both boxes and put them in the back of a closet, so I didn't need to encounter concrete evidence of their deaths each day.

Curiously, on the first and second anniversary of Matt's death, I had spells of "benign positional vertigo" that left me reeling, nauseous, ill. A specialist pronounced the timing of the annual onset a coincidence, the result of a virus, but I knew otherwise; clearly this was an embodied disorientation, grief, and memory problem, as my body itself struggled with Matt's death.

The cycles of nature have figured in my mourning and recovery. I live in Southern California, the land of perennial spring, and hadn't had much opportunity to observe the changes of season in the ways that those who reside in less friendly climates do. I thought about the Greek flower myths, which go back to the seventh or eighth century, BC, on an emotional rather than literary level, and the sorrow and joy that they symbolize in their narratives about the origins of wildflowers like the anemone, narcissus, and hyacinth. The cycle of death, rebirth, and resurrection is probably the most widespread of all ritual associations,[3] and I am reminded of them each year as I watch a white potted hydrangea lose its leaves, "die," and sprout to life again. A post-surgery gift from a colleague to Matt, those flowers were important to him and he asked me nurture them until he could plant them in the garden of the beach cottage he planned to buy. When Jerry, an elderly neighbor who fed the songbirds that live in the canyons that surround our community, died, I bought a bird feeder and bath. Jerry had fed 40 generations of these joyful singing birds, and I wanted to keep up the tradition, understanding that their little lives were important to them just as Matt's was important to him.

My death studies were transformed as I was forced to face up to the fact that death is not an abstract problem, it is a part of life. Before Matt died, death had been somewhat depersonalized for me; it was an idea, an aesthetic problem to

---

[3]   See Napier, *Masks, Transformation, and Paradox*, 1986.

explore, rather than something to experience, feel, or grieve. It is an axiom of feminism that the personal is political, so when I gave a public lecture in February 2006 at Bath's Centre for Death and Society, about the commodification of death imagery, I ended the talk by confessing that I had been unprepared for the sight and feel of Matt's corpse body, was moved by its vulnerability, and was disgusted by defilement of simulated human remains in pop culture as a form of amusement. Matt's death haunted my imaginative mind, and in July 2006, I presented an essay at the Paris Writer's Workshop about the day I picked up his cremains. For a death studies anthology I was invited to write a chapter about the prevalence of brutalized corpse images in forensics news, drama, and reality programs, and noted in the piece that "after Matt's death, I could not stomach them anymore."[4] I served as guest editor for a special issue of the journal *Mortality, The Corpse in Contemporary Culture* (2008: 13.2), a volume with an editorial viewpoint, troubled by the various ways that dead bodies are misused. My studies led to an appearance on BBC4 and a role as a commentator during a 2009 *CBS New 48 Hours Special* about the death of Michael Jackson. Most recently, I have written critically about the "skull style" fashion trend and "corpse chic" imagery, the styling of death to sell fashion in mainstream lifestyle and fashion magazines.[5]

With Matt's blessings, the journey we embarked on in the last six months of his life has provided rich fodder not only for the way I approach death imagery but also new research interests. As I pondered my role in Matt's end of life drama, I realized that I had become an individual with a difficult to articulate social identity. I took note of stories about divorced individuals who take on caretaking roles of their mortally ill ex-spouses. As I reviewed the literature, I learned that my status was classified as an "unusual bereavement situation," a "double-loss," "loss within a loss," or "hidden sorrow."[6] Most commonly, it was referred to as a form of "disenfranchised grief," mourning that is not culturally legitimized or supported. Every society has conventions about socially permissible grief, including some bereft and excluding others. It was galling to learn that I fell under an excluded form.[7] The articles about grieving ex-spouses' were few in number, often written by journalists or bloggers, and for me this was a seeming confirmation of my marginal status – at least to academics. I read about the complicated grief of ex-spouses; reasons for mourning, and ambivalent relationship to the deceased. There were pieces about ex-spouses being barred from visiting and caretaking roles;[8] lack of access to medical information;[9] exclusion from funerals, headstones, and

---

[4]   See Foltyn, "Dead Sexy: Why Death is the New Sex," 2008, p. 48.

[5]   See CBS, "Michael Jackson: The Last Dance," 2009. See also: Foltyn, "To Die For," 2010, and Foltyn, "Corpse Chic," 2011.

[6]   See Beder, *Voices of Bereavement*, 2004.

[7]   See Doka, *Disenfranchised Grief*, 2002.

[8]   Ibid.

[9]   See Hospice of the Valley, in *Grief Healing Discussion Groups*, March 20, 2004.

obituaries;[10] current spouse reactions;[11] dealing with offspring from the marriage;[12] financial implications;[13] lack of social support;[14] feelings of closure;[15] and the ways in which counselors, educators, and the community can assist with grief management.[16] I dug deeper and learned that as the divorce rate has risen, death educators, academics, grief counselors and clinicians, have come to appreciate that the divorced are likely to feel bereaved when an ex-spouse dies and may need help dealing with profound sorrow.[17] I reflected upon how the hospice counselors where Matt had died had sought me out to console.

While some of what I read partially explained my experience as an ex-spouse, in some cases it contradicted it. Many times, Matt and I had discussed how ending our marriage had not dissolved our emotional attachment. Our non-legal union was recognized by others, including my then husband, and while Matt and I were no longer legal partners, I was enfranchised rather than marginalized throughout his passage to death, an atypical finding in the death studies literature. I came to think of myself as a "quasi-wife" and then a "quasi-widow," as I carried out – and others let me carry out – social, cultural, and institutional roles traditionally associated with a wife and widow. Only occasionally did someone remark that I was not obligated to help Matt, claiming that "most people would not." I understood that these remarks were not meant to marginalize me but rather to socially locate me in what for them was an unfamiliar role. As an ex-spouse and a married woman, I was breaching social norms about marriage and divorce in western contemporary culture. In the fall of 2008, I presented a paper about the subject at a dying and death conference and published it in 2009, noting, "while they were correct that I was not socially or legally obligated to assist Matt, not doing so was not a morally or emotionally viable option for me." I explained that "I was unwilling to disenfranchise myself … first love, first wife, and first ex-wife, I was transformed into something more than all of these statuses when I became Matt's quasi-wife

---

[10]   See Doka, *Disenfranchised Grief*, 2002.

[11]   See Hospice of the Valley, in *Grief Healing Discussion Groups*, March 20, 2004. See also Scott, "Grief Reactions to the Death of a Divorced Spouse," 1987.

[12]   See Glazer, "How Do You Mourn an Ex-Spouse?" 2007.

[13]   See Doka, *Disenfranchised Grief*, 2002.

[14]   See Kamerman, "Latent Functions of Enfranchising the Disenfranchised Griever," 1993.

[15]   See Beder, *Voices of Bereavement*, 2004; and Mel Glazer, "How Do You Mourn an Ex-Spouse?" 2007.

[16]   See Beder, *Voices of Bereavement*, 2004. See Doka, *Disenfranchised Grief: Recognizing Hidden Sorrow*, 1989. See also Kamerman, "Latent Functions of Enfranchising the Disenfranchised Griever," 1993.

[17]   See Doka, "Loss upon Loss: The Impact of Death after Divorce," 1986. See also Scott, "Grief Reactions to the Death of a Divorced Spouse," 1987.

and quasi-widow, a person with a difficult to articulate social status in a society where social relations are so fragile that people too often die alone."[18]

As Matt's quasi-wife and then quasi-widow, I am part of a growing, little understood or documented trend discussed anecdotally by hospice workers and medical personnel.[19] As the institution of the family grows more fragile and smaller, families are dispersed geographically, individuals have few or no children, and people are unwilling to take on a caretaking role of a dying family member, mortally ill individuals may find themselves without a loved one present to provide them with a secure sense of family and "home." Because of the growing number of individuals who are in Matt's position, hospice personnel are training an army of volunteers to comfort individuals who might otherwise die alone.[20] At the hospice I met such volunteers, who helped not only those who were dying but those who were caretakers. My experience underscores the need for more research into this subject, for individual circumstances, I have learned, matter extremely, enfranchising some while disenfranchising others. It was the urging of the hospice grief counsellors that inspired me to write about quasi-wifedom and widowhood, and I am pleased that my work is now used by hospice educators.

Today is September 4, 2010. It is five years to the day that Matt died and my mother's 78th birthday. Only after I called my mother to wish her a happy birthday did I remember that it is Matt's death day. As I think about my "forgetting" I am surprised that I don't feel guilty. I look in the mirror and understand that the person reflected back in the image is alive. I need to move forward with life the way that the living do. Matt would want that too.

For Matt and me, his final days were a time of suffering, grieving, healing, and working through of a complicated history. Through that period of heightened emotion, we revisited our youths and established a satisfying mid-life relationship and new sources of identity. His dying didn't end our story, but it did end his life, and in doing so it transformed my work and my life. I eventually ended my second marriage as it became clear that the years of trying to revive that union had failed and giving more years to a "dead" marriage was a throwing away of the life I have left.

My relationship with Matt lives on in my work, in memory, and in family history. A portrait of Matt, cocky, grinning, full of professional success and happiness, resides with other family photos on the piano in my study. Another hangs on my parents' family picture wall – it was never taken down.

---

[18]   See Foltyn, "Quasi-Widowhood: Crossing Boundaries of Marriage, Divorce, and Death," 2009, p. 300.

[19]   See Richtel, "When an Ex-Spouse Returns as Caregiver," 2005.

[20]   See Roan, "So They Don't Die Alone: Some Dying Patients Have Neither Friends Nor Family. Increasingly, Volunteers are Filling In," 2007.

References

Ariès, Philippe. *Western Attitudes toward Death: From the Middle Ages to the Present*. Patricia M. Ranum (transl.). Baltimore: Johns Hopkins University Press, 1974.

Beder, Joan. *Voices of Bereavement: A Casebook for Grief Counselors*. New York: Brunner-Routledge, 2004.

CBS. Jacque Lynn Foltyn, interviewed by Paul LaRosa. "Michael Jackson: The Last Dance." *CBS National News Katie Couric Special/48 Hours: Michael Jackson: The Last Dance,* CBS, July 7, 2009.

Doka, Kenneth J., ed. *Disenfranchised Grief: New Directions, Challenges, and Strategies for Practice*. Champaign: Research Press, 2002.

Doka, Kenneth J., ed. *Disenfranchised Grief: Recognizing Hidden Sorrow*. Lexington: Lexington Books, 1989.

Doka, Kenneth J. "Loss upon Loss: The Impact of Death after Divorce," *Death Studies*, 10 (1986): 441–9.

Foltyn, Jacque Lynn. "Dead Sexy: Why Death is the New Sex." In *Making Sense of Death, Dying and Bereavement: An Anthology*, edited by Sarah Earle, Caroline Bartholomew, and Carol Komaromy. Thousand Oaks, London, and New Delhi: Sage, 2008, pp. 47–51.

Foltyn, Jacque Lynn. "Quasi-Widowhood: Crossing Boundaries of Marriage, Divorce, and Death." In *Re-Imaging Death and Dying: Global Interdisciplinary Perspectives*, edited by Dennis R. Cooley and Lloyd Steffen. Oxford: Inter-disciplinary Press, 2009, pp. 295–305.

Foltyn, Jacque Lynn. "Corpse Chic: 'Dead' Models and 'Living' Corpses in Mainstream Fashion Magazines." In *Fashions: Exploring Fashion through Culture*, edited by Jacque Lynn Foltyn. Oxford: Inter-Disciplinary Press, 2011, pp. 269–94.

Foltyn, Jacque Lynn. "To Die For: Skull Style and Corpse Chic." Special Issue*: Fashion Media Journal of Media Arts Culture*, 8, no. 2 (2010), edited by Alex Munt and Susie Khamis. Available at:www.scan.net.au/scan/journal/display php?journal_id=151 (accessed January 31, 2011).

Glazer, Mel. "How Do You Mourn an Ex-Spouse? Self-Improvement/Grief-Loss," *Ezine Articles,* February 18, 2007. Available at: http://ezinearticles.com/?How-Do-You-Mourn-An-Ex-Spouse?&id=459347 (accessed October 4, 2008).

Hospice of the Valley, in *Grief Healing Discussion Groups*, March 20, 2004. Available at: http://hovforum.ipbhost.com/index.php?showtopic=175 (accessed October 3, 2008).

Kamerman, Jack, "Latent Functions of Enfranchising the Disenfranchised Griever," *Death Studies*, 17 (1993): 281–7.

Napier, David Masks. *Transformation and Paradox*. Berkeley: University of California Press, 1986.

Richtel, Matt. "When an Ex-Spouse Returns as Caregiver," *New York Times*, May 19, 2005. Available at: www.nytimes.com/2005/05/19/fashion/

thursdaystyles/19DIVORCE.html?_r=1&pagewanted=print&oref=slogin (accessed July 19, 2005).

Roan, Shari. "So They don't Die Alone: Some Dying Patients Have Neither Friends nor Family. Increasingly, Volunteers are Filling In," *The Los Angeles Times*, June 4, 2007. Available at: http://articles.latimes.com/2007/jun/04/ health/he-dyingalone4 (accessed May 4, 2008).

Scott, Shirley. "Grief Reactions to the Death of a Divorced Spouse." In *Death: Completion and Discovery*, edited by Charles A. Corre and Richard Pacholski. Lakewood: Association for Death Education and Counseling, 1987, pp. 107–16.

Chapter 8
Seeing Differently: Place, Art, and Consolation

Christina Marsden Gillis

"You are fortunate that you have a place," my friend remarked to me. She was referring to the fact that my family and I had a *place* – more than a burial plot per se – to bury the ashes of our son who had been killed in a freak flying accident in East Africa. The place is a small island off the northeast coast of the United States where our family has spent at least a part of every summer for more than four decades; the burial plot lies close to a white wooden fence in the northwest quadrant of the small cemetery that was established by the original islanders, fishing and farming people, in the late eighteenth century. Occupying the brow of a hill overlooking the sea, the cemetery is a favorite spot of the island's summer community of about 50 people; it is a place of broad vistas, both spatial and temporal.

But it's not just "having" a place, a physical site for a burial: perhaps more important, it's the place we *make* that offers consolation in the face of loss. Place gives us the capacity to "see differently" the awful gap that the death of a loved family member, in our case an adult child, leaves in our lives. Elizabeth Hallam and Jenny Hockey have astutely pointed out in *Death, Memory and Material Culture*, that death tends to create a "heterotopia": a site of layered meanings that bespeak our connections with a remembered past.[1] As archaeologists of loss then – and is not loss central to the archaeologist's task? – we "excavate" the layers, the details of the physical landscape, but also the stories, histories, myths, perhaps even fragmented objects, that create a particular place in both personal and social memory. The work at hand is no less than the attempt to transform the pain sustained by loss such that it can be viewed "differently."

Place, sight, and memory are essential elements in this quest. Like narratives of transformation over time, metaphors of memory, Frances Yates told us in her classic text, *The Art of Memory*, published a half-century ago, are usually spatial.[2] Akin to other animals, we humans depend in good measure upon a physical environment, but we relate to that physical world, and we "know" it, in ways that depend in turn upon what we bring to it. In a book titled *Escapism*, geographer Yi-Fu Tuan argues

---

[1] Elizabeth Hallam and Jenny Hockey, *Death, Memory and Material Culture* (New York: Oxford University Press, 2001), p. 84.

[2] Frances Yates, *The Art of Memory* (London: Pimlico, 1992[1966]), p. 120; discussed in Hallam and Hockey, p. 31.

that "Humans not only submit and adapt [to 'nature,' or 'reality']; they transform it in accordance with a preconceived plan. [They] 'see' what is not there. Seeing what is not there lies at the foundation of all human culture."[3] Pointing out that we must consider who we are as human "in productive tandem with the real and imagined," Tuan asserts that the "transformation of the environment is an essential theme in human geography."[4]

Nature is for Tuan both a "responsive 'thou'" and an "indifferent 'it.'" To counter its undependability and violence – and surely the experience of death and loss is central to that "undependability" – we attempt to distance ourselves by establishing a "mediating and more constant world of [our] own making."[5]

In Tuan's dynamic view of the human encounter with the physical world, the line between so-called "nature" and "culture" is always ambiguous:

> The cultural trumps the natural by appearing not so much human made as
> spiritual or divine … The poem is more real than vague feeling. The ritual
> is more real than everyday life. In all of these is a psychological factor that
> enhances the sense of the real and couples it with the divine, namely, lucidity …
> When I am thinking and writing well, I feel I have escaped to the real.[6]

If the "poem" or other created form is more real, sites and spaces, and the relationships among them, give us language for the "poem" or prose narrative that conveys the emotions we experience in times of death or loss. In this process, one story may take the place of another. And all is equally "real." "Loss," poet and writer Barbara Hurd has observed, "is, after all, mostly a story about what happens next."[7]

But "what happens next" depends in good measure on what came before, what we remember. Memory is self-affirming – we are what we remember – but in a much larger sense, and in ways suggestive of Tuan's argument, it engages us in a dynamic relationship with the place and its multiple associations with our loss. In active memory, in active imagining, the heterotopic "layers" that Hallam and Hockey have identified become more knowable, even more visible. They are, after all, the malleable stuff of transformation, offering consolation not only for all that we do not know, cannot explain, about the loss we have suffered, but also for the very experience of not knowing.

In a recent study of grieving, psychologist George Bonanno argues persuasively for human resilience in the face of loss through death. Eschewing Freud's notion that the reclamation of psychological energy can be achieved only through what

---

[3]   Yi-Fu Tuan, *Escapism* (Baltimore: The Johns Hopkins University Press, 1998), p. 6.

[4]   Ibid., p. 8.

[5]   Ibid., p. 10.

[6]   Ibid., p. 22.

[7]   Barbara Hurd, *Walking the Wrack Line: On Tidal Shifts and What Remains* (Athens, Georgia: University of Georgia Press, 2008), p. 7.

he calls a "bit by bit" view of "each single one of the memories [associated with the lost person]."[8] Bonnano promotes what he sees as a more dynamic conception of memory. "Memories of people and places are not objects in our heads," he says. "They are clusters of snakelike neurons, arranged in branching pathways through the brain. The strength of a memory has to do with the connections of the neurons, their links to other ideas and other memories."[9]

Certainly, this language of linkage and connection bespeaks a kind of heightened – and he would probably say, therapeutic – mental activity in Bonnano's assertion, but the reference to the "cluster of neurons" seemingly leaves out the transformational energy of "people and places," the power that Yi-Fu Tuan would ascribe to the creation of the "real" or the "poem." Writing, as critic and poet Susan Stewart has pointed out, "gives us a device for inscribing space, for inscribing nature"; it helps us survive the "terror of the unmarked grave."[10] Poet Alan Shapiro may have something similar in mind when he explained to an interviewer that for him the act of writing following the death of his brother was not in itself "therapeutic," not a form of grieving; rather, creating poetry meant the "transformation of what [he] passively suffered into something [he] could actively *make*" (my italics).[11] Where Tuan theorizes, however, a process where we "see what is not there" and then embark upon a process of transformation that conforms to such "sight," Shapiro suggests, rather, that the "sight" – and in my terms, ultimate consolation – comes about *through* the process of transformation: through the "making." In a related vein, Peter Turchi has observed that "like maps, [the making of] fiction and poetry enable us to 'see' what is literally too large for our vision."[12]

"The author must know his countryside, whether real or imaginary, like his hand; the distances, the points of the compass, the place of the sun's rising … should all be beyond cavil," Robert Louis Stevenson once wrote.[13] Knowing one's "countryside," we could also say, is requisite to seeing the metaphorical value of a physical environment. Thinking of the physical (and "natural") world as if it were a human-only zone, "threatens to take away not only the imaginative solace of a world beyond us, but the very language of the mind," environmental writer Rebecca Solnit has observed in *A Book of Migrations*; for metaphor, Solnit asserts,

---

[8] George Bonanno, *The Other Side of Sadness: What the New Science of Bereavement Tells Us About Life After Loss* (New York: Basic Books, 2009), p. 15.

[9] Ibid., p. 16.

[10] Susan Stewart, *On Longing: Narratives of the Miniature, the Gigantic, the Souvenir, the Collection* (Baltimore: The Johns Hopkins University Press, 1984), p. 31.

[11] Alan Shapiro, "An Aesthetics of Inadequacy," *Atlantic Unbound* (May 30, 2002), www.theatlantic.com/past/docs/unbound/interviews/int2002-05-30.htm.

[12] Peter Turchi, *Maps of the Imagination: The Writer as Cartographer* (San Antonio, Texas: Trinity University Press, 2004), p. 151.

[13] Quoted in ibid., p. 231.

is the "transportation system of the mind" that enables us to "make connections between disparate things."[14]

Yi-Fu Tuan's reading of place as both natural and culturally constructed, "real" and "imagined," all at the same time, is also about "making connections." It's about imagining wholes in parts, even valuing the substitutions and surrogates. Engagement in such construction, especially in time of loss through death, is suggested in the very title of critic Mark Allister's book, *Refiguring the Map of Sorrow: Nature Writing and Autobiography*, a study of the work of several contemporary prose writers for whom a physical environment is integral to the process of life telling in the face of loss.[15] Following the death of a beloved companion, Gretel Ehrlich, for example, uses, in *The Solace of Open Spaces*, a winter spent in the remote rugged mountains of Wyoming as the vehicle for "grief work." The book she writes recounting this experience, Allister comments, "consciously and carefully in an extended way [does] what all humans do in their minds – using language to express what is remembered and observed, structuring memories and observations into story." But, in an echo of poet Alan Shapiro, Allister emphasizes that writing can alter that memory, can turn disabling loss into "manageable sorrow." In a sense, then, Ehrlich writes *about* Wyoming and her memories of that place; but more accurately, she creates or *constructs* Wyoming. The chapters, Allister concludes, "function as pieces of a puzzle that, once put together, display a newly written dramatic story, one that heals and shows healing."[16]

Through the "healing" that Allister describes, the natural landscape in Ehrlich's book, I want to emphasize, is far more than a "projection of consciousness." The physical environment – "nature" – hardly sits inertly there passively awaiting its moment of usefulness to the perceiving eye (recall Tuan's allusion to "undependabiltiy and violence"). Recent work in the field of literature and the environment has emphasized – as have environmental historians and geographers like Tuan – the complexity of interactions between the human – us – and our so-called natural worlds. In a chapter called "Mind the Gap," Timothy Morton seemingly re-asserts the culture/nature binary when he stresses the "emptiness" pertaining between experiences of place and of mind.[17] But if nature, as one reviewer of Morton has observed, is seen as something "over there," while art is a "human production closer to hand," art and art-making may be seen as a place of "intersection between physical matter and conscious being."[18]

[14]   Rebecca Solnit, *A Book of Migrations* (New York: Verso, 1997), p. 25.

[15]   Mark Allister, *Refiguring the Map of Sorrow: Nature Writing and Autobiography* (Charlottesville, Virginia: University of Virginia Press, 2001).

[16]   Ibid., p. 155.

[17]   Timothy Morton, *Ecology Without Nature: Rethinking Environmental Aesthetics* (Cambridge, Massachusetts: Harvard University Press, 2007), p. 169.

[18]   Vince Carducci, review of *Ecology Without Nature*, in *PopMatters* (May 21, 2007), www.popmatters.com/pm/review/ecology-without-nature-by-timothy-morton.

Environmental critic Kent Ryden makes a similar point when he says that "maps, like landscapes themselves, represent an inextricable blending of the earth's non-human surface with the transforming force of human thought and action."[19] For Ryden, place is "equal parts geography and imagination; it is a complex intermingling, and ultimately, fusion of mind and landscape, so that neither is finally separable from or meaningful without the other."[20] In such "fusion," the so-called emptiness is not empty after all. The gap disappears.

Given its climate and location, the small Atlantic island I share with fewer than 50 people, my "heterotopia" and personal "countryside," site of my son's grave, could be seen to intensify a sense of nature separated from, and uncontrolled by, mere human existence: this was abundantly apparent in the summer of 2009, for example, when giant waves created by a fierce Atlantic storm washed over the granite belt of rock that binds and defines the island, destroying the once familiar and protective edge between land and ocean. At such moments, the island is hardly the *locus amoenus* of the classic pastoral tradition that seeks to mitigate the threat of a harsh, even violent or malevolent, nature that simply goes about its business. This is the case even though that "delightful place" of pastoral – the place supposedly free of the relentless forces of time, nature, and mortality – derives its power not from static form or convention, but rather, from the staging the latter provides for transformational activity: the dynamic process that is the essence of art-making.

Paradoxes and contradictions that force our attention to distinctions in scale, small and large, close and proximate, are integral to that process. A small speck of land, floating as it were in a large ocean (the island is one mile across and three miles round), powerfully concentrates experience, condenses or distills it. Despite the disruptions of the storm that broke down the familiar categories for understanding our physical environment, we can still feel protected on a small island. It's as if the granite that appears to bind the island forces an absorptive attention to detail – to tiny lichens, bits of shell, tiny pebbles. In constructing minuscule "elf villages," successive generations of island children in a sense only replicate the adult's delight in the creation of what Tuan called the "real" place.

At the same time, even as I stand in the small island cemetery, a well-defined fenced quadrangle of ground, I look out to 40 miles of ocean and other islands. "The smaller and more enclosed [small islands] are, the larger the window on the infinite," Maine environmental writer Philip Conkling has observed.[21] Just as an artist friend used his hands like a lens to view a spot on the distant horizon, the island is my frame; it is my lens. I know its rocky edges and its meandering

[19]   Kent Ryden, *Landscape with Figures: Nature and Culture in New England* (Iowa City: University of Iowa Press, 2001), p. 97.

[20]   Kent Ryden, *Mapping the Invisible Landscape* (Iowa City: University of Iowa Press, 1993), p. 254.

[21]   In Carl Little, *Art of the Maine Islands* (Camden, Maine: Down East Books, 1997), p. 55.

pathways through dark and mossy woods. I know the old stone foundations, remains of the year-round fishing and farming culture that once flourished here; I know the marble and granite stones that populate, like the stone on my son's grave, this community of the dead that seems always to be with us, part of our daily lives. As for mortality, on a small island with a very small, seasonal, community, we are even more acutely aware of the passing of generations: those who were once the just-marrieds with young children are now the grandparents; and the people I once looked to as the generation considerably senior to my own have now joined the company of "names in stone" in the village cemetery.

In the landscape of memory, in the "heterotopia," the absent and distant play as important a role as the present and the proximate. For a young child, as Rebecca Solnit has pointed out, the absent is "impossible, irretrievable, unreachable." Only as adults does the "blue of distance" become available to us, "the discovery of melancholy, of loss, the texture of longing, of the complexity of the terrain we traverse."[22] Perhaps this is merely the acquisition, with age, of a sense for the aesthetic that "redeems the losses time brings." But Solnit concludes her meditation on distance and absence with a profoundly moving statement: "Some things," she says, "we have only as long as they remain lost, some things are not lost only so long as they are distant."[23]

On a bright day in July, already gathering up our gear to disembark from the lobster boat that takes us out to our island, I saw on the western horizon an island that I had never seen before. Suddenly it rose up into view; in the local Maine language, it "loomed." A trick of certain atmospheric conditions, I later learned. But as Solnit would seem to suggest, the imaginary island, the small landmass that is not really there, is just as real as our more familiar and apparently solid ground.

The physical environment we know – small details, broad visual expanses, physical remnants of the past human community – reflects, refracts, and informs our experience of loss. We are not just changed ourselves by loss, made "different," though that certainly may be the case; we also acquire another framework wherein the "not there," the absent, asserts its own special presence. Discussing the ways that material culture mediates Westerners' relationship with death, Hallam and Hockey suggest that the absence occasioned by death and experienced by survivors is filled in by "cultural materials and strategies, including objects, visual images and texts that constitute a system of recall."[24] That is, as humans dealing with loss through death, we "fill in" the empty space, and the place of the absent and the unknown, of incomplete traces, becomes a necessary element in the constructive, and transformational, work of memory.

Writer Barbara Hurd movingly evokes the role of absence in the "world between grains of sand" on a beach. Without the so-called negative space, she

---

[22] Rebecca Solnit, *A Field Guide to Getting Lost* (New York: Viking Press, 2005), p. 39.

[23] Ibid., pp. 40–1.

[24] Hallam and Hockey, p. 3.

says, "a poem would look on the page like prose, balustrades would appear as wall." The spaces between the grains of sand "shift and reconfigure but never disappear. [They are] *interstitial*, from the Latin root meaning to *stand between*." The word suggests "occupancy."[25]

In her attraction to what she calls the "mystery of vacancy," the "evidence of disappearance," Hurd searches out the traces of what has gone before: the lines of seaweed left by a receding tide on the beach, the "wrack line," are for her a fitting site for an investigation of landscape and loss. The beach, never a sharp edge or end point, is, rather, what philosopher Edward Casey, in a discussion of French philosopher Merleau-Ponty, described as a porous band or region in which "continued movements of transition occur."[26] While the sand of the beach, unlike the granite that marks the shore of my island, is impressionable, both are markers of the edge or the "littoral." While the sand may be seen to take the human trace, it offers also a "site for the imaginative grappling with temporality, and the reality and representation of flux." Change and ambiguity, Shauna McCabe points out, are "inherent to the shore."[27] On a beach such a this, the Cuban artist Ana Mendieta, who died at the tragically young age of 37 in 1985, created in her *Silueta* series of photographs, "silhouettes" of her own body pressed into, or superimposed upon, the sand. In physical form and in remarkable images, Mendieta transforms an ostensibly empty beach, a border, with a silhouette that is itself a signifier of absence: she creates presence out of absence even as she is aware that that presence will also physically disappear with the rising water of the next full tide.

The constantly moving waters that meet the beach both conceal and reveal. New patterns emerge as we see differently the physical environment that we inhabit and fill in what appears empty. That particular sense of what Barbara Hurd calls "occupancy" within apparent vacancy describes also the traditional Japanese "dry garden," whose most famous exemplar is Kyoto's Ryoan-ji. "The senses provide only one part of the experience [of Ryoan-ji]," landscape architect Marc Treib points out; "the other part is provided by the mind." The reduction of materials, Treib contends, is intended to "achieve the definition of space through suggestion." Space and its definition, as opposed to mass and materials, is the major concern in a garden inspired by the Shinto notion that space is sanctified through the presence of spirits dwelling there. Hence a list of the physical elements does little to convey the essence of a garden like Ryoan-ji, for "it is not the materials in isolation that form a garden but these fragments in relationship to one another."[28]

---

25 Hurd, pp. 35–6.

26 Edward Casey, "Borders and Boundaries: Edging into the Environment," in *Merleau-Ponty and Environmental Philosophy*, edited by Suzanne L. Cataldi and William S. Hamrick (Albany, New York: State University of New York Press, 2007), p. 74.

27 Shauna McCabe, *Littoral Documents* (Charlottetown, Prince Edward Island: Confederation Centre Art Gallery, 2004), p. 12.

28 Marc Treib and Ron Herman, *A Guide to the Gardens of Kyoto* (Tokyo: Shufunotomo Company, Ltd, 1980), pp. 3–4.

Consolation derives from putting the "fragments" together in a new relationship, a new "gestalt." The "segregation of parts is independent of knowledge and meaning," psychologist Wolfgang Kohler wrote in his classic 1947 work on gestalt cognition. "In darkness or mist, we see an unknown something, detached from its environment, as a particular object, but we cannot say what it is."[29] But we want to understand, to "say what something is," to identify a pattern. My imaginative construction of a new geography of self, loss, and physical world will include the landscape elements we know – fields, forest, marshes, meadow, and rock – as well as the fragmented remains of objects that have lain for decades in a dusty attic, bits and pieces of lives lived before us. Whether or not directly allied with the lost and absent beloved friend or family member – as, for example, a piece of clothing or a lock of hair encapsulated in a locket would be – memory, as Hallam and Hockey point out, takes on "substance" through metaphor. The remains of a fishing weir that is visible only at the lowest tide and even then in pieces, the old broken rocking chair, the oil lamp with the missing chimney – all belonged to earlier generations, to ghosts or spirits of the past, as much as to us; but they become part of our lives, the more valuable in that they are not property in the usual sense of that term.

Here are the constitutive elements, like those in the Kyoto garden Ryoan-ji, that, in the aggregate, give substance to memory. They enable us to make our own mark or what Yi-Fu Tuan would have called the "poem." We create our trace, "substantiate" ourselves, and come to know who we are both within ourselves and in relation to those we have lost.

Traces can take many forms depending on the medium. Not a site of sand beaches, my island is a place dominated by stone, by granite formed of violent volcanic eruptions. Stone, literally the bedrock of my heterotopia, is an important "layer" and a central building block, in my narrative of loss. Late eighteenth-century Maine islanders used smooth round rocks called "popplestones" to ballast the holds of homemade sailing vessels; later such stones were used to pave the streets of growing cities in the American northeast. The change in function, like a re-organization of parts, is integral to the meaning and significance of the stone. Carrying within them a history, each a fragment of pre-history in fact, the stones figure metaphorically for the written pieces that together form, for me, the new story, or the new landscape, occasioned by loss.

"The rocks tell how old is old," Ruth Moore, a writer and poet who grew up in the island house now owned by my family, once wrote.[30] But the rocks are not the sole historians; theirs is not an isolated telling. Nor is stone less malleable than sand. Rather, joined to all the much younger constituents of the place – other physical landscape elements, the fragmented human-made objects left in a house,

---

[29]   Wolfgang Kohler, *Gestalt Psychology* (New York: Liverwright Publishing, 1947), p. 140.

[30]   Ruth Moore, "Rocks," in *The Tired Apple Tree* (Nobleboro, Maine: Blackberry Books, 1990), n.p.

and the stories and myths passed down through generations – it lends itself to human memory and imagination.

New creations, new visions, of landscape are never literally "new" of course. We also cling to what we know and can imagine as endowed with a certain permanence. It is tempting to think that our small island in Maine simply sits there, "empty" in that it is bereft of all habitation through the long winter; that the scattered houses, the objects stored in attics and barns, the fields and woods, the stones in the cemetery – all may be thought of as waiting to spring to life only when we return each June. But this, surely, is not the case. One could perhaps more accurately take Ruth Moore's view of an distanced, even inimical, natural world when she wrote that "compassionate" summer days are only "leased" to us, "less than smoke, / Less than a flight of sparrows in the air." For a New England poet whose physical world offers little solace, the "flinty" landscape and spring are marked only by "The slow, reluctant blooming out of stone."[31]

But stone may "bloom" in many ways. Tiny petals will re-appear and tell us that despite a stark wintry climate the wild flowers will nonetheless defy the "wild wet winds." They will bloom, even "out of stone." And like the tiny harbingers of spring, we too return. We come back to the familiar site, to the landscape and physical objects we know, but in T.S. Eliot's famous formulation, we will also "know the place for the first time."[32]

References

Bonanno, George. *The Other Side of Sadness. What the New Science of Bereavement Tells Us About Life After Loss* (New York: Basic Books, 2009).

Casey, Edward. "Borders and Boundaries: Edging into the Environment," in *Merleau-Ponty and Environmental Philosophy*, edited by Suzanne L. Cataldi and William S. Hamrick (Albany, New York: State University of New York Press, 2007).

Eliot, T.S. "Little Gidding," *Four Quartets*, in *Collected Poems* (New York: Harcourt, Brace, and World, 1963).

Hall, Elizabeth and Jenny Hockey. *Death, Memory and Material Culture* (New York: Oxford University Press, 2001).

Hurd, Barbara. *Walking the Wrack Line: On Tidal Shifts and What Remains* (Athens, Georgia: University of Georgia Press, 2008).

Kohler, Wolfgang. *Gestalt Psychology* (New York: Liverwright Publishing, 1947).

Little, Carl. *Art of the Maine Islands* (Camden, Maine: Down East Books, 1997).

---

[31] Ruth Moore, "The Mountain of Snow–1934," in *Time's Web* (New York: William Morrow and Company, 1972), p. 39.

[32] T.S. Eliot, "Little Gidding," *Four Quartets*, in *Collected Poems* (New York: Harcourt, Brace, and World, 1963), p. 208.

Mark, Alister. *Refiguring the Map of Sorrow: Nature Writing and Autobiography* (Charlottesville, Virginia: University of Virginia Press, 2001).

McCabe, Shauna. *Littoral Documents* (Charlottetown, Prince Edward Island: Confederation Centre Art Gallery, 2004).

Moore, Ruth."The Mountain of Snow–1934," in *Time's Web* (New York: William Morrow and Company, 1972).

——. "Rocks," in *The Tired Apple Tree* (Nobleboro, Maine: Blackberry Books, 1990).

Morton, Timothy. *Ecology Without Nature: Rethinking Environmental Aesthetics* (Cambridge, Massachusetts: Harvard University Press, 2007).

Ryden, Kent. *Mapping the Invisible Landscape* (Iowa City: University of Iowa Press, 1993).

——. *Landscape with Figures: Nature and Culture in New England* (Iowa City: University of Iowa Press, 2001).

Solnit, Rebecca. *A Book of Migrations* (New York: Verso, 1997).

——. *A Field Guide to Getting Lost* (New York: Viking Press, 2005).

Stewart, Susan. *On Longing: Narratives of the Miniature, the Gigantic, the Souvenir, the Collection* (Baltimore: The Johns Hopkins University Press, 1984).

Shapiro, Alan. "An Aesthetics of Inadequacy," *Atlantic Unbound* (May 30, 2002).

Treib, Marc and Ron Herman. *A Guide to the Gardens of Kyoto* (Tokyo: Shufunotomo Company, Ltd, 1980).

Tuan, Yi-Fu. *Escapism* (Baltimore: The Johns Hopkins University Press, 1998)

Turchi, Peter. *Maps of the Imagination: The Writer as Cartographer* (San Antonio, Texas: Trinity University Press, 2004).

Yates, Frances. *The Art of Memory* (London: Pimlico, 1992[1966]).

Chapter 9

'Sacramentality' and Identity Transformation: Deathbed Rituals in Dutch Spiritual Care

Thomas Quartier

Spiritual care in the context of dying requires special attention by professionals. In the Netherlands, spiritual caregivers act as ritual guides to support people's transformation of identity in a personal, interpersonal and trans-personal sense. Though these rituals are often performed outside traditional religious repertoires they still try to help dying persons and their loved ones with the reorientation required by the farewells they have to make. This chapter seeks to clarify both the nature of these rituals and the competence of spiritual caregivers by exploring the concepts of 'sacramentality' in its symbolic and performative dimension.

Death often leaves people around a deathbed feeling confused and insecure. Emotions like fear, hope, attachment or severed ties are typical and occur simultaneously.[1] Life has been turned topsy-turvy and they no longer see themselves clearly – who they are, who they are to others and of what larger whole they form a part. When such an identity crisis arises, it takes place at three levels. Firstly, one loses touch with oneself when life is in the balance. That applies equally to patients, their relatives and friends, and sometimes even to professionals. Secondly, one finds it awkward to relate to others: social relations are disrupted and communication and interaction with significant others are complicated. Thirdly, it is not easy to relate to life at a deeper level. In religious terms one could say that one has to rediscover one's relationship with God. One's identity has to be transformed in a way that faces up to human mortality at a personal, interpersonal and trans-personal level. But, in present-day secularised and individualised society, such a transformation, which presupposes a rediscovery of frameworks of meaning, is difficult at times of grave illness or death, albeit all the more necessary. Still, however tentatively, many people feel a need to find meaning.[2]

Spiritual caregivers are among the principal guides of people who need to reorient themselves to their identity at a personal, interpersonal and trans-personal

---

[1]   C.M. Parkes (2009). *Love and loss: The roots of grief and its complications*. London and New York: Routledge.

[2]   T. Quartier (2010). Symbolische en performatieve dimensies van sacramentaliteit. *Tijdschrift voor Geestelijk leven* 66 (2), 59–70.

level. This makes the creation of ritual space a key element of spiritual care. The term refers not only to space in the literal sense of a chapel or meditation centre but also in a metaphorical sense, where space refers to the possibility to be truly present to oneself (*habitare secum*). Such self-awareness is conducive to spiritual well-being, an explicit goal of spiritual care.[3] Especially when faced with serious illness, dying and death, such a space cannot be taken for granted.[4]

Ritual is, par excellence, a space in which the three levels I have outlined are realised, and this has to do with the meaning of ritual, involving the setting apart of something and of encountering the Holy,[5] an encounter I describe here as 'sacramentality'. And here it must be said that the hesitancy many people feel when they hear the words 'holy' and 'sacramentality' is unwarranted for, functionally, the Holy can be given highly personal meaning at various levels and can manifest itself in 'sacramental' acts – rituals – without necessarily forming part of classical liturgy or of a church service. But it can certainly entail religious reorientation. The meaning attached to these words depends partly on the client's background, hence I ask readers – irrespective of their own perspective – to interpret the terms 'Holy' and 'sacramentality' as used in this chapter very broadly.[6]

In the Dutch context an open-minded approach is essential, since it is very distinctive in two respects. Firstly, the Netherlands is one of the most secularised countries in the world while possessing, at the same time, widely divergent religious and spiritual trends: Dutch religiosity is stronger than church affiliation. This means that, when it comes to ritual formalisation round a deathbed, one often has to feel one's way without clear-cut guidelines. Secondly, Dutch care institutions are legally obliged to offer patients spiritual care that accords with their worldview and background. Since that background is often not denominational, a new kind of spiritual care is called for.[7] Training courses and hospitals respond by developing a 'neutral' form of spiritual care: spiritual caregivers draw freely from diverse traditions, *inter alia* to evolve rituals together with patients that will help them to ponder their identity anew. As a result the Holy and 'sacramentality' no longer have any fixed meaning but remain vital for the transformation of people's identity in the face of death.

Against this background this chapter seeks to cast light on the question of how 'sacramentality' furthers the reorientation of people confronting serious illness or

[3]   J. Vreeman, T. Quartier and W. Smeets (2009). Geestelijke verzorging in het kader van geestelijk welbevinden. *Tijdschrift Geestelijke Verzorging* 12 (53), 44–9.

[4]   T. Quartier (2010). Deathbed rituals: Roles of spiritual caregivers in Dutch hospitals. *Mortality* 15 (2), 105–19.

[5]   T. Quartier (2007). Ritual studies: Een antropologische bezinning op de liturgie. *Tijdschrift voor Liturgie* 91, 218–29.

[6]   M. Riesebrodt (2007). *Cultus und Heilsversprechen: Eine Theorie der Religionen.* München: C.H. Beck, 240.

[7]   W. Smeets (2007). *Spiritual care in a hospital setting: An empirical theological exploration.* Leiden: Brill.

death at a personal, interpersonal and trans-personal level. Though rooted in the Dutch context, this topic may well be of interest in other contexts that encounter comparable, albeit less explicit, questions.

Ritual Practice in Hospital

Life in a hospital ward is busy and very much governed by medical procedures.[8] In addition, the stress situation of the sick or dying person is often such that her personal, interpersonal and trans-personal identity is not always properly recognised. Thus it may happen that for personal, institutional or social reasons insufficient attention is paid to the process of illness and dying.[9] As a result there is no scope for reflection on what the loss means or for those meaningful experiences which are preconditions for identity transformation. In modern conceptions of care that is vitally important if the transition that severe illness or death implies is to be a good one.[10]

The comment, 'The Holy has to be mediated in human life', which I recently heard a Dutch spiritual caregiver make, perfectly describes the role that rituals can play in the confrontation with serious illness or death, as mentioned above. By 'the Holy' the speaker did not mean a traditionally prescribed God concept, but an experience that transcends our tangible, functional, reality and helps us find meaning in apparently meaningless situations. The caregiver's comment could translate into 'creating space for transformation', a transformation occurring at the three – personal, interpersonal and trans-personal – levels.

Formerly, Christian rituals were obvious means of creating such space. When a Roman Catholic priest entered a room where a person lay dying he was manifestly going to administer the sacrament of extreme unction, thereby helping the patient to come to terms with himself, the people around him, and God. It was a prescribed space for bidding farewell and reorienting at all three levels.[11] In present-day Catholic practice extreme unction still often serves this purpose, only the ritual is no longer performed automatically. Yet the need for ritual space in a situation of serious illness or death is as real as ever. Indeed, Dutch authors like Lukken indicate a new openness to and need for rituals since the 1990s.[12] How, then, can one create such a space in a modern hospital? To my mind this is an important task

[8] M. Walsh and P. Ford (2001). *Nursing rituals: Research and rational actions*. Oxford: Butterworth-Heinemann.

[9] S.B. Nuland (1994). *How we die: Reflections on life's final chapter*. New York: Vintage.

[10] A. Narayanasamyr (2001). *Spiritual care: A practical guide for nurses and health care practitioners*. London: Quay.

[11] W. von Arx (1979). *Das Sakrament der Krankensalbung*. Freiburg i.Ue.: Canisius.

[12] G. Lukken (2005). *Rituals in abundance: Critical reflections on the place, form and identity of Christian ritual in our culture*. Liturgia Condenda 17. Leuven: Peeters, 3.

of spiritual caregivers who can enhance patients' spiritual well-being in a difficult situation by guiding them in the transformation they have to undergo.

Below I try to show how ritual provides opportunities to do this in spiritual caregivers' repertoire: creating space that enhances well-being through reorientation and transformation in the process of illness or dying. My premise in dealing with this ritual space lies, as already mentioned, in the concept of *'sacramentality'* with its *symbolic* and *performative* dimensions. That is because I consider it an apt term to express the special nature of the spiritual caregiver's contribution, as distinct from that of other professionals such as social workers and psychologists. I do not use the term in a strictly theological sense, but adapt it specifically to spiritual care, as Van der Geest did in the case of medical care.[13]

Ritual Transformation: Enacting 'Sacramentality'

From a ritual studies perspective the need to ritualise illness and dying is perfectly understandable. Special situations have always called upon people to reassess their position in life, to affirm it, or to embark on new ways or to take their leave. But this reorientation does not necessarily happen of its own accord and one may have to consciously deal with situations that potentially call for reorientation and transformation – only then will they enhance well-being and bring people closer to what life ultimately is about: a new orientation to oneself, to those with whom we share our lives, and to that which transcends physical existence.[14] The personal, interpersonal and trans-personal reorientation I have in mind takes place in ritual spaces: moments and situations that do not arise spontaneously but have to be created, drawing on ritual repertoires. Following the classical works by Victor Turner, who defined it as liminal space,[15] such rituals are in the tradition of rites of passage at pivotal moments in life.[16]

Pivotal moments, traditionally set aside for reorienting one's life, have the potential to transform people.[17] However, it is by no means guaranteed that they will actually be experienced that way, not least because liminality primarily means insecurity – 'anti-structure' in Turner's sense – and only secondarily involves possible new potential. Ritual helps to open up that potential.

---

[13]   S. van der Geest (2005). 'Sacraments' in the hospital: exploring the magic and religion of recovery. *Anthropology and Medicine* 12 (2), 135–50.

[14]   T. Quartier (2010). Ritualisierungen des Sterbens. Rituelle Dimensionen der Seelsorge im Niederländischen Gesundheitswesen, *Jaarboek voor liturgie-onderzoek*, 135–48.

[15]   V. Turner (1967). *The ritual process: Structure and anti-structure.* Chicago: Aldine.

[16]   A. van Gennep (1999). *Les rites de passage.* Berlin: Campus Verlag.

[17]   T.F. Driver (1998). *Liberating rites: Understanding the transformative power of ritual.* Boulder: Westview.

'We undergo passages', Ronald Grimes maintains, 'but we enact rites'.[18] What Grimes means by rites in this case assumes the form, in Catholic tradition, of sacraments like extreme unction. But, if that classical repertoire is inapplicable, other forms of ritual space often emerge or the space is utilised differently. In hospital wards there are various reasons for this. There may be no suitably qualified clergy available to administer the Catholic sacrament of extreme unction,[19] or it may be non-Catholic patients who are in need of a ritual space. They may not be allowed to receive the sacrament but could benefit by the actions or symbols.[20] My concern is to determine the attributes of suitable rituals for different situations.

To my mind the concept of 'sacramentality' helps to clarify the ritualising task performed by and in conjunction with spiritual caregivers in such situations, because they focus on encounters with the Holy. 'Sacramentality' extends beyond the churches' traditional sacraments (although these embody 'sacramentality' in a special way). As noted already, I understand the term to refer to people's experience of being in contact with the Holy, more particularly at transitional moments in their lives when they have a need for reorientation at a personal, interpersonal and trans-personal level. Catherine Bell points out that the distinction between sacred and profane can be interpreted in many different ways. The common factor, however, is that a separate category is reserved for that which is sacred to people and affects the core of their existence.[21] Communication with that which touches the core of their existence, and which therefore lies beyond everyday life, opens up possibilities for the future.[22] When people are up against the limits of life that need becomes all the more urgent. Then, they need something that is meaningful in itself and does not have to be supplied with a particular meaning, as Rudolf Otto suggests.[23] In this sense 'sacramentality' has to do with limits and transitions. And in a religious sense these are the preserve of liturgical rituals. Liturgy is a concrete, formal expression of 'sacramentality', which is what I have in mind, although certainly not the only one.

Essentially liturgy is always in the nature of a minor or major 'rite of passage', for special (pivotal) moments arise not only at birth, the attainment of adulthood, marriage and, especially, death, but also in other cycles of life: the day, the week, the year – as well as at unexpected moments. The enactment, however, assumes

---

[18]   R.L. Grimes (2000). *Deeply into the bone: Re-inventing rites of passage.* Berkeley: University of California Press, 5.

[19]   K. Richter (1973). *Liturgie mit Kranken.* Essen: Driewer.

[20]   T. Quartier (2008). Voorbij de dood? Rituele stervensbegeleiding in het ziekenhuis. In E. Venbrux, M. Heesels and S. Bolt (eds), *Rituele creativiteit: Actuele veranderingen in de uitvaart- en rouwcultuur in Nederland.* Zoetermeer: Meinema, 59–74.

[21]   C. Bell (1997). *Ritual: Perspectives and dimensions.* Oxford: Oxford University Press, 156.

[22]   Riesebrodt, *Cultus und Heilsversprechen*, 109.

[23]   R. Otto (1958). *The idea of the Holy: An inquiry into the non-rational factor of the idea of the divine and its relation to the rational.* New York: Galaxy.

different forms in different cultures.[24] Just as symbols are only comprehensible in a particular context, so the performance and functioning of rituals vary from one culture to another. Take the symbol of an old-fashioned weighing-scale: whereas it used to have mainly practical connotations, nowadays people associate it with justice and judgment. Actions, too, change their meaning: in former times bowing or curtseying was a normal way to greet an acquaintance, today it will be experienced as far more ceremonious, even archaic. It is still meaningful, but it means something very different from what it meant 200 years ago.

Sacraments, as enactments of special moments that permit reorientation, must likewise – as Grimes puts it – be 're-invented' each time.[25] The theologian Edward Schillebeeckx pointed out that sacraments are shaped to some extent by their anthropological roots.[26] Yet they must never lose contact with the Holy lest they lose their transformative potential. They operate at the interface of our familiar life world and a promised world that we have not yet reached or have lost touch with in our crisis situation.

In a society that in many respects is ready for reorientation and is looking for it, there are many ways of highlighting special occasions in human life and turning them into opportunities for reorientation, because people's lives are so diverse. Old and new rituals can have a 'sacramental' dimension: an encounter with the Holy.[27] When looking for this dimension in our day two clues serve as important guides: the *things* people use and the things they *do*. Situations with 'sacramental' potential always include *symbols* and entail actions that can be termed '*performances*'.

When it comes to situations of grave illness and death, it implies that *symbolic performances* are essential for the well-being of the people involved, since they permit transformation at a personal, interpersonal and trans-personal level. This does not mean that words do not play an important role, but they need to be interpreted as 'communicative action' as Garrigan argues.[28] Deathbed rituals are performed everywhere: they support the dying person, strengthen those gathered round the deathbed, and in sense help people to transcend the barrier of death.[29] Here, too, the performance need not involve explicitly religious images. The hallmark of virtually all deathbed rituals, however, is the presence of some form of

---

[24]   M. van Endt-Meijling (2006). *Rituelen en gewoonten: Geboorte, ziekte en dood in de multiculturele samenleving*. Bussum: Coutinho. K. Garces-Foley (2006). *Death and religion in a changing world*. New York and London: Sharpe.

[25]   Grimes, *Deeply into the bone*, 87.

[26]   E. Schillebeeckx (2000). Naar een herontdekking van de christelijke sacramenten. *Tijdschrift voor Theologie* 40, 164–87.

[27]   T. Quartier and J. Wojtkowiak (2010). Nieuwe rituelen: Creativiteit en herontdekking. *Tijdschrift voor Geestelijk Leven* 66 (2), 19–28.

[28]   S. Garrigan (2004). *Beyond ritual: Sacramental theology after Habermas*. Aldershot: Ashgate, 97.

[29]   Quartier, Deathbed rituals.

transcendence.[30] The barrier of death can be transcended in various ways whether in the form of images of the hereafter, a memorial culture, or a reassessment of the mourners' identity.[31] That applies to extreme unction in the Catholic tradition as well as to parting rituals not directly associated with a religious system of meaning. Spiritual caregivers should have the symbolic and performative tools available and offer them to people so they can discover the space for 'sacramentality', issues we now examine in greater detail.

Symbolic Dimension of 'Sacramentality'

When faced with death people rediscover the importance of objects: personal objects, in particular, may become memorial symbols transcending death, embodying hope of life after death.[32] This touches the very core of the symbolic dimension of 'sacramentality' as predominantly concerned with *things*. While symbols exist in every area of human life, they are often not rated at their true value.[33] A symbol is not just a sign. Take a wedding ring. It not only signifies the love relationship between the two partners but actually embodies it, which they often realise only when one of them loses the ring. A new ring, even if identical, simply does not have the same value. The remarkable ambiguity of symbols that on the one hand refer to something and on the other have their own reality makes them super-cognitive objects. There is no purely rational reason why a lost wedding ring is irreplaceable. Its material dimension concerns the special celebration of lifelong love, both at the moment of making the marriage vows and afterwards. In a sense it eludes functional logic, but remains perfectly real and experiential. In recent years religious studies has shown renewed interest in the material dimension that underlies symbols. For a long time the focus was mainly on verbal expressions, but of late the accent has shifted to the materialisation of religious experience, more especially at pivotal moments in life.[34] How did this come about?

According to Louis-Marie Chauvet, who reflects on liturgical symbols in the French philosophical tradition, they are not confined to the places where they are physically observable but enable us to perceive another reality while, at the same

---

[30]   D. Chidester (2002). *Patterns of transcendence: Religion, death, and dying.* Belmont, CA: Wadsworth.

[31]   'J. Wojtkowiak and E. Venbrux (2010). Living through ritual in the face of death, in A. Michaels (ed.) *Ritual Dynamics and The Science of Ritual, Vol. II: Body, Performance, Agency and Experience.* Wiesbaden: Harrassowitz, 265–78.

[32]   H. Embsen and T. Overtoom (2007). *Hoe zou jij het willen? Persoonlijk afscheid nemen van je dierbare.* Kampen: Ten Have.

[33]   T. Quartier (2009). Personal symbols in Roman Catholic funerals in the Netherlands. *Mortality* 14 (2), 133–46.

[34]   A. Molendijk (2003). *Materieel christendom: Religie en de materiele cultuur in West-Europa.* Hilversum: Verloren.

time, such symbols are fully part of the observer's life world. In effect they exist in two places: they are recognisable elements of the life world but also transcend it. Chauvet calls this bipolarity of symbols 'heterotopy'.[35] According to him symbols featuring in 'sacramental' rituals display a symbolic rupture: they transcend what they are at a functional level. They are part of the Holy and have something sublime about them. Yet the sublimity is not such that people cannot recognise them in an experiential sense. The rupture in their heterotopy makes symbols vulnerable. They can easily become either too sublime or too trivial. Chauvet uses two concepts in this regard. When a symbol loses touch with the observers' life world he speaks of 'hieratism', the symbol is 'too sacred', but when it is too fully assimilated into the life world Chauvet calls it 'trivialisation', the symbol is now so close to people's experiential world that it loses its symbolic rupture and can no longer trigger reorientation.

It could well be this vulnerability of 'sacramental' symbols that explains why the symbolic dimension is so essential for 'sacramental' experience. Symbols are situated at an interface, where they may easily lose their experiential value. Yet one cannot experience 'sacramentality' without venturing to that interface. Transformation at a personal, interpersonal and trans-personal level presupposes putting one's life world at risk: on the one hand one makes it accessible, on the other one is ready to transcend it. That is quite a tall order and one must ask how far traditional liturgy allows diverse groups scope for such development.

Recent times have also seen a marked personalisation of symbols in church liturgy.[36] We have noted that this is particularly noticeable in the highly personal rituals concerned with illness and death. In addition to traditional symbols, personal objects belonging to the dying person often feature prominently. Grandpa's watch that he gives to his grandson in the space created for his parting; the coffee pot children bring to the hospital because it had stood on mother's breakfast table for decades and was subsequently used on special occasions – such objects become 'sacred', even after the death of the loved one. People find deathbed rituals valuable to experience life in symbolically condensed fashion and to draw hope from it.[37] At the same time the risk of trivialisation is ever present. Symbols must continually rupture to be able to actively trigger transformation at a personal, interpersonal and trans-personal level. Individual symbols have to be carefully selected to avoid trivialisation.[38] But traditional symbols call for equal circumspection if they are not to be hieratically eclipsed in the performance of

[35]   L.-M. Chauvet (1995). *Symbol and sacrament: A sacramental re-interpretation of Christian existence*. Collegeville: Liturgical Press.

[36]   Quartier, Personal symbols, 145.

[37]   E. Leach (1979). *Culture and communication: The logic by which symbols are connected – An introduction to the use of structuralist analysis in social anthropology*. 4th edn. Cambridge: Cambridge University Press.

[38]   C. Menken Bekius (2009). Men neme een symbool. *Handelingen* 1, 29–33. C. Menken-Bekius (2001). *Werken met rituelen in het pastoraat*. Kampen: Kok, 13.

a ritual. In the case of sickbed and deathbed rituals the Catholic rite of extreme unction again offers a good example. Are the symbols used – holy oil, sometimes communion – still sufficiently rooted in the life world of the patients and their significant others? If not, there is a danger that the ritual will not address them. But these risks do not mean that only strictly religious patients have a need for symbols. On the contrary, people of whatever ecclesiastic affiliation may feel a need for personal or traditional symbols, and a major task of caring for seriously ill or dying patients and their loved ones is to provide good guidance in this respect.[39] So it is that spiritual caregivers have to help people to find appropriate symbols, often entailing a combination of both traditional and personal symbols.[40] Personal symbols may be incorporated into extreme unction, and religious symbols from various traditions may be incorporated into personal rituals. The choice of symbols requires a primary ritual competence from spiritual caregivers especially since, in the stress associated with serious illness or death, people often cannot think for themselves what symbols would be appropriate.

Performative Dimension of 'Sacramentality'

Symbols are meaningful only if something is *done* with the representations of the 'other place' on which the parties are reflecting. That brings us to the performative dimension of 'sacramentality' – and that requires a second major ritual competence of spiritual caregivers. Edward Schillebeeckx emphasises the *dromenon* in liturgy: when at pivotal points in human life words, small or great, are inadequate, we need to *act*.[41] The really important things in life are *enacted*: words – the *legomenon* – may feature in them, but the words too are spoken in performative fashion and become speech *acts* which establish communicative action, as already mentioned.[42]

Again, although a sickbed or deathbed is, par excellence, the site where gestures and actions count, people often do not know how to conduct themselves there, their 'natural' repertoires of interaction are inadequate. In this liminal state – to invoke Turner again – there is a need for performative repertoires.[43] People feel a need for meaningful actions that will help them to re-enact their attitude to themselves, their significant others and the transcendent – in effect, a personal, interpersonal and trans-personal reorientation.

Performance studies are, for example, a recognised branch of sport research and there are many different conceptions of what performance entails. I shall

---

[39]   T. Quartier (2008). Voorganger of begeleider? Rituelen rond sterven en dood in de moderne geestelijke verzorging. *Tijdschrift voor geestelijke verzorging* 47 (11), 15–25.

[40]   Quartier, Personal symbols.

[41]   Schillebeeckx, Naar een herontdekking.

[42]   Garrigan, *Beyond ritual*, 71.

[43]   T. Quartier (2007). *Bridging the gaps. An empirical study of Catholic funeral rites.* Empirische Theologie 17. Münster: Lit Verlag.

not dwell on these, but focus on just one meaning of the term that in my view can help us to understand 'sacramentality'. Bell lists three dimensions that are essential for a meaningful performance that would permit reorientation. Firstly, the performance has to be *multi-sensory*, addressing more than only one sense organ: words alone do not constitute a performance. Secondly, a performance should enable people to become totally absorbed in it. Bell's term 'framing' refers to the phenomenon recognised by everyone who has ever had the experience after a theatre performance that the world around them has come to a standstill. For the duration of the show it was their only frame of reference. Thirdly, a performance must exceed its own limits: then its impulses direct life as a whole and become a *guideline* shaping people's ordering of the world. It orients our future living. Thus a film directs an ethical appeal that shapes people's future dealings with nature or other human beings.[44] We must stress that the performative aspect of a 'sacramental' situation is obviously not a stage show. A ritual is not a performance, but there are resemblances and one can avail oneself of insights from other genres.[45]

Bell's three dimensions provide food for thought over 'sacramental' performances aimed at promoting reorientation at a personal, interpersonal and trans-personal level. The multi-sensory dimension is apparent in the liturgy as well. In the wake of the *participatio actuosa* of Vatican II a Roman Catholic style of liturgical performance evolved which put the accent squarely on corporeality, for instance liturgical dance.[46] This invites us to adapt the frame of reference (Bell's second dimension) created in liturgy to our own day and age. We try to include sufficient stimuli to produce an exciting liturgy. New forms of community arise from physical togetherness in search of the Holy.

To many people this is valuable and may help them discover the third dimension of a performance in a guideline for living and ordering of the world. But it also calls for caution for, as with symbols, the way we participate in liturgy and the stimuli we derive from it can be experienced very differently. What strikes one person as a subtle form of physical involvement may make another person uncomfortable. Stimuli that excite one person are off-putting to another. Hence the same 'sacramental' performance that works for one person may be totally wrong for another. For one person it will trigger transformation, for another it will cut off access to the Holy altogether.

In the case of performative actions in the context of serious illness and death, in some Christian traditions it has become customary for relatives and friends of the dying person to participate actively in extreme unction, the ritual space. That is an instance of a rediscovery of personal involvement in rituals associated with the end of life. There are other examples after death: washing the body of the

---

[44] Bell, *Ritual*, 72f.

[45] R. Grimes (2006). *Rite out of place: Ritual, media, and the arts*. Oxford and New York: Oxford University Press, 90. T. Quartier (2009). Theologische en rituologische perspectieven op liturgie. *Tijdschrift voor Theologie* 49, 287–97.

[46] M.A. Friedrich (2001). *Liturgische Körper*. Stuttgart: Kohlhammer.

deceased, closing the coffin and many other gestures. But let us look at extreme unction. From a 'sacramental' point of view the performative aspect of the ritual could be greatly enhanced by letting people perform it themselves. It means that the senses of sight and hearing are augmented by the sense of touch. This could greatly enrich the framing of the ritual, because the sensory experience makes it all the more absorbing: a rite of passage that people perform together becomes a guideline beyond the actual moment of parting. But everyone knows from practice and personal experience that reality is more complex than that. The same applies to new rituals: not everybody will be capable of having the physical contact with a dying person that they might have had with her in their childhood. To others it would be an intense reorientation. What strikes one person as an intensified reorientation may, to someone else, be repulsive. That applies particularly to what people *do*, which touches their bodies to the very core.[47] That is why proper guidance – the second major competence of spiritual caregivers – is essential. People should be helped to find and perform actions that suit them. Feeling duty bound to participate or that they are not taken seriously puts paid to performance, and thus to 'sacramentality' as well.

Because 'sacramentality' is always embedded in some form of community it may be necessary to allow for different forms of participation: from active participation to being present in a community.[48] That may happen at a deathbed, for not everyone is involved in the same way. The performative quality of a performance that seeks to trigger reorientation and transformation is therefore neither fixed nor imposed. Circumspection in the first place means respect – respect for the way people can and want to shape a performance at the pivotal moment of serious illness or death. Because the personal, interpersonal and trans-personal experience of corporeality in modern-day culture is diverse, re-invention cannot be prescriptive but at most inviting, a possibility offered by, amongst other things, the spiritual caregiver.

Horizontal and Vertical Space for Transformation

Having briefly examined the symbolic and performative dimensions of 'sacramentality' I will now review the metaphor of ritual space alluded to in this chapter's introduction. To my mind the enactment of rituals at pivotal moments creates a space with a horizontal and a vertical aspect. Essentially 'sacramentality' entails a more conscious manner of living and experiencing and enacting

---

[47]   T. Quartier (2004). Het kwijnen van de katholieke devotie: Dialectische exploraties omtrent katholieke ritualiteit. In J. Jacobs and R. Nauta (eds), *Daarom toch katholiek: Opstellen rond een kentering*. Nijmegen: Valkhof, 112–40.

[48]   P. Post (2005). Gezocht verband: Een verkenning van nieuw opkomende rituelen. In S. Gärtner (ed.), *Bandeloos? Zoeken naar samenzijn in een individualistische cultuur*. Nijmegen: Valkhof, 82–97.

situations meaningfully. At a horizontal level people perceive life differently and behave differently. Self-perception and relations with oneself and others are a precondition for reorientation and transformation. That also means that in situations of serious illness or dying spiritual caregivers have to be alert to this personal and interpersonal dimension, bearing in mind that they themselves are part of it. In principle this means that every situation in life can be 'sacramental', as Wil Derkse puts it: everything from gardening and bookkeeping to a birthday party might become 'sacramental'.[49] But situations are not merely perceived differently – that in itself may have nothing to do with the Holy. Besides that a further dimension is added to our perception, which brings us to the vertical aspect of 'sacramentality' and the trans-personal dimension of ritual. For in hospital, too, not every situation in which ritual creates a 'sacramental' space may, when viewed objectively, be anything out of the ordinary. Symbolic performances sometimes happen spontaneously, sometimes in classical repertoires, but the common denominator is that they leave scope for transformation. That is what I call the vertical aspect of 'sacramental' space enacted at a trans-personal level.

Here, what Michael Casey understands by prayer is very pertinent to 'sacramentality' as conceived of in this chapter, for in it we add a new dimension to our human life world.[50] When it comes to the vertical aspect of 'sacramentality' it is not just a matter of structuring or remembering but, for Casey, it is a movement towards God, in which humans are often passive. They receive this additional dimension from life outside them. Above all they have to create openness. Viewed more broadly it implies creating space for the Holy, which can then enter into human life. It should be clear from the foregoing that people who are not classically religious also know this movement: forming a relationship with the Holy in a broad sense. The crux of this lies in a transformation that transcends the limits of personal identity, whether that of a seriously ill or dying patient or of a significant other.

To my mind the two concepts, 'symbol' and 'performance', are helpful in exploring the horizontal and vertical aspects of 'sacramentality'. Symbolically, the horizontal aspect entails being alert to the symbolic potential – what Chauvet calls heterotopy – of things we handle in everyday life. These can then be included in the repertoire that spiritual workers keep handy to offer to people. Performatively, the horizontal aspect requires them to do everything wholeheartedly and attentively. The vertical aspect can be experienced by means of carefully chosen symbols. People can participate fully by placing the performance in a frame of reference that is not overcrowded with an inordinate number of stimuli but actually leaves participants lots of free scope. Just like prayer in Casey's description, 'sacramentality' can be present everywhere and at all times, but people need guidance to experience it. That is the purpose of ritual, liturgy and sacraments, to assist people in their reorientation and transformation at a personal, interpersonal

---

[49]   W. Derkse (2003). *Een leefregel voor beginners*. Tielt: Lannoo, 123–4.

[50]   M. Casey (2007). *Toward God*. Missouri: Liguori.

and trans-personal level – to scrape off the grime of living so the Holy becomes visible. That makes 'sacramentality' a hallmark of rituals in spiritual care. Provided the term is given an interpretation that is neither too broad nor too narrow – that is, refraining from either hieratism or trivialisation – it is the very core of the spiritual caregiver's task. Rituals should not function as a straitjacket, but neither should their opportunity be missed.

Summary and Conclusions

Now that the reader has arrived in the ritual space for 'sacramental' transformation, both horizontal and vertical, I return to the question underlying this chapter, namely, how does 'sacramentality' contribute to people's reorientation at a personal, interpersonal and trans-personal level in the face of serious illness or dying? We have explored a number of concepts: reorientation and transformation, symbols, performances, ritual space in a horizontal and a vertical sense. The scheme below lists the key concepts, each accompanied by a question to guide the spiritual caregiver.

As is evident in the guiding questions, I do not mention any tradition or religion to which clients may adhere. For the purpose of this model of 'sacramentality' it is essential not to do so, at least at the outset. The Holy that people encounter at the personal, interpersonal and trans-personal level is neither fixed nor the same for everybody. People from traditions other than that of the spiritual caregiver or those without any religious affiliation are perfectly able to undergo the transformations I have described and experience the Holy as real. Naturally this does not detract from the importance of religious traditions.

As for the identity of the patient, the dying person and significant others, I believe that 'sacramental' rituals make it possible to touch the core of the person

Table 9.1   Symbolic-performative spiritual care

Element	Concept	Question
Transition	Liminality	How can situations of conscious transition be created at sickbeds and deathbeds?
Objects	Symbol	What objects are familiar to people and also have referential potential?
Actions	Performance	What actions suit people and how can they be motivated to perform them?
Horizontal space	Attentiveness	What issues pertaining to the person's identity and social relations play a role (personally and interpersonally)?
Vertical space	Transformation	What sacral dimension may open up to the client in the ritual space (trans-personally)?

at important levels and also to exceed its limits. Unfortunately the scope of this chapter does not permit lengthy discussion of this last conclusion, especially as regards the identity of the spiritual caregiver. Obviously his or her identity forms part of the ritual performance, but that does not establish any norm for the way clients experience the Holy. I cannot dwell on the question of the spiritual caregiver's confessional background, nor on what ritual roles are feasible for which spiritual caregivers. In my view the initial question in this chapter takes precedence over these issues. It also co-determines the flexible identity of many contemporary spiritual caregivers practising in the Netherlands who create space for encountering the Holy – for 'sacramentality' – by facilitating and enacting rituals. That often makes them, in effect, ritual guides.[51] Spiritual caregivers should have symbolic and performative competence, which enables them to support people in the crisis of illness and dying to undergo the identity transformation that helps them to accomplish the often painful transition associated with loss and parting.

References

Bekius, C. Menken. (2009). Men neme een symbool. *Handelingen* 1, 29–33. C. Menken-Bekius (2001). *Werken met rituelen in het pastoraat.* Kampen: Kok, 13.

Bell, C. (1997). *Ritual: Perspectives and dimensions.* Oxford: Oxford University Press, 156.

Casey, M. (2007). *Toward God.* Missouri: Liguori.

Chauvet, L.-M. (1995). *Symbol and sacrament: A sacramental re-interpretation of Christian existence.* Collegeville: Liturgical Press.

Chidester, D. (2002). *Patterns of transcendence: Religion, death, and dying.* Belmont, CA: Wadsworth.

Derkse, W. (2003). *Een leefregel voor beginners.* Tielt: Lannoo.

Driver, T.F. (1998). *Liberating rites: Understanding the transformative power of ritual.* Boulder: Westview.

Embsen, H. and T. Overtoom (2007). *Hoe zou jij het willen? Persoonlijk afscheid nemen van je dierbare.* Kampen: Ten Have.

Friedrich, M.A. (2001). *Liturgische Körper.* Stuttgart: Kohlhammer.

Garces-Foley, K. (2006). *Death and religion in a changing world.* New York and London: Sharpe.

Garrigan S. (2004). *Beyond ritual: Sacramental theology after Habermas.* Aldershot: Ashgate.

Grimes, R.L. (2000). *Deeply into the bone: Re-inventing rites of passage.* Berkeley: University of California Press.

---

[51]   T. Quartier (2008) Rituele stervensbegeleiding in het ziekenhuis. *Handelingen. Tijdschrift voor praktische theologie* 5, 57–62.

——. (2006). *Rite out of place: Ritual, media, and the arts*. Oxford and New York: Oxford University Press.

Leach, E. (1979). *Culture and communication: The logic by which symbols are connected. An introduction to the use of structuralist analysis in social anthropology*. 4th edn. Cambridge: Cambridge University Press.

Lukken, G. (2005). *Rituals in abundance: Critical reflections on the place, form and identity of Christian ritual in our culture*. Liturgia Condenda 17. Leuven: Peeters, 3.

Molendijk, A. (2003). *Materieel christendom: Religie en de materiele cultuur in West-Europa*. Hilversum: Verloren.

Narayanasamyr, A. (2001). *Spiritual care: a practical guide for nurses and health care practitioners*. Salisbury: Quay.

Nuland, S.B. (1994). *How we die: Reflections on life's final chapter*. New York: Vintage.

Otto, R. (1958). *The idea of the Holy: An inquiry into the non-rational factor of the idea of the divine and its relation to the rational*. New York: Galaxy.

Parkes, C.M. (2009). *Love and loss: The roots of grief and its complications*. London and New York: Routledge.

Post, P. (2005). Gezocht verband. Een verkenning van nieuw opkomende rituelen. In S. Gärtner (ed.), *Bandeloos? Zoeken naar samenzijn in een individualistische cultuur*. Nijmegen: Valkhof, 82–97.

Quartier, T. (2004). Het kwijnen van de katholieke devotie. Dialectische exploraties omtrent katholieke ritualiteit. In J. Jacobs and R. Nauta (eds), *Daarom toch katholiek: Opstellen rond een kentering*. Nijmegen: Valkhof, 112–40.

——. (2007). *Bridging the gaps. An empirical study of Catholic funeral rites*. Empirische Theologie 17. Münster: Lit Verlag.

——. (2007). Ritual studies: Een antropologische bezinning op de liturgie. *Tijdschrift voor Liturgie* 91, 218–29.

——. (2008). Voorbij de dood? Rituele stervensbegeleiding in het ziekenhuis. In E. Venbrux, M. Heesels and S. Bolt (eds), *Rituele creativiteit. Actuele veranderingen in de uitvaart- en rouwcultuur in Nederland*. Zoetermeer: Meinema, 59–74.

——. (2008). Voorganger of begeleider? Rituelen rond sterven en dood in de moderne geestelijke verzorging. *Tijdschrift voor geestelijke verzorging* 47 (11), 15–25.

——. (2008). Rituele stervensbegeleiding in het ziekenhuis. *Handelingen. Tijdschrift voor praktische theologie* 5, 57–62.

——. (2009). Personal symbols in Roman Catholic funerals in the Netherlands. *Mortality* 14 (2), 133–46.

——. (2009). Theologische en rituologische perspectieven op liturgie. *Tijdschrift voor Theologie* 49, 287–97.

——. (2010). Ritualisierungen des Sterbens: Rituelle Dimensionen der Seelsorge im Niederländischen Gesundheitswesen. *Jaarboek voor liturgie-onderzoek*, 135–48.

——. (2010). Symbolische en performatieve dimensies van sacramentaliteit. *Tijdschrift voor Geestelijk leven* 66 (2), 59–70.

——. (2010). Deathbed rituals: Roles of spiritual caregivers in Dutch hospitals. *Mortality* 15 (2), 105–19.

——. and J. Wojtkowiak (2010). Nieuwe rituelen: Creativiteit en herontdekking. *Tijdschrift voor Geestelijk Leven* 66 (2), 19–28.

Richter, K. (1973). *Liturgie mit Kranken*. Essen: Driewer.

Riesebrodt, M. (2007). *Cultus und Heilsversprechen: Eine Theorie der Religionen*. München: C.H. Beck.

Schillebeeckx E. (2000). Naar een herontdekking van de christelijke sacramenten. *Tijdschrift voor Theologie* 40, 164–87.

Smeets, W. (2007). *Spiritual care in a hospital setting: An empirical theological exploration*. Leiden: Brill.

Turner, V. (1967). *The ritual process: Structure and anti-structure*. Chicago: Aldine.

van der Geest, S. (2005). 'Sacraments' in the hospital: Exploring the magic and religion of recovery. *Anthropology and Medicine* 12 (2), 135–50.

van Endt-Meijling, M. (2006). *Rituelen en gewoonten. Geboorte, ziekte en dood in de multiculturele samenleving*. Bussum: Coutinho.

van Gennep, A. (1999). *Les rites de passage*. Berlin: Campus Verlag.

von Arx , W. (1979). *Das Sakrament der Krankensalbung*. Freiburg i.Ue.: Canisius.

Vreeman, J., T. Quartier and W. Smeets (2009). Geestelijke verzorging in het kader van geestelijk welbevinden. *Tijdschrift Geestelijke Verzorging* 12 (53), 44–9.

Walsh, M. and P. Ford (2001). *Nursing rituals: Research and rational actions*. Oxford: Butterworth-Heinemann.

Wojtkowiak, J. and E. Venbrux (2010). Living through ritual in the face of death. In A. Michaels et al. (eds), *Ritual dynamics and the science of ritual*. Mannheim: Harrsowitz. Forthcoming.

Chapter 10
Every Funeral Unique in (Y)our Way! Professionals Propagating Cremation Rituals

Meike Heessels

Introduction

As a result of processes of secularization in the Netherlands, the authority over the design and performance of death rituals is increasingly placed in the hands of funeral professionals replacing religious specialists. Funeral directors have increasingly professionalized and expanded their tasks (Howarth, 1996; Laderman, 2003; Parsons, 2003). Since the beginning of the twentieth century, professionals have become a self-evident part of dying, death and disposal in the Netherlands.

While professionals still have a substantial role, recently, from the 1980s and onwards the authority is increasingly also ascribed to the individual mourners creating their own death rituals. Walter (1996) demonstrated that despite the ideal of individual mourners creating personalized death rituals, death, dying and disposal are social processes, which are negotiated with other mourners, grief counsellors and funeral professionals. On a micro level, the declining authority of religious specialists and the increasing authority ascribed to the bereaved means that funeral professionals in negotiation with the bereaved manage not only the organizational aspects of death rituals, but also the ceremonial and symbolic aspects (see also: Davidsson Bremborg, 2006; Schäfer, 2007a, 2007b).

The professionals themselves are often unaware of this, as they identify their role as neutrally assisting the bereaved in arranging death rituals according to their personal wishes. I will show that, even if this is unintentional, professionals do not simply reflect their clients' wishes, but actively direct them by stimulating certain aspects and discouraging others. I contend that professionals do possess a sense of what constitutes a 'proper' death ritual. I maintain that these ideas form an influential context for the creation of cremation rituals, eventually also influencing the practices of the bereaved. Therefore, in this chapter I will explore which ideal images of cremation rituals are, implicitly as well as explicitly, pursued by funeral professionals in the Netherlands.

Here I will deploy Canadian sociologist Erving Goffman's dramaturgical principles for analysing social life within companies (1959). His work leads us to see how performers, in this case crematorium professionals, tend to offer their observers, in this case the bereaved, an impression that is idealized in several different ways. While professionals probably would not consider their work a performance, when closely examined their actions are not only practical, but also contain more implicit symbolic and performative messages that I identify as 'ideal images'.

These ideal images are conveyed on a company-wide level by means of promotional material for clients including websites, mission statements and commercial correspondence as well as instructions for employees contained in in-house manuals, task descriptions and branch magazines of which I conducted a discourse analysis. I take these documents as constituting an overt performance of company-wide ideal images.

However, because professionals do not always follow these directions, I will demonstrate that, besides company-wide ideals, the personal convictions of professionals regarding best practice trickle out through their individual performance. These personal convictions are inevitably harder to detect because they are not overt. Moreover, given their view of themselves as facilitators, these professionals are not always aware of their directive role. I have sought to resolve this potential conflict by comparing company-wide ideals with practices in the crematorium investigated through fieldwork from 2007 to 2009 in four Dutch crematoriums, those of Nijmegen, Driehuis, Almelo and Usselo.[1]

Ideal Image of a Personalized Funeral

The role of funeral professionals, of religious specialists and of the bereaved in organizing death rituals, changed throughout recent centuries. In the nineteenth century and beginnings of the twentieth century, the involvement of professionals in funeral practice was limited. To a large extent death rituals were arranged by the bereaved themselves together with their neighbours. Neighbours were obliged by city laws to assist in death rituals in the Netherlands. This practice was called *burenplicht* or neighbour duties. These duties slightly differed by community, but generally included the announcement of the demise, the washing of the body and placing it on a bier and the transportation of the body to the church and the graveyard (Kok, 2005: 144–71; Sleebe, 1994: 369). As a result of increased urbanization, industrialization, domestic migration and the economical crisis of 1929, these neighbour duties started to decrease (Kok, 2005: 217; Sleebe, 1994: 375).

In order to complement or even replace this dwindling communal assistance, cooperatives of labourers were established between 1900 and 1920 (Kok, 2005:

---

[1]   The crematoriums in Usselo and Almelo are the two establishments of an independent cremation company called Crematoria Twente in the northeast of the Netherlands. The crematoriums in Driehuis, in the northwest, and in Nijmegen, in the central east, are two branches of the company Facultatieve Groep that is a multinational company owning various crematoriums and cemeteries in the Netherlands and Germany, is world market leader in cremation ovens and owns a funeral insurance company.

218–21). Labourers contributed monthly to a communal fund that ensured funeral costs for every employee. As most organizations were organized according to three main 'pillars' in the beginning of the twentieth century, namely Protestant, Catholic or Socialist, so were these associations of labourers. For example DELA, which is an abbreviation of *Draagt Elkanders Lasten* or Carry Each Other's Duties, was a Catholic organization, while Monuta was protestant (Kok, 2005: 222). With the money from labourer organizations, a funeral director was hired who took care of the coffin, the transportation of the body, and the organization of the funeral. The ritual dimension of death however, was still firmly in the hands of religious institutions. For example in the Catholic Church, the dying received the anointing by a priest, the funeral mass took place in church and the grave was chosen and blessed by a cleric.

In the 1950s, and most strongly in the second half of the 1960s, the pillarized structure of Dutch society started to crumble. In the 1960s and 1970s, the religious base of the labourer funds was erased from the association's statutes (Kok, 2005: 222). The professionalization of the funeral director further expanded, now including the arrangement of clerical as well as non-clerical funerals. The task of professionals was perceived as saving the family from the task of arranging the funeral (Kok, 2005; Sleebe, 1994). For example, the motto of funeral company Dela was 'Alle zorg uit handen nemen', which could be translated as 'Relieving the bereaved from all worries'. The funeral directors made decisions about the funeral on the basis of their professional expertise and commercial interests and, by contrast with previous decades, the role of the family in funerary practices decreased considerably.

In reaction to this development, by the mid 1980s, protests arose claiming that the bereaved had practically no say in death rituals which, in turn, was described as impersonal, uniform and cold (Bot, 1998; Enklaar, 1995; Sax et al., 1989). Consequently, small funeral companies sprung up striving for personalized death rituals arranged in consultation with the family (Bot, 1998; Sax et al., 1989). These companies argued against the downside of the professionals' ideal of 'sparing the bereaved'. In 1995, several of these pioneers united themselves in a network of funeral innovators advocating the possibility of personalized death rituals for every citizen demanding that funeral companies and government officials, instead of taking over the rituals, should enable people's involvement in disposal. Approximately 100 years after the institution of an association propagating the right to be cremated, an association was founded fighting for a personalized funeral. This finally changed the perceived task of professionals in death rituals.

Today, the notion of 'a unique farewell' has become mainstream. Nowadays the wishes of the bereaved and/or deceased are centralized in the commercial communication of funeral businesses. Companies recommend their goods by means of slogans such as 'the wishes of the bereaved are our point of departure'.[2] The mottos of two big funeral businesses in the Netherlands are also telling, Monuta propagates 'the end of impossible wishes' and Yarden advertises with 'Every funeral unique'.[3]

The attention for a personalized and unique farewell accounts for the funeral, but also for the ash disposal. One to three weeks after a funeral, a letter informs the bereaved about the forthcoming ash disposal and presents the 30-day waiting period established as an opportunity to take the time and make a conscious choice regarding the means of ash disposal. The ash disposal is presented as a personalized ritual as the bereaved are invited at the crematorium for advice about 'a unique and personal disposal matching the life of the deceased'. The options offered vary and are motivated by differing personal characteristics, for example a scattering by boat, 'if the bereaved and/or deceased had a special bond with the sea'[4] or 'placing an urn in one of the columbaria that matches the deceased best'.[5]

From a content analysis of the presentation of funerary objects on the Internet (for more information see: Heessels, 2010) followed that these are also primarily praised as exclusive, handmade and one of a kind, all referring to a sense of personalization. The promotion of glass objects by Kroes company illustrates this perfectly: 'The objects are blown and shaped by hand into a product that has a *unique* character, making every object *unique*, just as every person is or was *unique*' [my italics].[6] On her website goldsmith Annahbelle puts it as follows:

> After the farewell comes the period of mourning. Annahbelle translates this into her designs that come into being after a conversation with the bereaved about the deceased. In this way every jewel acquires its own unique character that reflects the relation with the deceased.[7]

When turning to the daily practices in a crematorium, the overarching ideal image of a personalized funeral can be subdivided into the ideal image of 'cremation rituals as singular events' and of 'professionals as facilitators of the wishes of the bereaved and/or deceased'.

---

[2]   www.boskamp.nl/wensen-van-de-nabestaanden-staan-centraal (accessed 11 January 2011).

[3]   In 2010, the Netherlands counted over 700 funeral businesses, but only three companies dominated the market, namely Dela, Yarden and Monuta.

[4]   www.dela.nl/rondom_overlijden/na_de_uitvaart/asbestemmingen (accessed 11 January 2011).

[5]   www.crematoriumjonkerbos.nl/asbestemming-bijzetting (accessed 11 January 2011).

[6]   www.kroesglasblazerij.nl (accessed 11 January 2011).

[7]   www.annahbelle.nl/annahbelle.html (accessed 11 January 2011).

Ideal Image of Cremation Rituals as Singular Events in Practice

The daily routine, the architecture and the decoration of the building as well as the performance of professionals, underline the ideal image of a cremation ritual as a singular event. The professionals are instructed to present a unique and personal farewell, yet in practice they are managing up to 20 bereaved groups per day. This discrepancy created a constant tension between the ideal of singularity and the practice of engaging in numerous consecutive services throughout the day. In order to maintain the ideal image of singularity, a sharp contrast is made between what Goffman (1959) called front and backstage regions. When in the front region, professionals have to preserve the ideal image, while in the back region, they can temporarily relax without the direct presence of the bereaved.

Before the corpse arrives for the cremation service, the funeral is arranged by the funeral director together with the bereaved. Their choice of music, flowers, catering and the auditorium are communicated to the crematorium beforehand. The day of the funeral, the auditorium is prepared by cleaning, putting the book of condolence ready and placing a sign with the name of the deceased and the time of the service at the entrance. When the hearse arrives the crematorium host waits outside, bows in silence and points the way to the guests.[8] The body is driven to the rear access of the crematorium. There, the funeral director 'unloads' the coffin. Together with the host, the funeral director checks the death certificate and the permission to cremate. The deceased is given a unique cremation number, also called an identification number, this identifies the corpse and its subsequent ashes within the crematorium's administration. The coffin and the flowers are then placed on a trolley and moved into the auditorium of choice.

Crematoriums have introduced certain services and objects that help give an auditorium a personal 'touch', with the bereaved encouraged to choose their favourite music, to tell the life stories of the deceased and to use personal symbols, such as pictures, film or objects from home. Besides, crematoriums possess what I call situational religious symbols such as a cross that can be wheeled into and out of an auditorium. In some cases, symbols are even designed to fit different tastes and denominations. In Nijmegen, I encountered a crucifix – a cross bearing the image of Jesus Christ – that can also be turned displaying a plain cross. Generally speaking, most symbols are Christian, based on the Dutch Christian heritage. However, with the arrival of Hindustan immigrants and other religious groups these symbols have diversified. In Usselo a Hindu Ohm sign stands next to a crucifix in the backstage area.

Meanwhile, the mourners are received in two separate rooms. The direct family have coffee and refreshments in the family room, with decoration resembling a

---

[8] Generally, the work in the crematorium consists of different shifts simultaneously carried out by different employees, successively the oven shift, the hosting shift (also called 'being on reception'), the kitchen shift, the garden shift, the shift in the music room and the ash disposal shift (also called after-care).

living room, while the wider circle of mourners is invited into a waiting room. Professionals explained that the inner circle of bereaved is separated from the rest, 'to grant them a moment's rest before they are confronted with the condolences of all visitors'. While the guests assemble, the funeral director drinks a cup of coffee backstage and chats with his colleagues who constantly walk in and out. Although the conversation serves to check the details of the service, it may also contain anecdotes about the mourners, their special requests or conflicts as well as personal talk: behind the scenes the atmosphere is informal.

By then, in the music room, the musical pieces are prepared with the 'music employee' able to view the assembling mourners and the auditorium on a screen to check when the door is opened by the host. At that moment, the music is started. The host counts the number of visitors walking into the auditorium and after closing the door the employee discretely passes the number on to the kitchen through an intercom. Then the service takes place. Generally, 30 to 45 minutes are reserved for a cremation service, depending on the region, often less time is reserved in the bigger cities than in more rural areas. When requested the mourners can reserve more time for an extra fee. In most cases, three musical pieces are played and professionals or the mourners themselves tell stories about the life of the deceased and poems or prayers are recited. In the end, visitors pay their respect to the deceased by passing the coffin, often decorated with a picture. Sometimes the inner circle of bereaved stays behind to privately pay their last respects.

During the service, the catering is prepared and the foyer is put ready for the guests. The foyer is also called *koffiekamer*, meaning coffee room, because coffee is the main drink served. On their screen backstage in the kitchen, employees can see when the guests leave the auditorium to enter the coffee room. Again, the closest family members are separated from the other mourners, as a special table is reserved for them. In most cases, the funeral director asks the guests to allow the family a moment's rest. Then, a line is assembled by which the guests offer their condolences to the inner circle of mourners. In total, 30 minutes to an hour are reserved for coffee and condolences. In the meantime, employees roll hallstands from the entrance to the foyer enabling the guests to leave smoothly through the appointed exit, while a new group enters.

While the bereaved are having coffee, the host brings the coffin to the oven room. The flowers and/or ribbons are given back to the bereaved or placed at a monument in the crematorium grounds. Dutch law requires the body to be cremated the same day. In most cases, the coffin is entered without the bereaved present. The employee operating the oven, called the *ovenist*, manages and controls the cremation process. Subsequently, the employee collects the remains and puts them in a cremulator to crush the bones to ashes. After which the ash containers are placed in a general niche where the urns are organized by number. In the meantime, the auditorium is already being prepared for the next scheduled service.

As this description makes clear, employees arranging funerals have relatively little interaction with the bereaved, especially when compared with staff working

Figure 10.1   Ash disposal room in a Dutch crematorium
Source: Picture by Meike Heessels

in the department of ash disposal. Their work represents another world within the crematorium, with its own rhythm, objects and performances, often located in a separate wing or even a separate building appointed for the ash disposal. In Usselo this department was called 'the little ash house', in Driehuis the Department of Information and Aftercare. When the bereaved arrive for a scattering or an informative talk on the possibilities of disposal, they are received in a special room where urns and other ash objects that can be filled with ashes are displayed. The bereaved are invited to take a seat and are offered a drink. When their drinks are served, the employee goes away to give the mourners a chance to talk and acclimatize themselves to the scene.

The whole performance of cremation rituals is orchestrated so that every group of mourners perceives the ritual as a singular event. As Goffman (1959: 138) contends, one of the aims of every performance in daily life is to sustain the impression of a personal and unique event. During a funeral there is always an employee present supposedly to assist 'in case someone would be indisposed'. In fact, I argue that the main goal of this practice is to prevent people from wandering around the building, because, if different groups would bump into each other this would jeopardize the ideal image of a singular event.

Professionals are constantly aware of the whereabouts of the different groups of bereaved. Red and green lights above doors inform the employees where the families are situated. Throughout the building, posts and movable partitions are placed to lead the bereaved on the appointed route from entrance to exit (see also Chapter 11, this volume). The whole building is orchestrated to lead the mourners through the performance and prevent the different groups of mourners from meeting each other, as then the performance of singularity would ultimately fail. In one crematorium in Haarlem, the architect wanted to break this separation up by using glass walls for the auditorium through which different groups of bereaved could see each other. But the employees could not get used to this 'as they do not want the bereaved who leave the casket behind, to see how they remove the flowers and ribbons and move the casket to the cremator' (Klaassens and Groote, 2010).

The ideal image of a singular event also accounts for the disposal of the ashes. The bereaved are received in special rooms, filled with soft couches, painted in warm colours and decorated with candles and flowers in an attempt to replicate the atmosphere of a living room. However, in a similar fashion, the employees daily receive several small groups of bereaved persons and prevent these from meeting each other through receiving them in different rooms and carefully maintaining a schedule of appointments. Moreover, I noticed that it was not appreciated when bereaved people stopped by unannounced to collect the ashes. At first employees explained that this creates more work, as the ashes have to be promptly collected from the general niche where they are stored. But more importantly, it does not tally with the personal and exclusive service that employees want to bestow. While the appointments with an ash disposal employee are directed towards personal attention, with coffee, light candles and a warm atmosphere, behind the scenes there is a tight schedule.

Overall, employees got uncomfortable when mourners did not arrive or leave at the agreed time and I argue that this is not only because time is money and another appointment is on schedule, but also because a change in plan might jeopardize the ideal image of singular event. While the conversations with professionals are interspersed with metaphors of taking time: 'take the time to enjoy your coffee', 'we have all the time in the world', 'take your time deciding', or 'now we will quietly go to …'. From the overall description of the routine of services and ash disposal in a crematorium, it becomes clear that there is a constant tension between the tight schedule and the bereaved that have to be moulded into this.

Finally, while the funeral professionals project an ideal image of cremation rituals as singular events, the same pattern is inevitably repeated daily. While some of the smaller businesses go to great lengths to create a personal ritual every time, the work of the bigger companies mostly takes place along established lines with a step-by-step plan that is adapted to fit the wishes of their clients but which, nevertheless, always consists of the same steps. While the professionals initially underlined the ideal image of a singular event, after some time of co-working with them and sharing conversations backstage, they admitted that even though cremation rituals were personalized, they were never really unique. As I once heard an employee comment on a service, 'In some way it is like Duplo, the toy building brick'. However, the script of the performance is to present the ritual as a singular and personal event. This corresponds with another ideal image, concerning the role that is ascribed to funeral professionals in creating these personalized and singular rituals.

Ideal Image of Funeral Professionals as Facilitators in Practice

The mission statement of funeral company Yarden declares that: 'There are as many wishes as there are people. Self-determination does not stop with death, therefore we centralize the personal wishes and the individuality of every person in our way of working.'[9] In this quote, which is characteristic for most funeral companies in the Netherlands, the role of professionals is implicitly understood as discovering personal wishes and translating them into death rituals. In fact, the role of professionals is understood as facilitating these wishes. Consequently, mourners are ascribed a participative and even directive role in the performance.

Funeral directors are no longer called funeral directors, or in Dutch *uitvaartleiders*, which lays emphasis on their directing role. Rather, their name has changed to the Dutch term *uitvaartbegeleiders* or *uitvaartverzorgers*, which could be translated as funeral facilitators or funeral caretakers. The following quote from the homepage of funeral company Monuta makes this shift perfectly clear: 'With the funeral insurance from Monuta *you* make a conscious choice for *your* funeral. Because *you* decide how *you* want to be remembered' [my italics].[10] In the current ideal image, the directing role is thus no longer ascribed to the undertaker, but to the bereaved as they are invited to make their own 'unique' choices for a 'personalized funeral'.

Mourners are stimulated not only to choose consciously, but also to contribute actively to death rituals. This occurs even before death as people who possess funeral insurance (which was 69 per cent of the Dutch in 2009 (Van Keulen and Kloosterboer, 2009)) are invited to construct a scenario for their own funeral and memorial. In a funeral insurance package a funeral codicil is included on which clients can register their funeral wishes, pointing out their favourite flowers, music and way of disposal. Still this remains a kind of symbolic message more than an actual practice, as many clients have no such form prepared.

In other aspects, the ideal image of a ritual executed and developed by the bereaved themselves did influence actual practices. While the ashes used to be dispersed without notice to the bereaved, nowadays, this is done by the bereaved under the guidance of a professional. Based on quantitative data that I collected from Driehuis, Usselo and Nijmegen, I have found that approximately 50 to 60 per cent of the ashes are still placed within crematorium grounds. Considering these scatterings in crematorium grounds, approximately in 35 to 50 per cent of the cases, the bereaved are present. In promotion brochures the disposal is emphasized as a

---

[9] www.yarden.nl/Over-ons/Onze-missie.htm (accessed 11 January 2011).

[10] www.monuta.nl/uitvaartverzekeringen/ (accessed 11 January 2011).

Figure 10.2   Scattering ashes at crematorium grounds
Source: Picture by Meike Heessels

ritual or 'a ceremonious and solemn moment', in Dutch *een plechtig moment*. The bereaved are encouraged to do it themselves. It is put forward that bereaved carry the urn to the field and conduct the scattering themselves, in the presence of an employee. Professionals list several options in correspondence with the bereaved, emphasizing the necessity of 'doing something' with the ashes. Suggestions are made to take flowers or to recite a last word of goodbye. In addition, some crematoriums offer assistance if people cannot find a suitable text, in the shape of a library with appropriate texts that bereaved can choose from.

The rationale behind this ideal image of the bereaved as directors and the professionals as facilitators lies in adopted theories of grief. These psychological paradigms do not exist in isolation, but are historically and culturally defined (Stroebe et al., 1992) and in their turn influence psychological practices as well as those of professionals in related branches, such as funeral professionals. I will explain this by means of an example of professionals making funerary objects. For example, ash jewels are labeled 'objects full of emotion'.[11] Moreover, the jewels are said to assist in the mourning process, as advertised on the website of goldsmith Annahbelle: 'Welcome to Annahbelle. A lasting memory of your loved

---

[11]   www.annahbelle.nl/annahbelle.html (accessed 11 January 2011).

one in the shape of a jewel. You will carry him or her with you always and that provides comfort and strength in hard times.' Another producer of cuddle stones containing ashes claims: 'Sensory Shapes are designed as something that people can hold on to in the lonely process of letting go. When memories and longing for reunion arise they can literally as well as mentally feel by touching the Sensory Shapes.' This attitude among professionals reflects the prevailing psychological model of grief called continuing bonds (Klass, 2006; Laderman, 2003; Walter, 1999). In this paradigm, which Laderman (2003) aptly calls grief mythology, it is assumed that mourners are helped by 'working through grief' and keeping loved ones close instead of breaking bonds.

The professionals believe that through participating in death rituals the bereaved can 'work' through their grief. During my fieldwork at the ash disposal department I repeatedly heard employees express their opinion to the bereaved that it was good that they decided to come. As Suzanne said to a bereaved family: 'I would like to compliment you for the fact that you have come, despite the difficulty. I think it is very brave and that it will help you in the grieving process.' Funeral director Joke, who owns a small company together with her husband, explained this attitude:

> If people come to us, we try to challenge them. In the first instance, the bereaved often think they are not able to do something. They are scared and often do not want to admit that. We try to stimulate them, because it is a one-time affair. You cannot redo a funeral. We have our tricks to get people out of their shell. For example by inviting them to wash and clothe the deceased together with us. By concentrating on the deceased, people are forced to release their feelings. Another trick that I used with a lady last week is to invite them here [in the funeral home where the deceased is laid out]. Then they cannot get around it and have to visit the deceased. Eventually the lady thanked us. She said that she would never have been able to do that without us. That is beautiful, not to compliment us, but to see what it does to people to participate and keep the deceased close.[12]

As the quotation makes clear, with the best of interests, professionals even use 'tricks' to force mourners to take part, because they are convinced of the benefits of these grief practices. While professionals present themselves as facilitating in these cases they positively do direct the bereaved.

In line with the ideal image of giving the bereaved a directive role, openness is highly valued by professionals. The mourners are ascribed the 'right' to get to know everything about the crematorium's procedures. The bereaved are granted more

---

[12]   Another company, specializing in laying out the deceased or taking care of the deceased, as they call it, echoes this ideal in their advertisement: 'It is good to take care of your loved one yourself, or at least to be present. Because it contributes to the process of coming to terms with your grief.' www.overledenenzorghartman.nl.

Figure 10.3   A visitor inspecting a cremation oven during an open day

Source: Picture by Meike Heessels

access and control within the premises of the crematorium, instead of keeping them away from backstage areas, these are opened for the public, underlining the role of directors, for example by means of open days (Bolt et al., 2007). During these days the oven room is always the most popular area. Urban myths regarding the piling up of coffins and the burning of several bodies in one oven make people curious about the actual procedures (Newall, 1985). Behind these myths is a serious concern that professionals engage, namely the question about the identity of the ashes. Employees explain and show their control procedures over the oven.[13] The areas that can be entered by the bereaved are expanding, causing the lines between front and backstage areas to blur. While until the last decade the oven room was mainly a backstage area designed for technical purposes, increasingly crematoriums offer the possibility to accompany the coffin to the oven. Since 1970 Hindus in the Netherlands demanded to be present at the 'charging' or the entry of the coffin into the cremator (Swhajor et al., 2010), but more recently this custom has spread among other groups in the

---

[13]   One funeral company has found a solution for answering these questions 24/7 by putting images on their website of how a coffin is entered into the oven and how it is transformed into ashes. http://yardenprodweb01.lostboys.nl/Alles-over-uitvaart/Informatie/Cremeren-begraven/Crematieproces.htm (accessed 11 January 2011).

Netherlands. Accordingly, oven rooms are refurbished and painted in bright colours to 'transform' them into a frontstage area resembling the rest of the crematorium.

However, while professionals present themselves as facilitators, arranging the personal wishes of the bereaved and opening up their backstage spaces, some elements of cremation rituals are underplayed. As Goffman argues, a performer tends to conceal those activities, facts and motives which are incompatible with an idealized version of himself and his products (1959: 48). The counterparts of the ideal images of professionals as facilitators show the professionals' continuing, yet implicit, directive role as well as the contested singularity of the rituals.

A first and general concealed element is profit. The import prices of products sold by the crematorium are carefully tucked away. This is the case with many businesses, but in the crematorium there is a double taboo as profit is made from the dead. Sometimes professionals were even ashamed to admit that they tried to make a profit. Once, an employee explained that while they had to make profit, he found that difficult with his often emotional clients. His 'solution' was that he only tried to sell the more expensive urns to rich customers.

Secondly, throughout the whole routine from corpse to ashes, the work in the crematorium is riddled with control procedures. In fact, there were so many control measures that I believe that they actually functioned as symbolic actions to re-affirm the ideal image of singularity, not only of the cremation service, but also of the deceased among so many other urns. Because the identity of the ashes is highly valued by the bereaved and because uncertainties still often exist, these regulations function (as do the open days) to affirm the care of keeping the integrity of the identity of the cremated remains. Consequently, elements that would cast doubt on the wholeness and identity of the ashes were concealed. Despite all scrupulousness, ashes sometimes drifted up during work and ended on the floor. In one crematorium a vacuum cleaner was used especially for this. While this is insurmountable and the employees quickly assured me that the contents of the vacuum cleaner were also scattered in their grounds, the use of vacuum cleaner was kept secret from me for a long time.

A third and more implicit way of concealment is the fact that behind the ideal image of facilitating every personal wish, certain boundaries did exist. These boundaries were presented as 'natural' and as such mostly taken for granted. For example, in the Netherlands, the cremated remains are always sifted with a magnet, extracting the metals before crushing them into ashes. While I imagine that some people might want to obtain the remains as they leave the oven, meaning as partially crushed bones still containing artificial hips and other elements, this was not even negotiable. I was met with great disbelief, and even disdain, every time I suggested this in a crematorium to explore the boundaries of potential requests.

The fourth way of concealing also concerns the ashes. While the employees elaborately explained the control procedures using examples of ash containers and identification stones, the ashes themselves were scarcely shown. Only one employee, who fiercely supported her stance that it is better to have the bereaved participating in the ritual, always put the urn in the middle of the table and showed the ashes.

The general practice of implicit distancing of the ashes came to the fore in many ways. Employees repeatedly warned the bereaved of all kinds of 'mistakes', such as that the wind might catch the ashes when scattering, presuming that contact with the ashes would harm or scare them. Moreover, when the bereaved come to collect ashes at the crematorium, all four crematoriums supply special bags or boxes to carry the urn. While handing out the bag, one employee always said: 'Would you like a bag, that is more neutral when you go out', assuming that people would want to hide the ashes, implicitly directing rather than asking the bereaved.

The fifth and last way of concealing has to do with the physical placement of professionals. I observed that while there was space enough on the fluffy furniture in the department of ash disposal, the employees were inclined to choose a 'hard' wooden chair taken from the backstage region or to remain standing between the family members, instead of taking a place on the couches between them. Contrary to the ideal of personal service, facilitating among equals, the professionals thus physically maintained their position as director instead of participant between the mourners.

These concealed practices, the counterparts of the ideal images, demonstrate how professionals recommend certain practices and discourage or even deny others. This again shows that despite the ideal of professionals as facilitators, implicitly their directive role continues in some aspects.

Professionals Creating Personalized Rituals: Whose Values Reign?

Employees fiercely defend the ideal images of singularity and their role as facilitators. Yet, actual practice does not always fit the ideal image. During my fieldwork I gradually realized that, particularly with regard to ash disposal, employees had no idea how their colleagues operated. At every location where I worked, colleagues asked me about each other's way of working and were often surprised about each other's interpretations. When I explained to Nicole that Remco, another employee at the department of ash disposal, always asks *if* someone wants to scatter the ashes, she was surprised: 'Oh no, I always ask: *who* wants to scatter the ashes? And if they seem reluctant, I try it through the kids, who mostly react enthusiastically. Then the adolescents always follow. I think it is important for them to do this themselves, so I stimulate them.' Another colleague, Josien, who was also present during this conversation, looked up from her work and said: 'On the contrary, I think it is important to leave it up to them. If they do not initiate it, I never push people.'

All employees work within the company-wide framework of ideal images. Yet, in practice, they explain the ideal images differently. Josien reasons that the fact that people are present at a scattering already underlines the ideal of a participative ritual directed and carried out by the bereaved and decides to respect their wishes substantiating her choice with another ideal image, respectively of her role as a facilitator, instead of a director. Nicole, however, emphasizes the ideal image of the mourners taking part in the ritual and investigates ways of involving the bereaved by gently pushing them a little bit further as she believes this will help them in the grieving process.

Personal convictions of employees influence the way they explain and carry out the company's ideal images. Sometimes the ideal images can even conflict with their individual convictions, moving them to act on their own accord. Goffman (1959: 12) would probably have called this disruptive events, because they contradict, discredit or otherwise throw doubt upon the ideal image. In most cases, these events stay undiscussed as they remain hidden in seemingly trivial gestures. However, I found that they surface when employees disagree with the requests of the bereaved or when they have to improvise as a result of new services. It is precisely in such situations, I argue, that they reveal their 'personal cards' that usually remain implicit.

Such an event can occur when professionals have difficulty accepting the personal wishes of the bereaved and decide to act on their own accord. I assisted at a service in which the funeral director decided to alter the ritual. While at first sight, this seemed a minor event to me, later I realized that this was one of those moments where an employee decides to deviate from the wishes of the mourners as these were in conflict with his personal convictions. Before a service in the crematorium, the employee on auditorium shift normally goes through the details with the funeral director, as on this particular day: 'Three musical pieces, as usual?', the employee Jolanda asked the funeral director. 'Yep', he replied. 'But', he continued, 'it is a very modest funeral. They are simple people. I do not mean that in a wrong way. It is just a very simple funeral. Three musical pieces, no speakers, that is all'. Jolanda replied, 'What about obituary cards?' 'Nope', the funeral director replied shortly. 'A book of condolence?', she asked. 'No', and he shook his head. 'Not even that? Oh my, that is so poor', she replied. 'I agree', he said, 'they even requested me to speak as little as possible'. The woman turned her attention to the candles as if to at least prepare something for this service. After a while the funeral director said: 'Wait, do not light them yet. I have an idea. I will welcome them and after the first piece of music I will ceremoniously light the candles. This way I will have a little ritual to put her [the deceased] into the light so there is at least something for the poor woman.' Jolanda sighed as if she was relieved, and said: 'That is a good idea.' During the service Jolanda and I sat in the back of the auditorium. When the service was over and all the bereaved had left, she turned to me and said: 'Only twelve minutes, that is so sad!'

I experienced a similar spontaneous initiative, when I accompanied a man who arranged scatterings at sea.[14] On the deck, the ashes of approximately 300 deceased were piled up in boxes. Before leaving, the man explained his work, when he suddenly said: 'Wait, here comes the ceremonious part.' Swiftly he put on a black jacket and stood straight up on the deck with his hands formally folded in front of him. While taking off his jacket, he explained that he did this for the bereaved that might watch the boat depart from shore. Soon the atmosphere changed into one of unremitting labour. We threw the brown paper bags with ashes overboard through a pipe one after another, while he made a joke every now and then. Suddenly, I

---

[14]   With many thanks to Sophie Bolt who took me along on this adventurous trip.

saw him put away a bag. I asked him what he did. He said: 'The bags with only a tiny bit of ashes derive from deceased children. We scatter those at the very end. Today, accidentally, an extra bouquet of flowers was delivered for the people who ordered a separate scattering with flower greeting. We will use that for the babies.' He turned back to work, as we still had dozens of boxes to go. When everything but the two little bags was scattered, he took the two bags and said: 'We do not throw the little babies through the pipe, we scatter them freely. You can throw the bouquet afterwards.' Carefully he emptied the bags, while mumbling: 'Rest in peace little ones, now you are free.' I threw the flowers in the sea. Together we stood still, looking at the ashes and flowers lying in the water and getting further and further away. I was touched by the sudden gesture of this sturdy man who had just routinely scattered hundreds of bags of ashes. 'Sad isn't it', he said, and started to tidy up.

The employees thus do not only perform their tasks, but also evaluate and adapt the rituals on their own initiative. In the mind of the funeral director as well as the captain, the ceremonies did not honour the deceased's lives sufficiently. Therefore, despite the personal wishes of the bereaved, they decided to alter the ritual and conduct a small candle-lighting ritual and flower ritual, as they called it.

During one scattering appointment I witnessed another action by which a professional showed his own ideas about a proper ritual and how he tried to add that to the scattering. Since January 2008, the crematorium in Usselo introduced a red plastic candle with every scattering. As it was a new service the candle forced the professionals to improvise in presenting this object, and, in turn, the bereaved had to respond to this suggestion of lighting a candle. Before leaving for the field, Remco asked the bereaved if they took flowers, when they obviously did not have any with them. 'No', a bereaved woman answered, 'I did not think about that, I did not know we had to'. 'Well, I ask that', Remco said, 'because sometimes people have flowers in the car. But if you don't, it will probably be a bit meagre. So if you would appreciate it, I can offer you a funeral candle from our crematorium. It is no necessity of course, it is just an extra service from us'. 'Yes?' he asked. The bereaved, a niece and two neighbours of the deceased looked at each other. 'Okay then', one of them replied and accepted the candle. This event shows how Remco improvised to fit in the candle by building on his personal convictions of a good scattering being personalized and rich in ritual. I contend that the professionals, while acting out of their idea of what is proper, tend to overlook that the preference of a sober scattering can also be part of a personalized ritual. What professionals consider scant action might exactly be in the spirit of the deceased, and thus a personally meaningful ritual.

Overall, with regard to ash disposal professionals are often forced to improvise together with the mourners as there is no ritual script for an ash scattering for example. Improvising on the basis of personal convictions about ritual can work both ways. Sometimes employees' ideas were accepted by the bereaved, while other times they were ignored or rejected. The bereaved do not indiscriminately follow every idea of the professionals. This became clear when Remco suggested scattering the ashes in a particular shape. I had already seen these forms in the grounds of the crematorium and was very curious as to how these had come into being. One day, Remco handed

Figure 10.4   Ashes scattered in circles

Source: Picture by Meike Heessels

the ash container to a bereaved man and suggested that they could scatter the ashes in the form of a heart or a circle. But the man had already started to scatter the ashes in a line in the corner of the scattering field. Remco shook his head silently in disdain. Afterwards he explained to me that he had guided a scattering years ago where a family dispersed the ashes in the shape of a heart and then surrounded the ashes holding hands. He was so impressed by this gesture that he uses it, when he thinks a family is receptive to such a suggestion.

While this particular family did not respond to his suggestion, another family did follow it, albeit in their own way. A Chinese woman and her two children came to scatter the ashes of their husband and father. At the field, Remco said that they could scatter the ashes however they wanted. 'What do you mean?', the son said. 'Well sometimes people scatter in a certain form for example', said Remco. Afterwards, the children scattered the ashes in the shape of the initials of their father and a Chinese sign for tree, because he loved nature. On another occasion, a woman replied to Remco's suggestion to scatter the ashes in the shape of a heart: 'Oh no, not in the shape of a heart. That is way too sweet for our parents.' Remco stood still and after a while he said: 'Maybe two circles, like wedding rings?' 'Yes, that is a good idea', the woman replied, 'but overlapping only for a small area. Because they were together but also very much had their own life'. Just as the candle, the ritual gesture of scattering in a certain shape resulted in a discussion about suiting symbols in which personal convictions of both professionals and bereaved were central.

These new practices result in more than a process of professionals facilitating the wishes of the bereaved, but also in exploring and imagining together in which the professionals' individual convictions inevitably play an important role. This ultimately shows that professionals do not only reproduce the ideal images defined by the company they work for, but interpret these in their own way and add their personal ideas to the process.

Conclusions

In conclusion, we can see how the performance of funeral professionals is always idealized, conveying a message about 'a proper cremation ritual', displaying cremation rituals as singular, unique and with the bereaved as the directors of 'their ritual'. However by analysing promotional material alongside practices and personal convictions of funeral professionals, it became clear that despite the ideal image of a unique and personal farewell organized by the bereaved, professionals remain directors rather than facilitators. Ideally, the ritual is 'given back' to the bereaved, but I demonstrated that while the idiom has changed the structures are to a certain degree still the same. The directing role of professionals has only become more implicit. Moreover, professionals do not indiscriminately follow the company-wide ideals. Especially with regard to ash disposal, professionals have to improvise together with mourners, forcing them to rely on their individual convictions. Finally, we have seen that the bereaved are not a passive audience, rather they respond actively to the suggestions of professionals by acceptance, adaptation or rejection.

References

Bolt, Sophie, Meike Heessels, Janneke Peelen and Joanna Wojtkowiak (2007). Op zondag naar de uitvaartbeurs. *LOVA: Tijdschrift voor Feministische Antropologie* 28(2): 50–6.
Bot, Marrie (1998). *Een laatste groet. Uitvaart- en rouwrituelen in multicultureel Nederland*. Rotterdam: Marrie Bot.
Davidsson Bremborg, Anna (2006). Professionalization without dead bodies: the case of Swedish funeral directors. *Mortality* 11(3): 270–85.
Enklaar, Jasper (1995). *Onder de groene zoden. De persoonlijke uitvaart. Nieuwe rituelen in rouwen, begraven en cremeren*. Zutphen: Alpha.
Goffman, Erving (1959). *The presentation of self in everyday life*. New York: Doubleday.

Heessels, Meike (2010). From commercial goods to cherished ash objects. Mediating contact with the dead through the body. In *The body and food in ritual*. E. Venbrux, T. Quartier and J. Wojtkowiak (eds), pp. 249–63. Wiesbaden: Harrassowitz.

Howarth, Glennys (1996). *Last rites: the work of the modern funeral director*. Amityville, New York: Baywood.

Klaassens, Mirjam and Peter Groote. (2010). Post-modern crematorium Haarlem: A place to remember. Proceedings of the Dying and Death in 18th–21st Centuries Europe International Conference, Alba Iulja, 2010, pp. 99–26. Editura Accent.

Klass, Dennis (2006). Grief, religion, and spirituality. In *Death and religion in a changing world*. K. Garces-Foley (ed.). New York: M.E. Sharpe.

Kok, Henk (2005). *Thanatos. De geschiedenis van de laatste eer*. Heeswijk Dinther: Berne Boekenmakerij.

Laderman, Gary (2003). *Rest in peace: a cultural history of death and the funeral home in twentieth-century America*. Oxford: Oxford University Press.

Newall, Venetia (1985). Folklore and cremation. *Folklore* 96(2): 139–55.

Parsons, Brian (2003). The funeral and the funeral industry in the United Kingdom. In *Handbook of death and dying*. C.D. Bryant (ed.). Thousand Oaks, London and Delhi: Sage.

Sax, Marjan, Knaar Visser and Marjo Boer (eds) (1989). *Zand erover? Afscheid en uitvaart naar eigen inzicht*. Amsterdam: Van Gennep.

Schäfer, Cyril (2007a). Dead serious? Funeral directing in New Zealand. *Sites* 4(1): 95–121.

Schäfer, Cyril (2007b). Post-mortem personalization: pastoral power and the New Zealand funeral director. *Mortality* 12(1): 4–21.

Sleebe, Vincentius Cornelius (1994). *In termen van fatsoen: sociale controle in het Gronings kleigebied, 1770–1914*. Assen: Van Gorcum.

Stroebe, Margaret, Mary M. Gergen, Kenneth J. Gergen and Wolfgang Stroebe (1992). Broken hearts or broken bonds. Love and death in historical perspective. *American Psychologist* 47(10): 1205–12.

Swhajor, Anne, Meike Heessels, Paul Van der Velde and Eric Venbrux (2010). Aan de Ganges in Twente. Onderhandelen over vormgeven van hindoe-dodenrituelen in Nederland. *Quotidian. Dutch Journal for the Study of Everyday Life* 2: 83–102.

Van Keulen, Martijn and Michael Kloosterboer (2009). *Hoeveel vaart zit in de uitvaart in 2009?* Amsterdam: TNS NIPO.

Walter, Tony (1996). Facing death without tradition. In *Contemporary issues in the sociology of death, dying and disposal*. G. Howarth and P.C. Jupp (eds). London: Macmillan Press Ltd.

Walter, Tony (1999). *On bereavement: the culture of grief*. Buckingham: Open University Press.

Chapter 11

Designing a Place for Goodbye: The Architecture of Crematoria in the Netherlands

Mirjam Klaassens and Peter Groote

Introduction

Crematoria may be considered cultural places of death and remembrance where identities are (re)produced and communicated through architecture, interior design and landscaping. These influence emotions, either intensifying feelings of awe or anxiety or assuaging them. During most of the twentieth century, a Modernist design seemed a logical choice for crematoria, as it fitted with both modern societal ideas on coping with death through negation, as well as modern technology. In public discourse, however, modern crematoria were criticised for being impersonal and meaningless non-places. In post-modern times mourners allegedly prefer a more personalised environment that allows emotional reflections upon the identity of the deceased in order to 'celebrate' his or her lived life. This chapter discusses whether the architectural history of Dutch crematoria reflects these ideas.

The Design Problem of Crematoria: Plurality, Emotion and Modernity

Since 2002 cremation has become the dominant form of bodily disposal in the Netherlands with some 57 per cent of the dead cremated in 2009 (LVC 2009). This relative importance of cremation would suggest that the architectural field would have reached some level of convergence in the discussion on the architecture of crematoria. However, the discussion about best practices in crematorium design is still underdeveloped. There is little literature, let alone a monograph on the architectural history of crematoria in the Netherlands. The exceptions are Cappers (1999) with the history of the organisation that built the first crematorium, and Hulsman and Hulsman (2008, 2010), who are working on a series of books on funerary architecture in the Netherlands in general. Consequently, it is not possible to retrieve the names of the architects of the current 68 Dutch crematoria without delving into archival material. Perhaps potential architectural historians have been deterred by the – unjustified – assumption that buildings relating to death would not make comfortable reading for the general public, because of carrying too many negative emotional connotations? One might also argue that very few architects have been able to develop accumulated expertise given the relatively recent introduction of the building type as well as its enduring marginal status. Indeed, few architects having designed more than one crematorium, with one exception being the Povše architectural office and partners with four.

A consequence of the rise of the cremation movement in the 1870s was the creation of a new landscape of mourning and remembrance (Jupp and Grainger 2002). There was no architectural precedent; therefore a new building type had to be designed. And after that it remained consigned to the margins of the architectural discipline (Grainger 2005), mainly as a consequence of the marginalisation of death itself. The idea is that, in Modernity, (spatial) exclusion of the processes of death and dying has been used as a rational coping strategy for this most irrational transition in life. Places of death and dying were literally kept out of sight and as far as possible drained of emotions and meaning. By the 1950s, at the zenith of Modernity, the denial of death had become the reigning orientation (Ariès 1977). If modern society is defined as a society based on rationalisation, predictability, calculability and control (Ritzer 2004), this is not surprising. Modernity had fundamental problems in dealing with death, which is by definition irrational, unpredictable, non-calculable and uncontrollable. Baudrillard (1976: 126) supplied the most influential expression of such processes of spatial separation of the places of the living and the dead:

> There is an irreversible evolution from savage societies to our own: little by little, the dead cease to exist. They are thrown out of the group's symbolic circulation. They are no longer beings with a full role to play, worthy partners in exchange, and we make this obvious by exiling them further and further away from the group of the living. In the domestic intimacy of the cemetery, the first grouping remains in the heart of the village or town … but are thrown further and further from the centre towards the periphery, finally having nowhere to go at all, as in the new town or the contemporary metropolis, where there are no longer provisions for the dead, either in mental or physical space.

In fact, cremation itself may be seen as one of Modernity's strategies of dealing with death. Cremation was explicitly promoted as the most rationalised and 'clean' (hygienic, but also spiritually pure) way of dealing with a dead body, and as such with death itself. P.J.R. Bucknill's article illustrates this, published in *The Journal of the Royal Society for the Promotion of Health* in 1915 it was entitled 'Cremation: The Only Rational Means of the Disposal of the Dead' (Bucknill 1915). More recently, Pursell (2003) has described the delicate relations between cremation, modernity and architecture in the case of Hagen crematorium, Germany.

The crematoria resulting from this strategy of concealing death from social life have been criticised. A target of criticism was their functional rather than ritual character (Walter 1990). It proved logically difficult for architects to combine spaces for an almost sacred ritual with those for the utilitarian process of burning

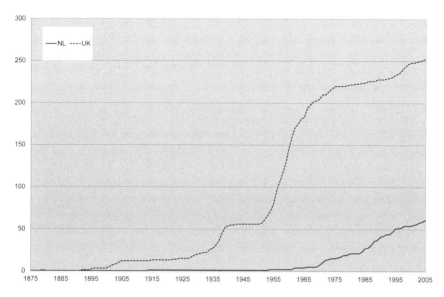

Figure 11.1   Number of crematoria in the Netherlands and the UK
Sources: Data for the Netherlands: authors' database; data for UK: Grainger Gazateer.

a corpse. A result of the utilitarian character of modernist crematoria was that visitors perceived a sense of being processed (Davies 1995). This was aggravated by the compelling presence of efficient routing through the building, which was a dominant feature of crematorium design to speed up the flow of congregations (Davies 1996). The results were described as self-effacing anonymous, discrete and modest buildings (Grainger 2005) that failed to fulfil basic human requirements (Hellman 1982). Because of the 'one door in and one door out' routing, the mourners had to exit the building through a different door in order to make way for the next group (Davies 1996). In the Netherlands, the presence of coffee rooms adds an extra element since the time spent in the coffee room is not easily controllable by crematorium staff and means that an efficient Dutch crematorium requires two coffee rooms if two consecutive groups are to be kept apart. The routine of services generates a constant tension between the tight schedule and the emotions of the bereaved. This is not only because time is money, but also because the mourners' perception of a unique service as a singular event is under threat (see Chapter 10, this volume).

When the Netherlands and the UK are compared, two differences are clear, namely, in timing (1878 and 1914, respectively) and in levels. Then, in the UK, fast growth took place between 1930 and 1970, interrupted only by the Second World War. Then, from the 1970s onward, it flattened off. The result was a difference in levels: in 1954, when the second Dutch crematorium was opened, the UK already had 72. In 2005, the figures were 61 and 252. Still, in the Netherlands, cremation has become the dominant way of bodily disposal since 2002 (LVC 2009).

The unclear legal framework surrounding cremation has already been mentioned as an explanation for this slow development in the Netherlands. Another explanation, however, might be that of dominant Calvinist attitudes yet the role of Protestantism is not entirely clear. While the idea of resurrection plays a central role in Protestant doctrines, as it does in Roman Catholicism, it is not unthinkable that the strong opposition against cremation in the Catholic Church may have created a contradictory view in Protestant circles, much in the same way as Freemasonry and Catholicism sparked opposite points of view in Italy (Davies and Mates 2005: 113). Bearing all these preceding points on crematorium building and architecture in the Netherlands in mind, this chapter will now suggest a four-phase model of development, with turning points centred around 1930, 1970 and 2000. Determined by dominant design choices these lead to phases described as 'pre-modern', 'shake hands modernist', 'sub-modernist' and 'post-modern.'

Phase 1: Pre- or 'Un'-Modernist

Before the first Dutch crematorium was opened in 1914, many plans and ideas concerning the design and layout had already been developed. The *Facultatieve* was explicit about the unsuitable styles for crematoria as a new building type: it was not to be in Neo-Gothic style, as often applied in the UK and the US, nor in any other style that would be reminiscent of religious buildings. Reminders of traditional burial practices and rituals did not fit with the movement's progressive ideology. Similarly, the *Facultatieve* explicitly rejected cemeteries as the location for a crematorium (Cappers 1999). Still, early plans, as well as the first crematorium to be realised were monumental, possessing a solemn atmosphere. Early plans for a crematorium in Hilversum were based on a full repertory of shapes and styles, such as a Roman theatre, early Christian basilica, Greek temple and Egyptian pyramid. In 1894 architect Salm designed a building in oriental style with a large dome, in which he cleverly hid the flue (Kuyt et al. 1997). However, Hilversum crematorium was never built because of shortage of money and differences of opinion within the *Facultatieve*.

The first Dutch crematorium that was built, in Driehuis-Velsen, also has a dome as its dominant feature (Figure 11.2). Other features also reflect solemnity: its location on the top of a dune in a large cemetery, its stained glass windows overlooking a sober interior, pews and the presence of an organ. Its relatively unknown architect, Marius Poel, has no other design to be found in any handbook on Netherlands' architecture, and seems to have been appointed thanks to his active presence in the pro-cremationist network, probably linked to Freemasonic or other spiritual circles. His design of the crematorium in some respects reflects the intriguing alliance of future oriented, progressive ideas (cremation as clean and purifying) and an apparent need for symbolism, sacrality and ritualism. Poel's relation with leading figures in

Figure 11.2   Crematorium Driehuis-Velsen (1914)
Source: Photo by Peter Groote

the *Facultatieve* deteriorated gradually, however, due to his lack of organisational ambition, and flaws in the engineering calculations (Cappers 1999).

The concluding assessment of this period now becomes clear with architects struggling with the proper design for this new building type but deliberately choosing not to use a modernist style. This seems surprising, but is also known from other countries, such as the UK and Germany: 'This persistent denial of Modernism has baffled those who have identified a credible link between the process of cremation ... and the philosophy behind Modernism' (Grainger 2005: 131). 'While cremationists espoused a potentially radical form of burial, they were not willing to embrace radical architecture, even when such an architect (as in the case of Behrens) supported their cause. Hagen's crematorium project became an uneasy alliance of future-oriented forces: architectural modernism and cremationism' (Pursell 2003: 234–5).

Phase 2: Shake-Hands Modernism

In the second phase, from around 1930 to 1970, a dozen crematoria were designed with most of them also built and, now, most of the chosen architects did select a modernist architectural language, albeit in a kind of softened version: functionalism with room for aesthetics. This was a familiar style in architecture in the Netherlands in this period and is often labelled shake-hands modernism (Colenbrander 1993). It resembles in many respects Scandinavian modernism as visible, for example in Gunnar Asplund's Woodland crematorium and cemetery in Stockholm. In his seminal book *Last Landscapes* Ken Worpole has convincingly shown why the softened version of Modernism was the logical choice for modernist architects in this period: 'Death ... appears at times so meaningless ... even the most hardened rationalist cannot avoid ameliorating the impact of death with comforting ... vocabularies: the "words against death"' (Worpole 2003: 195).

Arguably, one such shake-hands modernist architect was W.J.M. Dudok, the only Dutch architect who has a separate entry in the *Encyclopaedia of Cremation* (Davies and Mates 2005), although he never actually built a crematorium. He had, however, been involved in the design of crematorium Zwolle (1941), though that was not actually built, and in several extensions, including columbaria, at Velsen-Driehuis crematorium: he also designed a specific type of urn for Velsen-Driehuis.

One group of architects that sought to promote the ideology behind shake-hands was the so-called *Groep 32* (Bock et al. 1982). A member of this group was H.C.P. Nuyten, who became the architect of the second Dutch crematorium, at Dieren (1954). Nuyten is a relatively unknown architect, he was a personal friend of A.H. Wegerif, a board-member of the *Facultatieve* which commissioned the crematorium. The third crematorium (Groningen 1962) was designed by Wegerif himself (Figure 11.3). It is also built in shake-hands modernist style. Wegerif deliberately tried to link the inside and the outside of the building, just as Gunnar Asplund had done at Woodland. This meant that there was an open view from the coffee room to the front garden and lake. Later it was thought that this would allow sight of the next group to enter the building, so around 1985 an extra wall was placed to close the coffee room. Around 2005 the wall was removed again, in order to restore contact between the inside of building and the landscaped garden.[1]

Another friend of Wegerif was Jan Wils. They cooperated in the Masonic architectural advisory board, *vereniging tempelbouw*. In contrast to Nuyten and Wegerif, Wils was a well-known architect, who was, for example, responsible for the stadium for the 1928 Amsterdam Olympics. Wils designed Ockenburg crematorium in The Hague (1968), situated in a woody area, reflecting an open style with a great deal of glass that allows nature to become – symbolically speaking – part of the ceremony as people are given a view of the surrounding trees; a view thought to offer a calming and comforting experience (Bergeijk and Wagenaar 2007). This role of nature is important in crematoria design with large windows in the auditorium; frequently providing a view on a garden, fountain or pond. Nature has a symbolic significance as it exercises a compulsive hold on human emotions and invites a depth of human attachment (Grainger 2005). The sight of nature can provide a calm and serene feeling, which is often described in the literature of

---

[1]   Interview with the manager.

Figure 11.3   Crematorium Groningen (1962)
Source: Photo by Peter Groote

healing gardens. The idea that the physical environment influences human activity and behaviour is very much supported by designers of hospitals who believe that aspects of the environment can influence health outcomes (Hamilton 2006; Jencks 2006; Worpole 2009). The concept of a healing environment is often used in reference to stress reduction and the overcoming of undesirable conditions as, for example, in illness but perhaps also with grief.

While almost all crematoria built in this period were designed in the same style they were, surprisingly perhaps, built by relatively unknown architects. Some more illustrious and more robust modernist architects were interested in the building type but were not commissioned. The best examples are Gerrit Rietveld, prominent member of the *De Stijl* movement, and Mart and Lotte Stam. They participated in a design contest for a crematorium in The Hague organised by the *Facultatieve* to promote cremation but neither was awarded a prize by the jury that included Wegerif. Obviously, commissioners of crematorium buildings in this period, prominent among them board members of the *Facultatieve*, still kept to the ideology that cremation was part of the modernist movement in society, but without the brutality that postwar modernist architecture could sometimes exhibit. Buildings should be both expressive and impressive, in order to make the act of cremation a memorable event with room for emotional meaning-giving by the bereaved.

Phase 3: 'Sub'-Modernism?

During the 1970s, cremation really took off in the Netherlands, with a fast increase in the number of cremations and with a corresponding increase in crematorium building. There was, however, a corresponding tendency to decrease the scale of new crematoria that possessed a smaller as they served local or regional communities instead of the whole country (Driehuis-Velsen), or large areas (Dieren, Groningen, The Hague). If we compare cremations for each crematorium in 2004 (data from LVC, dated 24 January 2006), we find some 1,900 for the crematoria opened in the period 1914–1970, and some 1,200 for the ones opened after 1970.

This decrease in scale is reflected in the building design. The new design choices were already visible in Rotterdam crematorium (1970), although this was in fact one of the larger crematoria of the Netherlands, with almost 4,000 cremations annually in the 1980s. Its main architect, Dick Apon, was a member of the *Forum* group around Aldo van Eyck and Herman Hertzberger. Forum's ideology was that architecture should move back from large-scale, production-oriented and technological designs, to the human scale and social goals (Groenendijk and Vollaard 1998: 176). Worpole perfectly phrases Forum's ideology in his criticism of hard-line modernism: 'The human scale of design – and its attentiveness to the cycles and rituals of human life and vulnerability – has been squeezed into the edges' (Worpole 2003: 179). Unfortunately, in reality it did not always work out as the architects had planned. Often, the architecture was so downgraded that it resulted in the creation of places without any symbolic value or meaning, or any sense of place. Crematoria turned out to be anonymous suburban non-places, to use the label proposed by Augé (1995). They were almost indistinguishable from other utilitarian building types: 'it would be perfectly possible to describe crematoria in terms of … "non-places." Non-places are locations of transitions – places that people pass through but which carry no personal significance for those individuals' (Hockey 2007: 145). Common examples are airport waiting lounges and suburban railway stations. In the *Natural Death Handbook* (Wienrich and Speyer 2003: 153) British crematoria are described as just that: 'Who wants rushed funeral services in buildings which have been described as looking like waiting rooms in airports?' And in a review of Worpoles' *Last Landcsapes*, Curl does the same 'British crematoria are designed to pretend to be anything but what they are … entire ensembles are feebly suburban and meaningless' (Curl 2004). The same criticisms have also been levied against Dutch crematoria (Duijnhoven 2002; Hekkema 2002) (Figure 11.4). It is striking that the worn out version of modernism, which we label here as 'sub-modernism', with its low quality, indistinctive and unemotional buildings, has probably been a more effective negation of death than hard-line modernism, which would at least have created notable buildings!

Figure 11.4   Crematorium Stadskanaal (1998)
Source: Photo by Peter Groote

And Now the Fourth Phase: Post-Modernism?

If it is true, as stated earlier, that times may have changed and that post-modern architecture may be a suitable means to give room to new (post-modern?) mourning rituals (Venbrux et al. 2009), this should by now be visible in crematorium design. Indeed, some crematoria that are clearly 'different' in some elementary respects have been built more recently with the best examples being those of Haarlem (2002, by architect Herman Zeinstra), Leusden (2003, by Arnold Sikkel) and Zoetermeer (by Martijn de Gier of MYJ (now KBNG) architectural office). All incorporated the idea of sense of place in their building programme. There is, quite literally, room available for individual ritual experience. The design should allow emotions to flow freely, in order to ease the bereavement process. The incinerator is an integral part of building that is open to the public. This provides a solution for the open end problem of the cremation ritual. It allows a more personal and direct (ritual) interaction between the bereaved and the deceased. If new developments in the scattering of ashes (Heessels 2008) are linked to this, a new finalisation or culmination of the cremation ritual may finally have been achieved.

Haarlem's architect, Herman Zeinstra, designed a crematorium that most deliberately broke all design principles of modern crematoria (Groenendijk and

Figure 11.5   The auditorium surrounded by the arcaded courtyard of Haarlem
               crematorium (2002)

Source: www.crematoriumhaarlem.nl

Vollaard 2004: 59). It was opened in 2002 and won several prizes. Its basic ideas
were the total absence of a routing system and a reversed relation between the
outside and the inside. Zeinstra used the floor plan of a cloister with an open
auditorium at the centre of an arcaded courtyard that serves as an ambulatory.
The central auditorium is made almost completely of glass, its views from the
inside to the outside during a service allows mourners' minds to open up, come
into contact with nature and the weather, and emotions to be expressed (Figure
11.5). It also offers an alternative view during the ceremony and takes away
the obligation to focus on the coffin. This is reminiscent of England's Telford
crematorium by Haverstock Associates (Grainger 2005: 337–8). At the same
time, the glass auditorium allows views from the courtyard to the inside and it is
possible that strangers may be present in the courtyard, but only those that have
gained access to the inside columbarium. In modernist times this would be seen
as an infringement of the privacy of the bereaved but Zeinstra wondered why
it was such a bad thing to see other groups of mourners, just as that happens at
burials at a cemetery.

Zeinstra's ideas on routing are intriguing. The different events that constitute
the cremation process take place in different buildings arranged around the
inner courtyard. This stands in contrast with most existing Dutch crematoria in
which farewell ceremonies proceed within one building as smoothly as possible.

Figure 11.6   Façade of crematorium Zoetermeer (2006)
Source: Photo by Pieter Kers; courtesy KBNG architects

Figure 11.7   Crematorium Zoetermeer, view from the side (2006)
Source: Photo by Pieter Kers; courtesy KBNG architects

Zeinstra's idea is to allow walking between these events as part of the mourning ceremony. The act of passage itself provides time and distance to comfort people. It helps to recall the farewell ceremony, which is, according to Zeinstra, the central function of the ceremony, as with a traditional burial. Although the sequence of events and the passages between them are fundamental, they are not necessarily the same for all individuals. The ground plan of a courtyard with different surrounding buildings allows mourners to make their individual choices of where to go to at which moment in time. People can make positive choices on their specific (ritual) passages instead of feeling pushed through the process as a flock of passive sheep. Again, we have echoes of Telford crematorium: 'The intention at Telford was to create an open yet private landscape that will enable uninhibited movement around its spaces' (Grainger 2005: 338, original quotation from Moore 2000).

Then, in Zoetermeer crematorium, we encounter an extraordinary building thanks to its outer design and texture. Its main visible feature is a large 'second skin' in rusty Corten steel curving around the auditorium as a protective shell (Figure 11.6). Architectural office MYJ (now KBNG) found this symbolic for a crematorium; These architects see the gradual corrosion of the untreated sheets exemplifying the transitory nature of life. A bridge connecting the building and the adjacent cemetery (Figure 11.7), and a balcony are also made from Corten steel plates. The idea is that the remarkable shape and texture of the steel façade turns the crematorium into a conspicuous landmark and a natural component of the landscape at the same time.

As for the commissioners of Leusden crematorium, they wanted to design a multicultural and multifunctional crematorium that would fit the needs of diverse cultural and religious groups. Architect Arnold Sikkel worked together with representatives of these different groups, to discuss their needs and expectations. Consequently, the crematory, which is partly designed as a public space, is separated by a courtyard from the rest of the building making the auditorium suitable for burial services by Dutch Reformed people who oppose cremation. For Hindus it is possible to walk around the crematory as they traditionally walk around the pile with the body to perform religious rites in the open air at the courtyard.[2]

From the outside these post-modern crematoria moved away from the standardised 'non-places' towards unique buildings. A German example is the Treptow crematorium in Berlin, designed by Axel Schultes and Charlotte Frank. However, the question remains whether consumers choose between crematoria as if these were consumption goods? Will post-modern crematoria become more 'popular' than sub-modern crematoria? Thus far, the indications are that 'clients' seem rather conservative and that they choose crematoria that are near their places of residence, or the crematorium where a deceased loved one has been cremated. Despite the critiques that crematoria received because of their efficient routing,

---

[2]   Interviews with architect and manager.

it could arguably provide a sense of calmness as well, as people know where they have to go. Maybe what mourners need is the possibility to switch off their minds from making 'consumptive' choices at times of great emotional stress, so they can focus on the farewell service. People can at least pretend to themselves that at that very emotional moment the whole crematorium revolves around the farewell ceremony of their loved one, which seems to fit with contemporary death rites that remember and celebrate the identity of the deceased.

Conclusions

While this chapter has demonstrated how the Netherlands has shown a distinct momentum of its own in the development of crematoria and their building styles it has also indicated some resemblance in chronology with the attitude towards creating a specific sense of place with other European countries, for example the UK and Germany. The direction of an intended sense of place has developed from the sacred and solemn through a softened version of Modernism (called shake-hands modernism in the Netherlands) and suburban negation of death, to wider post-modern experiments. This resemblance seems to have been caused mainly by general societal developments in attitudes towards death as architects struggled in the same way as any ordinary citizen with the irrationality and incomprehensibility of death. The question stands as how best to create a sense of place for something so senseless? Here, the latest experimental developments that we have cautiously labelled post-modern look promising as sincere attempts at creating meaningful places where there is room for emotions. While it is difficult to know how to accomplish this in precise terms, having that goal as central to the building programmes seems essential. The success of these attempts remains to be seen, but crematoria have clearly appeared on the list of challenges for ambitious architects, and that is, definitely, good news.

References

Altena, M., 2009. Making memories: Film-makers, agency and identity in the production of funerary films in the Netherlands. *Mortality*, 14(2): 159–72.

Ariès, P., 1977. *L'homme devant la mort*. Paris: Éditions du Seuil.

Augé, M., 1995. *Non-places: Introduction to an Anthropology of Supermodernity*. London: Verso.

Baudrillard, J., 1976. *Symbolic Exchange and Death*. London: Sage Publications.

Bergeijk, V.H.D. and Wagenaar, C., 2007. *Jan Wils: De stijl en verder*. Rotterdam: Uitgeverij 010.

Bock, M., Fluks, M., Van Rossem, V. and Vink, M., 1982. *Van het Nieuwe Bouwen naar een Nieuwe Architectuur; Groep '32: Ontwerpen, gebouwen, stedebouwkundige plannen 1925–1945*. 's-Gravenhage: Staatsuitgeverij.

Bucknill, P.J.R., 1915. Cremation: The Only Rational Means of the Disposal of the Dead. *The Journal of the Royal Society for the Promotion of Health*, 36(1): 54–6.

Cappers, W., 1999. *Vuurproef voor een grondrecht. Koninklijke Vereniging voor Facultatieve Crematie 1874–1999*. Zutphen: Walburg Pers.

Colenbrander, B.W., 1993. *Style: Standard and Signature in Dutch Architecture of the Nineteenth and Twentieth Centuries*. Rotterdam: Nai Publishers.

Curl, J.S., 2004. Review of: Worpole (2003) 'Last landscapes: the architecture of the cemetery in the West'. *Architectural Review*, 215(1284): 97.

Davies, D.J., 1995. *British Crematoria in Public Profile*. Maidstone: Cremation Society of Great Britain.

Davies, D.J., 1996. The sacred crematorium. *Mortality*, 1(1): 83–94.

Davies, D.J. and Mates, L., eds, 2005. *Encyclopaedia of Cremation*. Aldershot.

Duijnhoven, D., 2002. Tegen de achteloosheid. *De uitvaart*, 5(May).

Grainger, H.J., 2005. *Death Redesigned: British Crematoria, History, Architecture and Landscape*. Reading: Spire Books Limited.

Groenendijk, P. and Vollaard, P., 1998. *Guide to Modern Architecture in the Netherlands – Gids voor moderne architectuur in Nederland*. Rotterdam: 010 Publishers.

Groenendijk, P. and Vollaard, P., 2004. *Guide to Contemporary Architecture in the Netherlands – Gids voor hedendaagse architectuur in Nederland*. Rotterdam: 010 Publishers.

Hamilton, K., 2006. Evidence-based design and the art of healing. In: C. Wagenaar, ed., *The Architecture of Hospitals*. Rotterdam: Nai Publishers, pp. 271–280.

Heessels, M., 2008. Mam, ik heb je thuisgebracht. Rituelen rondom asverstrooiing in Nederland. In: H.J.M. Venbrux, M. Heessels and S. Bolt, eds, *Rituele Creativiteit. Actuele veranderingen in de uitvaart- en rouwcultuur in Nederland*. Zoetermeer: Meinema, pp. 17–29.

Hekkema, H., 2002. Uitvaartcultuur als ontwerpopgave; 'De oesters zijn gegeten, de witte wijn is gedronken'. In: H. Hekkema, ed., *Uitvaartcultuur als ontwerpopgave: Situering en architectuur van funeraire functies in een veranderende samenleving; een ideeënprijsvraag voor studenten*. Zwolle: Esselink Stichting, pp. 59–76.

Hellman, L., 1982. Ashes to ashes: Crownhill Crematorium, Milton Keynes. *Architects' Journal*, 48.

Hockey, J., 2007. Review of Mates and Davies (2005) Encyclopaedia of cremation. *Mortality*, 12(3): 315–16.

Hulsman, R.N. and Hulsman, M., 2008. *Bouwen op de grens (deel zuid); Gids voor de funeraire architectuur in Nederland, Limburg – Noord-Brabant – Zeeland*. Rotterdam: Uitgeverij Ger Guijs.

Hulsman, R.N. and Hulsman, M., 2010. *Bouwen op de grens (deel midden en oost); Gids voor de funeraire architectuur in Nederland, Flevoland – Gelderland – Utrecht*. Rotterdam: Uitgeverij Godoy & Godoy.

Jencks, C., 2006. Maggie Centers and the architectural placebo. In: C. Wagenaar, ed., *The Architecture of Hospitals*. Rotterdam: Nai Publishers, pp. 448–59.

Jupp, P.C. and Grainger, H.J., 2002. *Golders Green Crematorium, 1902–2002: A London Centenary in Context*. London: London Cremation Company Plc, 141–154.

Kuyt, J., Middelkoop, N. and Van Der Woud, A., 1997. *G.B. Salm and A. Salm GBzn.: bouwmeesters van Amsterdam*. Rotterdam: Uitgeverij 010.

LVC, 2009-last update. Landelijke Vereniging van Crematoria: Aantallen. Available at: www.lvc-online.nl/aantallen (accessed 30 June 2010).

Pursell, T., 2003. The burial of the future: modernist architecture and the cremationist movement in Wilhelmine Germany. *Mortality*, 8(3): 233–50.

Ritzer, G., 2004. *The McDonaldization of Society*, revised new century edition. Thousand Oaks: Pine Forge Press.

Venbrux, E., Peelen, J. and Altena, M., 2009. Going Dutch: individualisation, secularisation and changes in death rites. *Mortality*, 14(2): 97–101.

Walter, T., 1990. Setting the style. *Resurgam*, 33(4): 126.

Wienrich, S. and Speyer, J., 2003. *The Natural Death Handbook*. London: Rider.

Worpole, K., 2003. *Last Landscapes: The Architecture of the Cemetery in the West*. London: Reaktion Books.

Worpole, K., 2009. *Modern Hospice Design: The Architecture of Palliative Care*. Abingdon: Routledge.

Chapter 12

New Identity of All Souls' Day Celebrations in the Netherlands: Extra-Ecclesiastic Commemoration of the Dead, Art, and Religiosity

Eric Venbrux

Introduction

Mortality makes people wonder about the meaning of life. It is hard to evade the question when faced with the death of a loved one. It invades our lives and leaves a pervasive sense of our own finitude. How to circumvent that innately human fate is the focus of many religions (Malinowski 1925: 46), especially Christianity. 'Mythical transcendence' (Chidester 2002) and the great Christian saga are attracting fewer and fewer adherents in the Netherlands (Arts 2009; Felling 2004), but death remains very much centre stage. In this chapter we look at the revival of the Catholic All Souls' feast, an annual ritual to commemorate the dead, but in a non-ecclesiastic context. According to William May (1972) death inspires awe because of our very inability to come to grips with it. He regards it as a source of religiosity. How true is that among participants in new All Souls' celebrations? How do they envisage life after death?

In recent times death has become a prominent theme in popular culture (McIlwain 2005; Walter 1994). Hubert Knoblauch (2009: 255–64) argues that this fascination with death is a major motivation of what he calls popular religion, a spirituality found among churchgoers and non-churchgoers alike, which makes no distinction between sacred and profane. In present-day society religious conceptions and practices are much more closely interwoven with people's private lives (Garces-Foley 2005; Quartier 2007), evidenced by the popularity of so-called personal funerals (Enklaar 1995). The form of these funerals is very much inspired by popular culture.

The same influence is noticeable in new commemorations of the dead on All Souls' day. These celebrations are 're-inventions' of the traditional rite of passage in the Catholic Church calendar (Grimes 2000; Myerhoff 1982). As funerary rituals they not only solve the problem of dealing with the loss of loved ones, but are also a way of making sense of death, and thus of life as well (Taylor 1989: 149). Before turning to the new All Souls' celebrations, however, we first take a look at the Catholic All Souls' feast, only then will I describe the burgeoning

Figure 12.1   Traditional All Souls' day celebration on the Roman Catholic
                graveyard in Beugen, the Netherlands, in 2006
Source: Photo by Eric Venbrux

tradition of extra-ecclesiastic celebrations and artistic forms of new rituals. After
that we shift the focus to the participants, who are mostly non-churchgoers. In
the penultimate section we present the findings of a questionnaire survey of their
religious ideas from which it appears that most participants do not see death as the
end station of life's journey. We conclude that these funerary rites help people find
new ways of transcending death, which according to Chidester (2002) are shaped
by cultural and experiential rather than mythical transcendence.

The Catholic All Souls' Feast

To Roman Catholics All Souls' day (2 November) is a feast day when one prays
for the souls of the dead. They are commemorated in the religious community
and their graves are visited (Beekman 1949: 27; Kors 1938: 28). The church's
celebration of All Souls' day was introduced by the Benedictine monks of Cluny.
In 998 Abbot Odilo stipulated that on the day following All Saints the monks of
the order would henceforth ring the bell, say an office for the dead and celebrate
a requiem mass. In the fourteenth century liturgical All Souls' services became
generally accepted throughout the Roman Catholic Church. After the Council
of Trent in the mid-sixteenth century the commemoration gave believers an
opportunity to pray for the salvation of the souls of the dead. Since the beginning

of the last century three masses are celebrated in Catholic churches on All Souls' day, or on the next Sunday. Believers are also promised plenary indulgence for the soul of a deceased person in return for their prayers on this day with a view to shortening its stay in purgatory (Beekman 1949: 27). The tradition includes a visit to the cemetery, putting chrysanthemums on the grave and lighting candles for the dead (see Figure 12.1).

According to popular belief in the Netherlands and other countries the souls of the dead visit the living at All Souls. In Flanders it was customary to bake special loaves or cakes for the returning souls. The confections were put outside at night so the souls could collect them. In Tyrol the souls were fed by leaving the remains of supper on the table for them on All Souls' eve (Schrijnen 1930: 242–3). The religious notion of returning souls was also evident in the advice not to close the door too abruptly on All Souls' day because of the danger of a soul getting jammed in it. In similar conceptions the howling of the wind was said to be the thunder of the souls' carriage wheels (Ter Laan 1949: 11). In Germany the light of candles that relatives lit on the graves of their dead served as beacons to guide these souls to their bodies' last resting place. The living were also warned against inadvertently stepping on a wandering soul or accidentally capturing one in an empty pot and to take care lest one of them sits down on the sharp edge of a knife (Sartori 1927: 268–72). Experts in folklore tend to see beliefs in the annual return of souls as relics of pre-Christian customs (Schrijnen 1930: 242–3). They may equally well have grown from interaction with official, ecclesiastically sanctioned portrayals. Both the All Souls' celebrations of the church and the religious ideas and practices of lay people form part of lived religion.

A typical notion is that on All Souls' day the living and the dead draw close to each other. They are the souls of the dead with whom some sort of bond is maintained. The rituals performed on All Souls' day bridge the divide between the worlds of the living and the dead. Although ecclesiastic celebrations of All Souls' day have lost some of their splendour and are moreover attended by a dwindling number of believers, we shall see below that the commemoration of the dead in the gloom of autumn continues to appeal to people. According to Peter Nissen, calendar feasts like All Souls' day, Christmas and Easter rarely have purely religious significance, for as a rule they are accompanied by all sorts of elements of profane festive culture. Nonetheless their inclusion in the Church calendar tends to make them points of 'crystallisation of the sacred' and, being vehicles of multiple meanings, they retain a very real 'sacred dimension' (Nissen 2000: 245–8).

That applies to Roman Catholics, who take the fate of the poor souls to heart and, on All Souls' day, listen to the names of fellow parishioners who have passed on in the past year. It also applies to neo-pagans who relate All Saints' and All Souls' day to the Celtic solstice feast, Samhain, when the souls of those that have died in the past year return in search of a body (Johnson 1968). It is closely associated with Halloween (All Saints' eve), a feast that has spread from the Anglo-Saxon world (Santino 1983). The feast inspired by the horror of death barely took root in Dutch popular culture and has, thus far, gained no purchase as a religious feast.

Yet, at the start of the twenty-first century we are witnessing renewed interest in All Souls' day as something of an emerging tradition in which institutionalised religion is of secondary significance. The major question now is whether we can discern notions of religiosity in it that are normally hidden from view.

All Souls' Day New Style

In 2005 new All Souls' celebrations took shape, initiated by two artists, Ida van der Lee and Mary Fontaine, who presented themselves as ritual mentors for artistic shows at cemeteries in which they explicitly involved the deceased's relatives. It is worth noting that both Fontaine and Van der Lee, although no longer practising, come from Roman Catholic backgrounds. Their envisaged revival of All Souls' day is also inspired by the Mexican Day of the Dead, which is deeply rooted in popular culture (Haley and Fukuda 2004). The two initiators took up various trends in funerary and mourning culture.

It would seem that ongoing secularisation and individualisation processes are accompanied by an undiminished demand for rituals, especially death rituals (Venbrux et al. 2009; Wouters 2002). In the undertaking business so-called personal funerals are catching on, in which the ritual centres on the person of the deceased, including the speeches, choice of music and ritual actions and objects. Relatives play a more active role than in traditional funerals, giving the ceremony an informal character, and seek to emphasise the unique person of the deceased, whose lived experience is celebrated. Not only are dead persons the main bond among an increasingly hybrid public, but they help highlight a memorable event.

The key word in these funerals is ritual creativity (Venbrux et al. 2008), wresting the deceased from oblivion and helping to mitigate death. Painting the coffin, using visual material, applauding the deceased, releasing balloons and the like underscore this climax, a grand finale that suggests that death can be transcended, at least in the here and now. Apart from invoking the creativity of relatives and other parties, new actors are entering the market with a supply of funerary art. In addition the undertaking business is being feminised. At first commemoration of the individual featured most prominently, but in due course it came to be placed in a collective context, such as mother's day celebrations in the crematorium and memorial concerts. Since 2005 the trend has manifested itself even more emphatically in All Souls' celebrations. That year Mary Fontaine (b. 1953) organised the first 'Night of the Soul' (*Nacht van de Ziel*) in Almere. Since then there have been five such occasions. At least 2,000 candles illuminate the cemetery. Participants go to the grave in procession. A bagpiper provides music. In the assembly hall there is always an open stage entitled 'live art', where people are invited to perform 'something personal'. These vary from recitals, poems and recounting memories of the deceased to visual presentations. Participants are given coffee and can enjoy delicacies (*lichtpuntjes*, 'pastry with light') prepared by a confectioner. Another standard feature is writing letters to the deceased that are then sent up in smoke. Sticks with bengal fire producing little stars are also lit and, as though to invoke the presence of people who were buried or cremated elsewhere, so-called 'soul flags' bearing portraits of the deceased are displayed. These ceremonies have also caught on in Belgium (www.doodenlevenskunst.nl; www.maryfontaine.nl). Also in 2005 Ida van der Lee (b. 1961) organised an 'All Souls' in all likelihood' (*Allerzielen Allicht*, also a pun: 'All Souls' all light') event at the Nieuwe Ooster cemetery in Amsterdam. Some 40 artists collaborated with relatives to enact a commemoration of the dead for All Souls' day. In similar vein Van der Lee followed it up with 'All Souls everywhere' (*Allerzielen Alom*, www.allerzielenalom.nl), which saw five performances in the province of North Holland in 2007 (see Quartier et al. 2008). The next year there were 10 spread countrywide and in 2009 'All Souls everywhere' celebrations were held at 21 locations.

After 2005 the Nieuwe Ooster cemetery continued these celebrations under their own management and with the title 'Memory lit up' (*Herinnering Verlicht*). Van der Lee's initiative was taken up in many other places, although the new All Souls' rituals were not necessarily designated 'All Souls everywhere'. Inspiration and guidelines for diverse situations culminated in the booklet *Allerzielen Alom. Kunst tot herdenken* (Van der Lee 2008; 'All Souls everywhere: Art for commemoration'), which Van der Lee compiled for this purpose. In 2008 she was awarded the biannual Yarden Prize by the undertaking business of that name in recognition of her innovative approach.

The two projects, 'Night of the Soul' and 'All Souls everywhere', led to a degree of institutionalisation. For the purpose of annual organisation and distribution, and to safeguard the 'intellectual property' of the initiators, foundations were set up. Since 2007 there has also been an annual 'Day of consolation for relatives'. Information about the new, extra-ecclesiastic rituals are available on the Internet. Within five years the projects to revive All Souls' day have evolved a distinctive structure and organisation. To some extent this has meant a loss of the spontaneity of the early efforts; at the same time, however, it guarantees annual repetition of the new rituals. The sense of solidarity or *communitas* (Turner 1969) engendered by the ritual gatherings appeared to be more intense at the newly initiated celebrations, although that could be partly because individual participants may have experienced the loss more acutely at that time. We should also appreciate that there is a steady increase in the number of visitors and locations where the new rituals are performed.

Although these new celebrations vary, their structure is comparable. They take place at night in the period around All Souls' day (late October/early November). After sunset the cemetery or memorial park is opened to the public. Thus the living enter a place that at that time of day is reserved for the dead. A warm and – according to some visitors – 'magical' atmosphere is created by illuminations ranging from candles, lanterns, artificial lights and torches to fire baskets. Candles, besides being a traditional element of All Souls' celebrations, provide light that contrasts with the darkness. The customary silence is broken by the sound of speeches and music recitals. Symbolically these contrasts lift the event out of the ordinary course of everyday life. They make it clear that this is a rite of passage.

Visual and performing artists, together with organisers and participants, contribute their imaginative talents. The artists' works represent new visual embodiments of commemorating the deceased. Individual works on graves or elsewhere on the premises form part of a larger whole (for numerous examples, see Van der Lee 2008). But artists do not have a monopoly in artistic portrayal. It is increasingly shared by cemetery staff and relatives in various places, with the result that the burgeoning tradition is spreading its roots. The intertwinement with popular culture has caused initiator Ida van der Lee some concern about artistic integrity. As a result by no means all celebrations inspired by her concept of a new All Souls' feast are held under the banner of 'All Souls everywhere'. Nonetheless these, too, are a new form of commemorating the dead, a revival of the seasonal ritual for the dead. Where cemetery officials and other people have taken charge of the celebration the role of individual, autonomous artists has moved into the background in favour of the collective creativity of other participants in the shaping of an emerging tradition (cf. Bogatyrev and Jakobson 1929). Some of these celebrations have been hugely successful, like 'Memory lit up' at Nieuwe Ooster cemetery in Amsterdam, where some 5,000 people attended in 2009.

Although the celebrations are richly varied certain elements appear to be common. These include displaying, singing or reading out the names of those who died during the past year, floating illuminated messages to the deceased or posting and burning such missives in fire baskets, listening to music and poetry, (communal) eating and drinking, the use of photographs and objects to evoke memories of the deceased, and visiting graves to place candles and other items on them. The new All Souls' rituals occurring right across the country demonstrate not only that the dead live on, but also that the living feel decidedly bound up with them.

Non-Churchgoers and the New All Souls' Day Celebrations

The five 'All Souls everywhere' celebrations in North Holland attracted remarkable numbers of non-churchgoers. This is evidenced by our questionnaire survey (n = 376) in the autumn of 2007. Almost two-thirds of the visitors (63.4 per cent) did not belong to any church or religious group. In addition the new All Souls' day celebrations attracted a solid contingent of Roman Catholics – a quarter of the respondents (27.7 per cent): clearly, the revival of a Catholic feast in an extra-ecclesiastic context appealed to them. The majority of respondents were middle aged people, half of them in the 40–60 age bracket. A substantial group (36.7 per cent) were over the age of 60, and a relatively small number were younger than 40 (13.3 per cent). More than four out of every five visitors (82.7 per cent) attended the celebrations in the company of one or more other person.

When asked about the purpose of their attendance the vast majority indicated that it was to commemorate their dead. A relatively small group (6.4 per cent) attended out of curiosity or an interest in art. Among those that used the organised celebrations to commemorate deceased loved ones 44 per cent had more than one person in mind. About a quarter of them (24.6 per cent) indicated that these were close relatives, such as a partner, parents or children. Another 10.9 per cent of visitors wanted to commemorate the dead generally. Most visitors, however, were recalling people to whom they were emotionally close. Up to two-thirds indicated that their relationship with the deceased was intense or very intense: 16.9 per cent defined it as fairly intense and 9.5 per cent indicated that it was superficial or very superficial. Respondents also expressed the emotions that they experienced during the celebrations. Warmth, love, peace, comfort and care were the most frequent responses, irrespective of whether the person had come on her own or in the company of others (mean = 3.6 on a 5-point scale). Hardly any (mean = 0.9 on the same scale) reported feelings of loneliness and helplessness, including those who had come on their own.

The new All Souls' rituals appeared to evoke a sense of commitment. In interviews and responses to open questions in the questionnaire the accent was often on solidarity. They enjoyed being part of such a large gathering and sharing their feelings about the loss of loved ones with others. Our observations confirmed this. Strangers walked around in groups, started conversations with each other and joined together as a public. This solidarity was reinforced by sharing food and other ritual activities. Earlier visitors often returned to subsequent annual celebrations. In our most recent questionnaire in 2009 at least 84.3 per cent of the respondents (n = 428) said that they planned to attend the event again the next year.

As already noted, the majority of participants in new All Souls' rituals comprised non-churchgoers. Declining church membership in the Netherlands relates to diminished social cohesion (Schmeets and Van der Bie 2009). Schmeets and Te Riele (2009: 8) rightly point out, however, that the important factor in social cohesion is not simply intra-group cohesion (e.g. among members of the same denomination) but also inter-group solidarity. In that respect the celebrations appear to unite non-churchgoers, lapsed members and churchgoers in a broader solidarity than separate religious persuasions. The authors of the Central Bureau of Statistics' recent report on religion in the Netherlands at the start of the twenty-first century (*Religie in Nederland aan het begin van de 21ste eeuw*, Schmeets and Van der Bie 2009) refers to Durkheim's classic work on the importance of religion for social cohesion (Schmeets and Te Riele 2009: 7), although they fail to mention that to Durkheim the socially cohesive function lies mainly in rituals.

Religious Notions

There is still a great need for rituals, but often not for traditional ecclesiastical ones. That is the verdict of Dekker (2007: 30) in the latest edition of the study

God in Nederland. The extra-ecclesiastic All Souls' rituals resonate with this need. The researchers of *God in Nederland* found that death, in particular, triggers experience of transcendence (Bernts et al. 2007: 134). In 2007 the All Souls' day celebrations modelled on Ida van der Lee's concepts were attended by people of whom the vast majority did not regard death as the end of life. Our survey showed an average of 4.1 on a Likert scale for those indicating that they believe in some sort of life after death.

This score might have been even higher if youths were not so under-represented in our sample. Bernts et al. (2007: 49) point out that among youths a proportionally higher percentage believe in life after death than is the case among older people. At all events, the finding confirms that belief in an afterlife – which appears to be equally prevalent among non-churchgoers – can no longer serve as the sole criterion of adherence to a Christian religious persuasion (Bernts et al. 2007: 49). Saler (2008: 222) does mention religious ideas and practices in relation to death as a hallmark of religion generally. It seems that religious activities and enactments in everyday life permit a greater measure of indeterminacy, pluriformity and development in people's religious notions (Venbrux 2007: 9). In other words, human religiosity is not necessarily constant but may fluctuate. Especially when confronted with the death of loved ones, and indirectly with our own mortality, this sensitivity appears to increase. Thus many people's conceptions cannot be linked directly to clearly defined religious tenets. It gives the impression that in practice doing things, performing rituals carries greater weight in people's enactment of their religiosity.

Visitors to the aforementioned All Souls celebrations felt, at an average rate of 3.6 on a 5-point scale, that there is a supreme power or 'something higher' that influences human life. A similar proportion (mean = 3.6) believed in the existence of 'something' which they could not or did not care to visualise in concrete terms. To a lesser extent (3.1 on our 5-point scale) they supported an anthropomorphic God concept – the notion of a God who intervenes in people's earthly lives and cares. The question regarding an afterlife obtained the highest score in this category: respondents indicated that to them death was not an absolute end to life (mean = 4.1).

The respondents based this on their experience of the commemoration of the dead that they attended. Hence one way or another the people who completed our questionnaire felt that they were relating to the dead. To many of them commemoration of the dead also implied retrospection. Personal commemoration of the lives of their loved ones appeared to be the key element of the All Souls' celebrations (mean = 4.2). If we combine this with the finding on belief in an afterlife (mean = 4.1), it suggests that bonds with the deceased transcend death. Two-thirds of the visitors indicated that they had an intense to very intense relationship with the deceased.

Various ritual activities in the new style All Souls' celebrations were aimed at communicating with the deceased. Thus every annual celebration of 'Night of the Soul' includes burning letters to the deceased in fire baskets. The messages are

Figure 12.2   The pond with floating urns, on which people released a written
message to their deceased loved one in a candle-lit float, during
'Memory lit up' at Nieuwe Ooster cemetery in 2009

Source: Photo by Eric Venbrux

thought to rise upwards with the smoke. At 'All Souls everywhere' ceremonies there is often a pond, on which people can release a written message to their deceased loved one in a candle-lit float. This also happened at 'All Souls in all likelihood' and is repeated annually under the name 'Memory lit up' in a pond with floating urns at Nieuwe Ooster cemetery (see Figure 12.2).

In 2009 this latter celebration included two official letterboxes, each supplied with two wings (see Figure 12.3), where relatives could post a message to their dead. They can also speak anonymously to their deceased loved ones on telephones connected with a device that plays back messages recorded at the receiving end.

In these and other ways the relationship between the living and the dead finds expression. The informal ritual activities of the new All Souls' celebrations allow people scope to enact their commemoration of their loved ones according to their own ideas and needs. The extra-ecclesiastic framework does not dictate rigid religious tenets, but expressions in the communal celebrations, such as ritual communication with the deceased, indicate broad agreement with the notion of life after death.

Figure 12.3   Official letterbox, supplied with two wings, where relatives could
post a message to their dead during the 'Memory lit up' celebration
at Nieuwe Ooster cemetery, in Amsterdam, in 2009

Source: Photo by Eric Venbrux

Conclusion

In the Netherlands one observes a burgeoning tradition of extra-ecclesiastic All Souls' commemorations of the dead in cemeteries. It started in 2005 as a simultaneous project by two female artists, who put their stamp on the 're-invention' of the ritual. The enactment of the new All Souls' ceremonies puts the accent on individual and collective creativity that makes these events memorable, wrested from oblivion, and thereby helping to mitigate death. The new cultural form of commemorating the dead concurs with the innovation of funerary ritual in the Netherlands and the distancing from church authorities. Participation in these ceremonies is less formal than membership of a church. Nonetheless the new rituals inspire a sense of solidarity both among the living and between the living and the dead. Hence they transcend individuality and the limits of the community of the living and in that sense entail a form of 'cultural transcendence' (Chidester 2002), the survival of a cultural group after the death of individuals. It seems that the participants' religiosity is not constant but fluctuates and, especially in the case of the death of a loved one, finds expression in ritual activities. These practices express something that cannot be articulated in words alone. Thus religious beliefs in terms of some concept of eschatology remain fairly vague, whereas concrete, symbolic acts bridge the divide between the living and the dead. Ritual communication with the deceased suggests that the latter live on in some way. The notion of transcendence of death lies in the performance of a ritual act. David Chidester (2002) refers to experiential transcendence. The very performance of ritual activities like those in the new All Souls' celebrations helps people to find meaning in life when confronting death.

Acknowledgements

I am grateful to my colleague Thomas Quartier and research assistant William Arfman, who participated in the research, and to Douglas Davies for editing the English text. Any shortcomings are mine.

References

Arts, K. (2009). 'Ontwikkelingen in kerkelijkheid en kerkbezoek (1999–2008)'. In: H. Schmeets and R. van der Bie (eds), *Religie aan het begin van de 21ste eeuw* (pp. 41–6). The Hague: Central Bureau of Statistics.
Beekman, A. (1949). 'Allerzielendag'. In: P.E. van der Meer (ed.), *De Katholieke Encyclopaedie*, part 2 (p. 27). Amsterdam: Van den Vondel.
Bernts, T., Dekker, G. and Hart, J. de (2007). *God in Nederland 1996–2006*. Kampen: Ten Have.

Bogatyrev, P. and Jakobson, R. (1929). 'Die Folklore als eine besondere Form des Schaffens'. In: St.W.J. Teeuwen, Baader, Th. and Baumstark, A. (eds), *Donum Natalicum Schrijnen. Verzameling van opstellen door oud-leerlingen en bevriende vakgenoten opgedragen aan Mgr. Prof. Dr. Jos. Schrijnen bij gelegenheid van zijn zestigsten verjaardag* (pp. 900–13). Nijmegen: Dekker & Van de Vegt.

Chidester, D. (2002). *Patterns of Transcendence: Religion, Death, and Dying.* Belmont, CA: Wadsworth.

Dekker, G. (2007). 'Het christelijk godsdienstig en kerkelijk leven'. In: Bernts, T., Dekker, G. and Hart, J. de (eds), *God in Nederland 1996–2006* (pp. 12–73). Kampen: Ten Have.

Enklaar, J. (1995). *Onder de groene zoden: De persoonlijke uitvaart.* Zutphen: Alpha.

Felling, A.J.A. (2004). *Het proces van individualisering in Nederland: een kwart eeuw sociaal-culturele ontwikkeling.* Nijmegen: Catholic University Nijmegen.

Garces-Foley, K. (ed.) (2005). *Death and Religion in a Changing Modern World.* New York: Sharpe.

Grimes, R.L. (2000). *Deeply into the Bone: Re-inventing Rites of Passage.* Berkeley: University of California Press.

Haley, S.D. and Fukuda, C. (2004). *The Day of the Dead: When Two Worlds Meet in Oaxaca.* Oxford: Berghahn.

Johnson, H.S. (1968). 'November Eve Beliefs and Customs in Irish Life and Literature'. *The Journal of American Folklore* 81: 33–42.

Knoblauch, H. (2009). *Populäre Religion. Auf dem Weg in eine spirituelle Gesellschaft.* Frankfurt am Main: Campus Verlag.

Kors, J.B. (1938). *Encyclopædisch Kerkelijk Woordenboek.* Bilthoven: Gemeenschap.

Laan, K. ter (1949). *Folkloristisch Woordenboek van Nederland en Vlaams België.* The Hague: Van Goor.

Lee, I. van der (ed.) (2008). *Allerzielen Alom. Kunst tot herdenken.* Zoetermeer: Meinema.

Malinowski, B. (1925). 'Magic, Science and Religion'. In: J. Needham (ed.), *Science, Religion and Reality* (pp. 19–84). New York: Macmillan.

May, W.F. (1972). 'The Sacred Power of Death in Contemporary Experience'. *Social Research* 39(3): 463–88.

McIlwain, C.D. (2005). *When Death Goes Pop: Death, Media and the Remaking of Community.* New York: Lang.

Myerhoff, B. (1982). 'Rites of Passage: Process and Paradox'. In: V. Turner (ed.), *Celebrations: Studies in Festivity and Ritual* (pp. 109–35). Washington, DC: Smithsonian Institution Press.

Nissen, P. (2000). 'Percepties van sacraliteit. Over religieuze volkscultuur'. In: T. Dekker, H. Roodenburg and G. Rooijakkers (eds), *Volkscultuur: Een inleiding in de Nederlandse etnologie* (pp. 231–81). Nijmegen: SUN.

Quartier, T. (2007). *Bridging the Gaps: an Empirical Study of Catholic Funeral Rites*. Münster: LIT-Verlag.

Quartier, T., Wojtkowiak, J., Venbrux, E. and Maaker, E. de (2008). 'Kreatives Totengedenken: Rituelle Erinnerungsräume in einem niederländischen Kunstprojekt'. *Jaarboek voor Liturgie-Onderzoek* 24: 155–76.

Saler, B. (2008). 'Conceptualizing Religion: Some Recent Reflections'. *Religion* 38: 219–25.

Santino, J. (1983). 'Halloween in America: Contemporary Customs and Performances'. *Western Folklore* 42(1): 1–20.

Sartori, P. (1927). 'Allerseelen'. In: E. Hoffmann-Krayer and H. Bächtold-Stäubli (eds), *Handwörterbuch des deutschen Aberglaubens*, vol. I (pp. 268–72). Berlin: De Gruyter.

Schmeets, H. and Bie, R. van der (eds) (2009). *Religie aan het begin van de 21ste eeuw.* The Hague: Central Bureau of Statistics.

Schmeets, H. and Riele, S. te (2009). 'Religie in het perspectief van sociale samenhang'. In H. Schmeets and R. van der Bie (eds) (2009), *Religie aan het begin van de 21ste eeuw* (pp. 7–11). The Hague: Central Bureau of Statistics.

Schrijnen, J. (1930). *Nederlandse volkskunde*, part 1 (second edition). Zutphen: Thieme.

Taylor, L.J. (1989). 'Introduction: The Social Uses of Death in Europe'. *Anthropological Quarterly* 62(4): 149–54.

Turner, V. (1969). *The Ritual Process: Structure and Anti-structure*. Chicago: Aldine.

Venbrux, E. (2007). *Ongelooflijk! Religieus handelen, verhalen en vormgeven in het leven van alledag*. Nijmegen: Radboud University Nijmegen.

Venbrux, E., Heessels, M. and Bolt, S. (eds) (2008). *Rituele creativiteit. Actuele veranderingen in de uitvaart- en rouwcultuur in Nederland*. Zoetermeer: Meinema.

Venbrux, E., Peelen, J. and Altena, M. (2009). 'Going Dutch: Individualisation, Secularisation and Changes in Death Rites'. *Mortality* 14(2): 97–101.

Walter, T. (1994). *The Revival of Death*. London: Routledge.

Wouters, C. (2002). 'The Quest for New Rituals in Dying and Mourning: Changes in the We-I Balance'. *Body and Society* 8(1): 1–28.

Chapter 13

A Dream of Immortality: Mahler's *Das Lied von der Erde* (The Song of the Earth)

Hyun-Ah Kim

Get well soon, my Luxerl, so you can soon keep pace with me, and we can enjoy life together like two good comrades. Life and love will seem to you like the blossom of a tree that grows ever taller – and sometimes ever broader; and even if the blossom may fall, and later the fruit – one can confidently expect the next spring, when everything germinates once again. (Vienna, 8 June 1910)[1]

Death, Mahler and *Das Lied von der Erde*

Gustav Mahler (1860–1911), a Bohemian-born Austrian composer, was best known as one of the leading conductors in his lifetime.[2] Mahler called himself a 'summer holiday composer', since it was the only time when he could devote himself to creative work at his 'composing hut'.[3] From Toblach (Dobbiacco), where his last composing hut was built, Mahler wrote to his closest colleague Bruno Walter (on 18 July 1908) as follows: 'It is only here, in solitude, that I might come to myself and become conscious of myself'.[4]

Existing studies of Mahler have centred on the subject of death, which was a preoccupation in his music throughout his life.[5] Mahler was fascinated by funeral marches ever since his childhood and often incorporated them into his symphonies.[6] *Das Klagende Lied* (The Song of Lament), which is the most

---

[1] *Gustav Mahler: Letters to His Wife*, edited by Henry-Louis de La Grange and Gunther Weiss in collaboration with Knud Martner, translated by Antony Beaumont (Berlin, 1995; London: Faber & Faber, 2004), 356–7.

[2] Mahler was born into a Jewish family in Kalischt, Bohemia, on 7 July 1860. Mahler famously states: 'I am thrice homeless, as a native of Bohemia in Austria, as an Austrian among Germans, and as a Jew throughout the world.'

[3] Henry Raynor, *Mahler* (London: Macmillan, 1975), 73. In 1893 Mahler began to devote his summer holidays to writing music in the Alps.

[4] Knud Martner (ed.), *Selected Letters of Gustav Mahler*, translated by E. Wilkins, E. Kaiser and B. Hopkins (London: Faber & Faber, 1979), 324.

[5] For a recent biographical study of Mahler, see Stuart Feder, *Gustav Mahler – A Life in Crisis* (New Haven: Yale University Press, 2004).

[6] As a child Mahler wrote 'a polka, to which he had added a funeral march as an introduction'. Stephen Johnson, *Mahler: His Life and Music* (Naperville: Sourcebooks

important of Mahler's early compositions, is a lament for his brother Ernst's death.[7] *Todtenfeier* (Funeral Rites), which Mahler completed in 1888, became the opening movement of his second symphony, *Resurrection*.[8] In memory of the premature, tragic deaths of his siblings, Mahler also wrote *Kindertotenlieder* (Songs on the Death of Children) in 1904, which he later regarded as foretelling of his own child's death.[9]

Mahler's lifelong struggle to come to terms with death reaches its peak in *Das Lied von der Erde*, which is his most loved and frequently performed work. While previous compositions concern deaths among his family and friends, *Das Lied von der Erde* is associated with his own, and reflects intensely emotional turmoil during his last three years, especially after a series of tragic events in 1907: Mahler was forced to resign from his post as Director of the Vienna Court Opera, and his elder daughter Maria (whom he called 'Putzi') died of diphtheria or scarlet fever in July, and shortly after Mahler himself was diagnosed with a fatal heart condition.[10] In her memoir of Mahler, Alma, Mahler's wife, notes that 'his whole attitude to the world and life in general had changed. The death of our child and his own personal sorrow had set another scale to the importance of things'.[11]

The unexpected diagnosis was almost like a death sentence for Mahler who was exceptionally athletic and considered his music-writing part of the 'antiquated life' he lived during the summer holidays. In his great despair, Mahler wrote to Bruno Walter in the summer of 1908:

> This time I must change not only my home but also my whole way of life. You can't imagine how hard it is for me. For years I have grown used to taking strenuous exercise, to walking in forests and over mountains and boldly wresting my ideas from nature. I would sit at my desk only as a peasant brings in his harvest, to give shape to my sketches ... Now I must avoid all effort, watch myself constantly, walk as little as possible ... I have never been able to work

---

Media Fusion, 2007), 67.

[7]   Mahler's brother Ernst, a year younger, died in 1874, aged 13.

[8]   Mahler, the second of 14 children (many of whom including the first-born died in infancy), became head of the family after his parents' death in 1889 which, alongside his friend Hans von Bülow's death (1894), served as a motivation for his second symphony completed three months after Bülow's funeral – the occasion for its inspiration.

[9]   In 1895 one of Mahler's two surviving brothers, Otto, committed suicide. Otto was just about to begin a career as a conductor and Mahler was very close to him.

[10]   Mahler married Alma Schindler (1879–1964), a daughter of the famous Austrian painter Emil Schindler. Twenty years younger than Mahler, their first child was born when Mahler was about 42 years old.

[11]   Alma Mahler, *Gustav Mahler: Memories and Letters* (rev. edn), edited by Donald Mitchell, translated by Basil Creighton (New York: The Viking Press, 1969), 136.

only at my desk – I need outside exercise for my inner exercises … This is the greatest calamity I have ever known.[12]

It was around this time that Mahler began writing *Das Lied von der Erde*. At first he entitled it *Das Lied vom Jammer der Erde* (The Song of the Earth's Sorrow); later, he deleted the word *Jammer* (sorrow). Mahler also gave it a sub-title, 'A Symphony for Tenor and Alto (or Baritone) Voices and Orchestra'.[13]

Das Lied von der Erde is of unique importance in the history of music as it is the first complete integration of song cycle and symphony.[14] In contrast to the posthumous glory both the composer and the music have enjoyed, it was written during the most miserable part of Mahler's life in the fearful awareness of death. While his physical vitality reached its lowest point, Mahler 'slaved' at *Das Lied von der Erde*, which was the only source of comfort for him under the dreadful circumstances. In a letter to Bruno Walter, Mahler described how he felt about the musical composition in progress: 'I have been hard at work (from which you can tell I am more or less "acclimatized"). I myself do not know what the whole thing could be called. I have been granted a time that was good, and I think it is the most personal thing I have done so far.'[15] As Walter recalls, Mahler was 'scarcely the same as a man or as a composer' when writing *Das Lied von der Erde*, which was 'written *sub specie mortis*': it is a totally new work, 'new in its style of composition, new in invention, in instrumentation, and in the structures of the various movements'.[16]

Music and Poetry in *Das Lied von der Erde*

To encourage Mahler after his daughter's death, a friend gave him a copy of *Die chinesische Flöte* (The Chinese Flute), a volume of ancient Chinese poetry

---

[12]   Edward Seckerson, *Mahler: His Life and Times* (New York: Midas Books, 1982), 119.

[13]   Stephen Hefling, '*Das Lied von der Erde*: Mahler's Symphony for Voices and Orchestra – or Piano?', *Journal of Musicology* 10 (1992): 293–341.

[14]   For an important monographical study of *Das Lied von der Erde*, see Hermann Danuser, *Gustav Mahler:* Das Lied von der Erde (Munich: W. Fink, 1986). See also Hans Tischler, 'Mahler's *Das Lied von der Erde*', *Music Review* 10 (1949): 111–14.

[15]   Cited in Donald Mitchell, *Gustav Mahler: Songs and Symphonies of Life and Death; Interpretations and Annotations* (London: Faber & Faber, 1985), 486. The letter was undated but has been assumed to be written in September, 1908 in Toblach. Martner, *Selected Letters of Gustav Mahler*, 326.

[16]   Bruno Walter, *Gustav Mahler*, translated by Lotte Lindt (London: Quartet Books, 1990), 108–9.

translated recently by Hans Bethge.[17] *Die chinesische Flöte* consists of 83 poems written by 38 writers. Among them Mahler selected seven poems for the music he was conceiving, and two of them were combined in the last movement, 'Der Abschied' ('The Farewell'). Mahler 're-titled, re-arranged, cut and added to the texts with such vigour that it is fair to call him co-author as well as composer' of *Das Lied von der Erde*.[18]

Table 13.1   The structure of *Das Lied von der Erde* (1908–1909)

1. *Das Trinklied vom Jammer der Erde* – The Drinking Song of Earth's Sorrow (Li, Tai-Po)
2. *Der Einsame im Herbst* – The Lonely One in Autumn (Chang Tsi)
3. *Von der Jugend* – On Youth (Li, Tai-Po)
4. *Von der Schönheit* – On Beauty (Li, Tai-Po)
5. *Der Trunkene im Frühling* – The Drunken Man in Spring (Li, Tai-Po)
6. *Der Abschied* – The Farewell (Mong, Kao-Yen/Wang Wei)

The text of *Das Lied von der Erde* has received significant attention from scholars.[19] It has been interpreted in the light of the philosophy of Arthur Schopenhauer (1788–1860), to which Mahler was attracted greatly as a young artist. One of Mahler's favourite quotations was from Schopenhauer's *Die Welt als Wille und Vorstellung* (The World as Will and Imagination): 'How often have the inspirations of genius been brought to naught by the crack of a whip!'[20] Schopenhauer's philosophy of withdrawal and transcendence, often expressed in pessimistic terms, reflects many Buddhist ideas. On the surface, this philosophy appears to resemble the melancholic mood of the poems selected by Mahler. As generally observed, however, the poetic sentiment of *Das Lied von der Erde* is more complicated than this, and there remains a difficulty interpreting the poems which imply many contradictions; the tones are bitter and pessimistic, while at the same time expressing 'sensuous hedonistic ecstasy of living', 'a hedonistic delight in the beauty of nature'.[21]

In an attempt to clarify this ambiguous work, a leading Mahler scholar, Donald Mitchell, went even further to consult native Chinese scholars for translating the

---

[17]   Hans Bethge, *Die chinesische Flöte* (Leipzig: Insel-Verlag, 1907). Bethge's translation is based on a French translation of the original Chinese poems.

[18]   Jonathan Carr, *The Real Mahler* (London: Constable Press, 1997), 190.

[19]   For a recent study of the text, see Teng-Leong Chew, 'The Identity of the Chinese Poem Mahler Adapted for "Von der Jugend"', *Naturlaut* 3/2 (2004): 15–17.

[20]   Alma Mahler, *Gustav Mahler: Memories and Letters*, 47.

[21]   Deryck Cooke, *Gustav Mahler: An Introduction to his Music* (Cambridge: Cambridge University Press, 1980), 106–7.

original into English.[22] None of the native scholars who participated in this project, however, provided any better clue for interpreting the poems, and the so-called 'Oriental mysticism' which underlies the poems have been invariably explained in Schopenhauerian terms (with Buddhist connotations) and, more recently, in terms of Nietzschean philosophy. As is well known, Nietzsche was heavily influenced by Schopenhauer's thought. A Dutch musicologist Nikkels argues for the Nietzsche/Mahler relationship and, in particular, she shows how, in modifying Bethge's titles for use in *Das Lied von der Erde*, Mahler consistently adopts Nietzschean models after the style of *Also sprach Zarathustra* (Thus Spake Zarathustra): for instance, 'Der Pavillon aus Porzellan' becomes 'Von der Jugend' and 'Am Ufer' becomes 'Von der Schönheit'.[23]

Nikkels's argument for the influence of Nietzschean imagery on Mahler is convincing. Though it is hard to know how deeply Mahler appreciated Nietzsche's ideas, he did draw on Nietzsche even in his earlier musical composition: the fourth movement of Mahler's third symphony was set to the famous lines from *Also sprach Zarathustra* in which Nietzsche first presented his conception of the 'Übermensch' ('Overman') – a goal for humanity to achieve, the self-overcoming of man who embraces life to its full, confronting both the beauty and the horror of existence.[24] As we discuss later, a more fundamental parallel between *Das Lied von der Erde* and the Nietzschean philosophy may be drawn by reading the poems in the light of their underlying philosophical perspective to which Mahler was highly sympathetic.

With regard to the music of *Das Lied von der Erde*, Mahler utilizes the technique of 'word painting' throughout the six songs and straightforwardly depicts words and moods of the poems in every detail, and one can readily notice

---

[22]   Mitchell, *Gustav Mahler: Songs and Symphonies of Life and Death*, 455–6; 461–2. According to the Chinese scholars' research, writers of the two poems, 'Der Einsame im Herbst' (Chang Tsi)/'von der Jugend' (Li, Tai-Po), are unidentifiable. See also Fusako Hamao, 'The Sources of the Texts in Mahler's Lied von der Erde', *Nineteenth-Century Music* 19/1 (1995): 83–94.

[23]   Eveline A. Nikkels, '*Licht, Leben, Lust*: Three Fundamental Concepts of Nietzsche Incorporated into Texts used by Gustav Mahler', a paper delivered to the Mahler Colloquy held in Paris at the Musée d'art moderne in January 1985. Mitchell, *Gustav Mahler: Songs and Symphonies of Life and Death*, 351. Mitchell notes, 'If I am correct in perceiving a Nietzschean influence on Bethge, then this itself would have made a further appeal to Mahler'. Ibid., 351.

[24]   Johnson, *Mahler: His Life and Music*, 73. Although Mahler's music is related to Nietzsche's work, his attitude to Nietzsche seems ambivalent, given Alma's statement: 'My taste appeared to please him, except for a complete edition of Nietzsche, at which his eyebrows went up in horror. He demanded abruptly that it should be cast then and there into the fire. I refused and said that if his abhorrence had any justification it would be easy enough to convince me; and it would be more to his glory if Nietzsche stayed where he was and I refrained from reading him than if I consigned him to the flames'. Alma Mahler, *Gustav Mahler: Memories and Letters*, 18–19.

the sonic portrayal of the textual meanings. In the first movement, 'Das Trinklied vom Jammer der Erde' ('The Drinking Song of the Earth's Sorrows'), the narrator sings that life is beautiful but so short, and recommends drinking wine as the best comfort in acknowledging human mortality. The phrase 'Dunkel ist das Leben, ist der Tod' ('Dark is Life, Dark is Death') is used only once in the original poem, but Mahler uses it as a refrain, which sets a gloomy mood for the rest of the song. The scale of the first song (for tenor solo) is overwhelmingly wide, as if portraying the expansive landscape of Chinese continent. Although *Das Lied von der Erde* was meant to be a song cycle in its basic format, the existing German style of art song (*Lied*) is hardly traceable in the first movement. Rather, it sounds more akin to the realistic expression (half-crying/half-singing) of the contemporary Italian *verismo* operas such as the famous aria of Leoncavallo's *Pagliacci*, 'Recitar! ... Vesti la giubba' ('To perform! ... Put on the costume').[25] While the first song pours out the emotion of sorrow in dramatic, loud and strenuous tones with maximum force, the second, 'Der Einsame im Herbst' ('The Lonely One in Autumn'), is delivered in contemplative, subdued mood. Mahler makes no alteration to the original poem.

'Von der Jugend' ('On Youth') is the shortest of the six songs and portrays the scene of the young drinking and chatting in the jolly mood at the summer pavilion. 'Von der Jugend' and the following 'Von der Schönheit' ('On Beauty') sound most Chinese in terms of musical style, being characterized by the pentatonic scale. In 'Der Trunkene im Frühling' ('Drunkard in the Spring'), the narrator is already drunk; he again says 'Let me be drunk!'. Brilliant use is made by Mahler of tempo changes, especially of the dotted rhythms to portray the stumbling drunkard; indeed, the tempo changes every few measures, shifting unpredictably. The incorporation of the solo violin indicates a confused mental state of the drunkard who tries forgetting the misery of reality in drinking and in sleeping (daydreaming) in spring time. The last movement, 'Der Abschied' ('Farewell'), is the longest movement and lasts over half an hour. It reflects most strongly Mahler's attitude to death through the image of eternity which is mirrored every spring in the blossoming earth.

---

[25] In 1907 *Pagliacci* became the first entire opera to be recorded. It became very popular, especially due to Enrico Caruso who was the greatest superstar of the Metropolitan Opera House at that time; one of Caruso's recordings of 'Vesti la giubba' was the first record to sell one million copies. Mahler made his New York debut at the Metropolitan on 1 January 1908 with Wagner's *Tristan und Isolde*. During his term at the Metropolitan, Mahler was responsible for engaging such famous artists as Caruso. Italian operas and singers were notably dominant at the Metropolitan while Mahler was there. It appears that Mahler's music, consciously or unconsciously, was influenced by this environment. See Zoltan Roman, *Gustav Mahler's American Years 1907–1911: A Documentary History* (Stuyvesant, NY: Pendragon Press, 1989), 21, 102.

Wie Ein Naturlaut and *Wu-Wei* (無爲)

Both chinoiserie and Orientalism were popular in *fin-de-siècle* Vienna.[26] Mahler's interest in ancient China appears to have developed significantly during his time in New York (1908–1910), as suggested by his close acquaintance with the famous sinologist, Friedrich Hirth.[27] Mahler emerges as a pioneer in merging Western music with Chinese musical styles, indeed, *Das Lied von der Erde* most successfully conveys the universal sentiment of life, death and nature, through both its music and words.[28] It is interesting that the seven poems selected by Mahler, by accident or intention, are the key Daoist poems of the Tang dynasty (618–906 CE) written by Li, Tai-Po (the famous wandering poet); Changzii (one of the major Daoist sages); and Wang-Wei and Mong, Kao-Yen, two key landscape poets of Tang dynasty. Daoism is essentially non-theistic, human- and nature-centred, and is regarded, often disapprovingly, as the 'philosophy of the retired', the philosophy of hermits. During the Tang dynasty it became the state religion of China; one should distinguish Daoism as a philosophy centring on ancient Laozii and Changzi's teachings from its later corrupted religion on the institutional level. It is also important to note that Chinese Buddhism itself is an amalgam of Daoism and Buddhism. Daoist thinking, like all mysticism, is full of paradox, as in the key scripture, *Dao De Jing* (Tao-Te-Ching):[29] 'He never does anything great. Therefore he can accomplish his greatness.' 'He seems to find things difficult. Therefore he never finds difficulties.'[30]

---

[26]   For Orientalism in nineteenth-century German culture, see Jennifer Jenkins, 'German Orientalism: Introduction,' *Comparative Studies of South Asia, Africa and the Middle East* 24/2 (2004): 97–100.

[27]   Friedrich Hirth was Professor of Chinese in Columbia University and his major publications include *The Ancient History of China to the End of the Chóu Dynasty* (New York: Columbia University Press, 1908). Mahler invited Hirth to his house on Christmas Eve of 1908 and the Mahler couple enjoyed hearing about ancient China from him. Alma Mahler, *Gustav Mahler: Memories and Letters*, 146; cf. *Gustav Mahler: Letters to His Wife* (Mahler's letter dated on 14 June 1909), 320, 348.

[28]   For a discussion of Orientalist aspect of *Das Lied von der Erde*, see Francesca Draughon, 'The Orientalist Reflection: Temporality, Reality, and Illusion in Gustav Mahler's The Song of the Earth' in *Germany and the Imagined East*, edited by Lee Roberts (Newcastle: Cambridge Scholars Publishing, 2005), 159–73. See also idem, 'Mahler and the Music of *Fin-de-siècle* Identity'. PhD dissertation (University of California, Los Angeles, 2002).

[29]   For a recent English edition of *Dao De Jing*, see Laozi, *Tao Te Ching*, translated by D.C. Lau (Hong Kong: Chinese University Press, 2001).

[30]   Quoted in Günther Debon, *Oscar Wilde und der Taoismus; Oscar Wilde and Taoism* (Bern: Peter Lang, 1986), 96. Daoism is a philosophy which is in essence environmentally friendly in the sense that the human is understood as part of nature rather than having sovereign power to rule it. N.J. Girardot et al., *Daoism and Ecology: Ways within a Cosmic Landscape* (Cambridge, MA: Harvard University Press, 2001).

Intriguingly enough, the text of *Das Lied von der Erde* characterizes the Daoist poetic imagery of nature, dream, wandering and death – the themes which were equally popular in the poetry of the Romantic era that was set to music, notably in Schubert's *Winterreise*. Comparative scholarship has examined the impact of Daoism on Western thinkers such as Oscar Wilde[31] and the affinity between Daoism and Western thought, especially Spinoza's *Deus sive Natura* ('God or Nature') and Nietzsche's conception of the Overman; Spinoza was among Mahler's favourite readings from his youth, though his work is not related to Mahler's as it is to Nietzsche's. There is no evidence for Nietzsche's contact with Chinese philosophy; recent studies have effectively demonstrated the affinity between the Nietzschean philosophy of nature/humanity and Daoist ideas.[32] Furthermore, an appreciation of this affinity sheds a fresh light on *Das Lied von der Erde* and more fundamentally on Mahler's own philosophy of musical composition – music as the spontaneous expression of human assimilation to nature.

It is well-known that Mahler had a passionate love of nature, especially of trees, which he called 'my favourite' in the world.[33] For many artists and writers of the Romantic era – the disciples of Goethe – nature was a major source of inspiration; for Mahler and his music, it meant everything and, indeed, his passion for nature was a driving force for his creative work:

> Nature embraces everything that is at once awesome, magnificent and lovable … It seems so strange to me that most people, when they mention the word Nature in connection with art, imply only flowers, birds, the fragrance of the woods, etc. No one seems to think of the mighty underlying mystery, the god Dionysus, the great Pan; and just that mystery is the burden of my phrase, *Wie ein Naturlaut*.[34]

Mahler's rationale for composing music can be best summarized by his own phrase '*Wie ein Naturlaut*', that is, 'as though spoken by Nature', which he wrote over the first bar of his first symphony (*Titan*).[35] During the nineteenth century 'programme music'[36] was much in vogue among composers but Mahler was not so sympathetic

---

[31]   Debon, *Oscar Wilde und der Taoismus*.

[32]   Graham Parkes, 'Human/Nature in Nietzsche and Taoism', in *Nature in Asian Traditions of Thought: Essays in Environmental Philosophy*, edited by J.B. Callicott and R.T. Ames (Albany: State University of New York Press, 1989), 79–97.

[33]   Gabriel Engel, *Gustav Mahler: Song Symphonist* (New York: Bruckner Society of America, 1932), 26.

[34]   Ibid., 69.

[35]   Ibid.

[36]   The term 'programme', coined by Franz Liszt (1811–1886), was defined as a 'preface added to a piece of instrumental music, by means of which the composer intends to guard the listener against a wrong poetical interpretation, and to direct his attention to the poetical idea of the whole or to a particular part of it'. Roger Scruton, *The New Grove*

to this type of music as his profession in musical composition developed. If there is anything that may be identified as Mahler's 'programme', as he articulates it to a prominent critic, it is *Wie ein Naturlaut*:

> *My music is always the voice of Nature sounding in tone*, an idea in reality synonymous with the concept so aptly described by Bülow as 'the symphonic problem'. The validity of any other sort of 'programme' I do not recognize, at any rate, not for my work ... for music and poetry together are a combination capable of realizing the most mystic conception. Through them the world, Nature as a whole, is released from its profound silence and opens its lips in song.[37]

For Mahler, then, a 'symphony' as a musical form was the most suitable medium for expressing what he perceived in nature, as he claims to the Finnish composer Jean Sibelius in 1907: 'The symphony must be like the world. It must embrace everything.'[38] Most extraordinary in Mahler's musical world, as American composer Aaron Copland expressed it, is 'the special quality of his [Mahler's] communings with nature'.[39] It is, then, unsurprising, that Mahler was deeply touched by the Chinese poems that described human life in great empathy with nature – its oneness with nature.

Although Mahler did not know Chinese, nor mention Daoism anywhere in his writings, his strategy for writing music (*Wie ein Naurlaut*) is in tune with the key principle of Daoist philosophy, *wu-wei*, which is, literally, 'not doing'; but 'not doing' does not mean 'doing nothing' but 'doing by not doing', that is, 'action through non-action'. That is, *wu-wei* does not imply laziness or inaction but spontaneous, natural, effortless actions in realizing oneness with nature, ultimately, with the *Dao*.[40] Spontaneity is of essential importance in relation to the literary, musical world of Romanticism, which is especially true of Mahler's, as he writes to Alma (8 June 1910): 'In art, as in life, I rely entirely on spontaneity. If I were obliged or compelled to compose, I know for sure that I couldn't put a single note to paper'.[41] Indeed, *Das Lied von der Erde* embodies most fully Mahler's notion of *Wie ein Naturlaut*, which centres on the spontaneity of art and life, not only in terms of the 'poetical music' Mahler pursued but also in terms of the way it came into being as a musical composition.

Dictionary of Music and Musicians, edited by Stanley Sadie, 29 vols (London: Macmillan, 2nd edn, 2001), 20: 396–40.

[37]   Cited in Engel, *Gustav Mahler: Song Symphonist*, 69. My italics.

[38]   Donald Mitchell, *Gustav Mahler Volume II: The Wunderhorn Years: Chronicles and Commentaries* (London: Faber & Faber, 1975/1995; Woodbridge: Boydell Press, new edn, 2005), 286.

[39]   Johnson, *Mahler: His Life and Music*, 12.

[40]   A literal translation of 'Dao' is 'way' or 'path'; often interpreted as the fundamental 'principle' of world in a metaphysical sense.

[41]   *Gustav Mahler: Letters to His Wife*, 356.

It is not always the case that composers write what they really want; rather, they tend to be driven by the ambition for writing something 'great'. In this respect, the young, successful Mahler was no exception. Despite his hectic schedule as a music director at one of the most prestigious opera houses, he compelled himself to write large scale symphonic works, notably, his eighth symphony (*Veni creator spiritus*), known as the *Symphony of a Thousand*, most of which was written in the summer of 1906. As Mahler himself put it, however, *Das Lied von der Erde* is the 'most personal' of his work, which he distinguishes from the rest of his output.[42] Indeed, anyone who listened to Mahler's music would agree with Bruno Walter about the dramatic change in his musical world: *Das Lied von der Erde* is 'more subjective than any of his previous works … Every note carries his individual voice; every word, though based on a poem a thousand years old, is his own, *Das Lied von der Ede* is Mahler's most personal utterance, perhaps the most personal utterance in music'.[43] According to Alma, almost daily, Mahler played part of *Das Lied von der Erde* on the piano. It was music into which he poured out his agony and sorrow, with no intention of producing a *magnum opus*. Ironically, however, this was the music that made Mahler most successful as a composer in later centuries, something which, itself, may be regarded as 'doing by not doing'.

Beyond Mortality – *Catharsis*

Mahler had already finished eight symphonies before writing *Das Lied von der Erde*, which, though calling it a symphony, he did not number. Later, when writing a symphony which he called the ninth, he said to his wife, 'Actually, of course, it's the tenth, because *Das Lied von der Erde* was really the ninth'. When composing the tenth he said, 'Now the danger is past'.[44] This superstitious act is often seen as 'cheating death'; Beethoven, Schubert, and Bruckner – the three key Viennese composers – had not outlived their ninth symphonies, hence generating a sort of superstition, the 'Curse of the Ninth'. In fact, the symphony numbered 'nine' by Mahler was the last symphonic work he completed; most of his tenth symphony remains un-orchestrated.

   Death, as expressed to Bruno Walter (summer 1908), was a fact to be recognized and accepted: 'You do not know what has been and still is going on within me; but it is certainly not that hypochondriac fear of death, as you suppose. I had already realized that I shall have to die.'[45] It is in the last movement, 'Der Abschied'

   [42]   For a comparison between the Eighth Symphony and *Das Lied von der Erde*,' see Christian Wildhagen, 'The "Greatest" and the "Most Personal": the Eighth Symphony and *Das Lied von der Erde*,' in *The Cambridge Companion to Mahler*, edited by Jeremy Barham (Cambridge: Cambridge University Press, 2007), 129–42.
   [43]   Walter, *Gustav Mahler*, 109.
   [44]   Mahler, *Gustav Mahler*, 115.
   [45]   Martner, *Selected Letters of Gustav Mahler* (dated on 18 July 1908), 324.

('The Farewell'), that Mahler's determination to face death is most compellingly expressed. While the original poems describe leaving one's friend behind, Mahler took this imagery of farewell as adumbrating his own death. His reflection on death is not, however, simply about 'the end of life'. Mahler highlights the image of spring – 'der Lenz' (a poetic term which refers to spring) – that provokes the image of renewal, through the endless 'rebirth' which is inherent to the seasonal cycle of the earth. Where Bethge ended the piece with 'The earth is everywhere the same, / And eternal, eternal the white clouds ...', Mahler changed this with a strong sense of eternity: 'The dear earth everywhere / Blossoms in spring and grows green again! / Everywhere and forever the distance shines bright and blue! / For ever ...for ever ...' ('Die liebe Erde allüberall Blüht auf im Lenz und grünt aufs neu! Allüberall und ewig blauen licht die Fernen! Ewig ... Ewig ...').[46] This longing for eternity is articulated musically too in the unprecedented rhythmic pattern of the last movement, set in long, unmeasured cadenzas, expressing time that is endlessly flowing. The last notes of 'Der Abschied' are set in D for a solo part, while the orchestra's notes are A and E, which signify the openness of eternal time, rather than the final destination. At the last section of the song, which highlights the image of the renewed earth, the lonesome, sorrowful mood of farewell is thus led into the state of *catharsis* (relieving the emotional tensions surrounding the farewell – death).

Das Lied von der Erde was poetico-musical consolation for the composer himself, an artistic expression of overcoming the fear of death. Through a combination of music and poetry, which, in Mahler's terms, was 'capable of realizing the most mystic conception', it embodies his contemplation on human mortality in aspiring to the immortality of nature – the endless renewal of the earth. Mahler loved the poems behind which lies the mystic tradition of seeking human longevity and the 'immortality of the body', but expressing them in highly paradoxical terms. He may have dreamed about physical immortality, or at least more enduring vitality: in a letter sent from New York to Walter (undated; beginning of 1909), Mahler wrote, 'I am thirstier for life than ever before and find the "habit of existence" sweeter than ever'.[47] Mahler's philosophical speculations on the heavenly, eternal world, which are strongly reflected in his previous music, may have lost their appeal while struggling with the horror of his death. Deryck Cooke remarks in his introduction to *Das Lied von der Erde* that 'Mahler's hard-won religious faith had deserted him, and left him with only the certain facts of earthly life and death'.[48]

---

[46]   The last line was added by Mahler himself. Arthur Wenk, 'The Composer as Poet in *Das Lied von der Erde*', *Nineteenth-Century Music* 1 (1977–1978): 33–47.

[47]   Martner, *Selected Letters of Gustav Mahler*, 329. For more on the Daoist practice of physical immortality as a religion, see Isabelle Robinet, *Taoism: Growth of a Religion*, translated by P. Brooks (Stanford: Stanford University Press, 1997).

[48]   Cooke, *Gustav Mahler*, 106.

Although *Das Lied von der Erde* reflects the dramatic change of Mahler's view of life and world during his last years, his preoccupation with the image of the *liebe Erde* (dear Earth) as an eternal entity persists: almost 30 years prior to writing *Das Lied von der Erde* Mahler writes to his friend Joseph Steiner (17 June 1879) as follows:

> O, earth, my beloved earth, when, ah, when will you give refuge to him who is forsaken, receiving him back into your womb? Behold! Mankind has cast him out, and he flees from its cold and heartless bosom, he flees to you, to you alone! O, take him in, eternal, all-embracing mother, give a resting place to him who is without friend and without rest![49]

Mahler died on 18 May in 1911 and the début performance of *Das Lied von der Erde* was given on 20 November 1911, in Munich, with Bruno Walter conducting. During his lifetime Mahler's music received mixed opinions; as he foretold, his 'time' as a composer did come, if posthumously, and *Das Lied von der Erde* has proved to be the immortal work of Mahler. Yet, according to Mahler, what is truly everlasting is not any outcome of one's life activity: his attitude toward mortality/ immortality is *existentialist*, like that of his favourite thinkers – but perhaps in a more optimistic way – seeking the will power and the freedom to choose and to love life as such:

> Now perhaps you [Alma] will guess, or know, what I think of the 'works' of this person or that. They are, properly speaking, the ephemeral and mortal part of him; but what a man makes of himself – what he becomes through the untiring effort to live and to be, is permanent.[50]

References

Bethge, Hans, *Die chinesische Flöte* (Leipzig: Insel-Verlag, 1907).
Carr, Jonathan, *The Real Mahler* (London: Constable Press, 1997).
Chew, Teng-Leong, 'The Identity of the Chinese Poem Mahler Adapted for "*Von der Jugend*"', *Naturlaut* 3/2 (2004): 15–17. Available at: http://mahlerarchives. net/archives/dlvde.html.

---

[49]　Martner, *Selected Letters of Gustav Mahler*, 56.

[50]　Mahler's letter to his wife, dated on 20 (?) June 1909, Toblach. The letter goes on: 'This is the meaning, my dear Almschi, of all that has happened to you, of all that has been laid on you, as a necessity of the growth of the soul and the forging of the personality. And you still have a long life before you. Persist in exerting this inner force (as indeed you do); claim as your very own your utmost of beauty and power (more than this none of us can do) … exercise yourself in beauty, in goodness; grow unceasingly (that is the true productiveness)'. Mahler, *Gustav Mahler*, 322–3.

Cooke, Deryck, *Gustav Mahler: An Introduction to his Music* (Cambridge: Cambridge University Press, 1980).

Danuser, Hermann, *Gustav Mahler: Das Lied von der Erde* (Munich: W. Fink, 1986).

Debon, Günther, *Oscar Wilde und der Taoismus; Oscar Wilde and Taoism* (Bern: Peter Lang, 1986).

Draughon, Francesca, 'Mahler and the Music of *Fin-de-siècle* Identity'. PhD dissertation (University of California, Los Angeles, 2002).

Draughon, Francesca, 'The Orientalist Reflection: Temporality, Reality and Illusion in Gustav Mahler's The Song of the Earth', in *Germany and the Imagined East*, edited by Lee Roberts (Newcastle: Cambridge Scholars Publishing, 2005), 159–73.

Engel, Gabriel, *Gustav Mahler: Song Symphonist* (New York: Bruckner Society of America, 1932).

Feder, Stuart, *Gustav Mahler – A Life in Crisis* (New Haven: Yale University Press, 2004).

Girardot, Norman, Miller, James, and Xiaogan, Liu, *Daoism and Ecology: Ways within a Cosmic Landscape* (Cambridge, MA: Harvard University Press, 2001).

Hamao, Fusako, 'The Sources of the Texts in Mahler's *Lied von der Erde*', *Nineteenth-Century Music* 19/1 (1995): 83–94.

Hefling, Stephen, '*Das Lied von der Erde*: Mahler's Symphony for Voices and Orchestera – or Piano?', *Journal of Musicology* 10 (1992): 293–341.

Hirth, Friedrich, *The Ancient History of China to the End of the Chóu Dynasty* (New York: Columbia University Press, 1908).

Jenkins, Jennifer, 'German Orientalism: Introduction', *Comparative Studies of South Asia, Africa and the Middle East* 24/2 (2004): 97–100. Available at: http://cssaame.com/issues/24_2/jenkins.pdf.

Johnson, Stephen, *Mahler: His Life and Music* (Naperville: Sourcebooks Media Fusion, 2007).

Laozi, *Tao Te Ching*, translated by D.C. Lau (Hong Kong: Chinese University Press, 2001).

Mahler, Alma, *Gustav Mahler: Memories and Letters* (rev. edn), edited by Donald Mitchell, translated by Basil Creighton (New York: The Viking Press, 1969).

Mahler, Gustav, *Gustav Mahler: Letters to His Wife*, edited by Henry-Louis de La Grange and Gunther Weiss in collaboration with Knud Martner, first complete edition, revised and translated by Antony Beaumont (Berlin, 1995; London: Faber & Faber, 2004).

Mahler, Gustav, *Das Lied von der Erde in Full Score* (New York: Dover, 1988).

Mahler, Gustav, *The Song of the Earth (Das Lied von der Erde): A Symphony; Orchestral Score* (New York: Boosey & Hawkes, 1939).

Martner, Knud (ed.), *Selected Letters of Gustav Mahler*, translated by E. Wilkins, E. Kaiser and B. Hopkins (London: Faber & Faber, 1979).

Mitchell, Donald, *Gustav Mahler: Songs and Symphonies of Life and Death; Interpretations and Annotations* (London: Faber & Faber, 1985).

Mitchell, Donald, *Gustav Mahler Volume II: The Wunderhorn Years: Chronicles and Commentaries* (London: Faber & Faber, 1975/1995; Woodbridge: Boydell Press, new edn, 2005).

Parkes, Graham, 'Human/Nature in Nietzsche and Taoism', in *Nature in Asian Traditions of Thought: Essays in Environmental Philosophy*, edited by J. Callicott and R. Ames (Albany: State University of New York Press, 1989), 79–97.

Raynor, Henry, *Mahler* (London: Macmillan, 1975).

Robinet, Isabelle, *Taoism: Growth of a Religion*, translated by P. Brooks (Stanford: Stanford University Press, 1997).

Roman, Zoltan, *Gustav Mahler's American Years 1907–1911: A Documentary History* (Stuyvesant: Pendragon Press, 1989).

Scruton, Roger, *The New Grove Dictionary of Music and Musicians*, edited by Stanley Sadie, 29 vols (London: Macmillan, 2nd edn, 2001).

Seckerson, Edward, *Mahler: His Life and Times* (New York: Midas Books, 1982).

Tischler, Hans, 'Mahler's *Das Lied von der Erde*', *Music Review* 10 (1949): 111–14.

Walter, Bruno, *Gustav Mahler*, translated by Lotte W. Lindt (London: Quartet Books, 1990).

Wenk, A., 'The Composer as Poet in *Das Lied von der Erde*', *Nineteenth-Century Music* 1 (1977–1978): 33–47.

Wildhagen, Christian, 'The "Greatest" and the "Most Personal": the Eighth Symphony and *Das Lied von der Erde*', in *The Cambridge Companion to Mahler*, edited by Jeremy Barham (Cambridge: Cambridge University Press, 2007), 128–42.

Chapter 14

De morte transire ad vitam? Emotion and Identity in Nineteenth-Century Requiem Compositions

Wolfgang Marx

The requiem is one of the older musical genres; its earliest surviving compositions stem from the late fifteenth century. For more than 500 years, composers set the Latin text of the mass of the dead to music – with certain variations before 1570, when the text was codified in the aftermath of the Council of Trent, and also since the late nineteenth century, when a tradition of setting poems, other vernacular texts and instrumental pieces entitled "Requiem" was established alongside the continuing engagement with the Latin mass text. But, by and large, the 500-year-old tradition of setting the same or almost the same text to music, allows us to compare the different ways the text has been treated over time. These comparisons give us a chance to assess the attitudes of certain composers, societies and epochs towards death. The original function of requiem compositions was intercession on behalf of the dead; it was believed that the efforts of the living (including commissioning and performing a dedicated, elaborate requiem mass) might ease or shorten the deceased person's stay in purgatory. Since requiems were mainly composed for the rich and powerful, their performance was always simultaneously a representational event. For example, a new king could use its performance not only to celebrate his predecessor, but also to showcase the power and splendour of the dynasty and establish himself more firmly on the throne. A good example of this would be Luigi Cherubini's Requiem in C minor, commissioned for a mass in January 1816 held to honour the memory of Louis XVI, the king beheaded in 1793 during the French revolution. When the Bourbon dynasty in the person of his brother Louis XVIII returned to power after Napoleon's fall, they turned the day of the king's execution into a state occasion, with a festive requiem mass in the basilica St Denis at its centre. Every year (until the next revolution in 1830) a new requiem composition was commissioned from a different composer (Cherubini being the first one) to highlight the grandeur and importance of this occasion. Intercession on behalf of Louis XVI was certainly not a main issue here. This use of a requiem composition to remember and celebrate an important national personality can, however, play an important part in the shaping or maintaining of national identity. Cherubini was well aware of this when writing his requiem, as his unusually extended treatment of the line "quam olim Abrahae promisisti et semini eius" (as you have promised Abraham and his offspring) in the offertory clearly shows. The fact that god promised his blessing to follow a bloodline was certainly relevant to an already rather unpopular king whose dynasty stood on shaky ground in post-Napoleonic France. Yet not only kings but also other public figures regarded as important for a nation's identity were honoured in this way as in the requiem settings by Berlioz (commissioned in 1837 in memory of the soldiers fallen during the revolution of 1830, but later also utilised to commemorate a French general who had died in battle in Algeria) or Verdi (first performed in 1874 in memory of the novelist Alessandro Manzoni, alongside Verdi himself one of very few cultural icons in an only recently unified Italy to be recognised and admired nationwide).

In general, in the early nineteenth century, intercession on behalf of the dead had been replaced as a main function of requiem compositions by consolation of the living. At a time of increasing secularisation in the aftermath of the enlightenment, people were less worried about the fate of dead loved ones, but rather required comfort for themselves and their own loss. In this context the emotional function of requiem compositions has to be stressed. Their music can help channel grief and provide comfort and consolation. The two requiem settings by Gabriel Fauré and Antonín Dvořák that I want to focus on in this chapter represent the comforting and the representational function, the focus on emotion and on identity, that a requiem can provide.

The Requiem in the Church and in the Concert Hall

As part of continuing secularisations throughout the nineteenth century, performances of sacred music moved increasingly from the church to the concert hall. To my knowledge, the first requiem to be played outside a church was Mozart's, performed in February 1793 in a Viennese palace for the benefit of the composer's family (even though it had been conceived for liturgical use), while the first one genuinely written for the concert hall was Antonín Dvořák's requiem from 1890. Differentiating between liturgical and concert hall use is important, for it impacts on the way the composer approaches the text. The concert hall was the right place to enter into a more intellectual dialogue with a concert audience, a tendency originating in the nineteenth century but becoming far more important in the twentieth.

A liturgical work is written for a group of people close to the deceased and performed in close temporal proximity to the loss of a loved family member or friend. In the concert hall, few members of the audience are likely to have been very close to the one for whom the requiem is written, and there can also be a large temporal and geographic distance from this dedicatee. In an article published in 1993, Philip Tagg discusses the structure of the funeral musics of different cultures.[1] In Western Africa he observed funerals that look and sound more like parties, with quick tempi, loud talk, dancing and singing and large numbers of people in attendance. These events are neither organised by nor undertaken for the sake of the nuclear family (who grieve as much as Western families do); but instead are meant to give the whole village or peer group a chance to celebrate the deceased and their achievements. Tagg names three questions as relevant in this context.

- Who is responsible for organising the funeral?
- Whose relationship to the deceased is ritualised?
- Which emotions are ritualised?

These questions remain relevant when it comes to assessing requiem compositions and here I will consider two such requiems, one showing how emotional support and comfort may be provided for a grieving family, and the other exemplifying how a requiem may be used to unfold an aesthetic discourse, contributing to the development of the audience's identity in the face of death.

The Cathartic Function of Requiem Compositions

In 2004, Linda and Michael Hutcheon published a monograph entitled *Opera: The Art of Dying*.[2] In it, they develop a specific theory about the cathartic function of death in opera, particularly in relation to operas in which there is not just someone dying at the end, but in which death is a main topic throughout (such as *L'Orfeo*, *The Flying Dutchman* or *The Macropulos Case*). They claim that

> when people go to the theatre, at times and in part, they will find themselves participating in a ritual of grieving or experiencing their own mortality by proxy through an operatic narrative ... they can feel both identification and distance as they – safely – rehearse their own (or a loved one's) demise through the highly artificial, conventionalised form of opera.[3]

This conventionalised form allows the audience to get acquainted with and used to the notion of death in a way that is unique to this art:

---

[1]   Philip Tagg, "'Universal' Music and the Case of Death" *Critical Quarterly* 35/2 (1993): 54–98. Also available at www.tagg.org/articles/deathmus.html (accessed 20 July 2010).

[2]   Linda and Michael Hutcheon, *Opera. The Art of Dying*. Cambridge, MA and London: Harvard University Press, 2004.

[3]   Ibid., 11.

> Watching these operas ... is analogous to imaginatively experiencing the
> emotions associated with dying and, in a sense, even working through your own
> death or that of a loved one ... so we rehearse death in order to give life meaning
> ... Our aesthetic pleasure in the closure these operas afford is paralleled by a
> sense of psychological fulfilment and even ethical completion.[4]

Could this interpretation of the operatic experience be applied to the requiem? In
its original liturgical function this might be difficult as the element of identification
is certainly there, but the aspect of "intellectual distancing" might not. While we
know that what happens on stage is not real, the faithful believe that what they are
told in church is. However, a performance in a concert hall is a different matter.
The element of ritual that we know from both opera and liturgy is present there
too. In the concert hall as well as in the opera house we know that the emotions
we experience are not "real" ones – no one has actually died (as would be the
case in a requiem mass in church), and we can therefore afford the intellectual
distance required as part of this dialectic experience. Concert-hall performances
of requiems thus may be comparable to opera in this particular respect and help us
getting acquainted with death and the afterlife.

"Repetitive Consolation" in Gabriel Fauré's Requiem

Gabriel Fauré's requiem had a complex genesis. Its first version was finished in
1887 and first performed early in 1888, shortly after the loss of both his parents –
his father had died in 1885, his mother in 1887. Fauré was choirmaster at the Paris
church of St Madeleine and – unlike many other composers at this time – wrote
the requiem not with the concert hall in mind, but dedicated it entirely to liturgical
use. This is indicated not only by its relatively short duration (even shorter than
today as two of its movements – "Domine Jesu Christe" and "Libera me" – were
still missing in 1888), but also by the small forces required to perform it. The
orchestra has no violins (just a solo violin for some exposed passages), which
results in a darker, more subdued sound, and in the first version there was only one
solo part. The requiem's success prompted the composer to expand the work and,
in its second version from 1893, the two now well-known extra movements had
been added (which brought in the bass solo part), while the orchestra was enlarged
(adding mainly brass instruments, although they only double the already existing
string and organ parts). A third and final version was published in 1900; now, it is
set for full orchestra, yet this does not materially change the substance of the piece.
It is the second version, however, that is probably the most popular today.

I would like to focus on one particular aspect of Fauré's requiem which usually
receives little attention. It is a detail prevalent not in the vocal parts (on which most

---

[4]   Ibid., 186.

listeners naturally focus) but rather in the instrumental section. The following first example shows a detail of the viola part in the first movement.

Example 14.1   Fauré, *Requiem*, "Requiem aeternam", violas, bars 18–21[5]

It is not necessary to be able to read music in order to understand my point. The violas play this line after a slow introduction while the solo tenor presents the "Requiem aeternam" text for a second time (it is later repeated in the "Kyrie" section). It is obvious that the third and fourth bar repeat the first and second one. The first two bars display a wave-like shape, with the upward movement in the first bar, followed by the downward equivalent in the second one. While it is melodically "inverted", the second bar is rhythmically an exact copy of the first one: both begin with a long note (a minim tied to a quaver), followed by a quaver and a crotchet. This two-bar pattern is not just repeated once as indicated in this example but more often; after a number of repetitions it usually moves up or down to another pitch in order to be subjected to further repetitions.

Let us now look at another example from the same movement.

Example 14.2   Fauré, *Requiem*, "Introit and Kyrie", violas, bars 49–52[6]

This line accompanies "Exaudi orationem meam", one of the psalm verses of the introit. Again we can see that the first two bars are immediately repeated. We also notice the wave pattern stretching across each two-bar unit; this time the overall structure is rhythmically simpler that in the previous example as the entire line is a chain of dotted crotchets and quavers. This ensures that again the second bar is rhythmically identical to the first one while being melodically inverted – wherever the melody goes up in the first bar it goes down in the second one and vice versa. Finally, again the wave pattern is not just four bars long but is repeated at the same or another pitch much more often in the composition.

---

[5]   Gabriel Fauré, *Requiem* (1893 version), John Rutter (ed.), Oxford and New York: Oxford University Press, 1984, 3.

[6]   Ibid., 6.

The final example from the opening movement is the viola line accompanying the "Christe eleison", the middle section of the "Kyrie eleison".

Example 14.3   Fauré, *Requiem*, "Introit and Kyrie", violas, bars 70–3[7]

The features dominating the previous examples are present again: the overall wave-like *gestalt*, the motivic two-bar units, the combination of melodic inversion and rhythmic repetition in the second bar. The general rhythmic structure of the second example is repeated here, even though the upper and lower peaks of the wave now coincide with the first rather than the second note of each bar.

Let us now look at an example from another movement. The beginning of the "Sanctus" in the violas looks as follows.

Example 14.4   Fauré, *Requiem*, "Sanctus", violas, bars 1–2[8]

The wave pattern is evident again, but there are also some difference compared to the previous examples. The pattern is shorter here; each wave pattern is only eight notes long and then repeated. The eight notes are semiquavers, and since this section is set in 3/4 time, each pattern is shorter than a bar. The repetition of the wave thus stretches across a barline; there are altogether three renditions of the wave pattern in the two bars represented here. This obscures at least temporarily the listener's sense of metre as the beginning of the wave patterns does not always coincide with the usually strong first beat of the bar. The wave pattern is here present in two viola parts which complement each other: both play the same pattern, yet not in unison as whenever one of them moves up the other one moves down and vice versa. Unlike in the previous examples, the instruments here begin alone, while the voices follow a little bit later. The listener has thus a better chance

---

[7]   Ibid., 10.

[8]   Ibid., 29.

to notice the pattern, although once the voices have joined in one will find it very difficult to consciously keep following the viola line.

The final music example is a section from the offertory.

Example 14.5   Fauré, *Requiem*, "Offertory", violas, bars 35–8[9]

Again the basic repetitive structure is present: the first two bars are identical with the following ones, while all four bars are identical in terms of their rhythmic structure. However, in this case there is no wave pattern since the melodic pattern in all bars is not unidirectional. The line moves up and down in steps, while there clearly is no melodic inversion in the second bar; it is rather an almost literal repeat of the first one transposed up one note. In this respect the example is different from all the previous ones.

Let us, now, summarise what all these examples have in common.

- They occur only in the orchestra.
- They are in most cases (bar the last one) based on broken chords, i.e. the notes of a major or minor triad played not together as a chord but in succession.
- The patterns are in most cases two bars long.
- The second half of each pattern (bar the last one) is a rhythmic repeat yet a (literal or approximate) melodic inversion of the first half.
- The patterns are usually repeated a few times, then transposed up or down and repeated again.
- This results in a continuous wave-like movement.

In many ways this structure anticipates minimal music by composers like Philip Glass or John Adams. It is rhythmically and melodically repetitive and harmonically stable. The main difference is that in Fauré's case all this happens very much in the background since the voices of choir and soloists which stand very much in the limelight act quite differently. In minimal music this "background" is all there is, while Fauré has it operating at an almost subconscious level. The wave-like repetitive patterns feature extensively in five of the work's seven movements – the ones written as part of the requiem's first version in 1887. The offertory with the non-wave-like repetitive patterns (Example 14.5) was written in 1889, a year after the first performance, when the composer began to expand the work to

---

⁹   Ibid., 19.

prepare it for the concert stage. The only movement without any repetitive pattern is the "Libera me". This movement, however, is 10 years older than the rest of the requiem; it was originally written as a self-standing piece in 1878. Like the offertory, Fauré added it to the requiem after the first performance; he presumably found it easier to insert an already existing setting of the required text, rather than having to write a new movement. This explains its lack of repetitive patterns.

Yet why has Fauré used them so extensively in his requiem? It has to be admitted that he uses repetitive patterns not just in this composition; they can be found elsewhere in his œuvre too, including orchestral and chamber music. Yet in those other pieces the patterns usually do not occupy as much space as in this work (the "Sanctus" and the "In Paradisum" are more or less completely accompanied by them). They are also not wave-like, which creates the link between most of them in the requiem.

The fact that pseudo-minimalist repetitive patterns only ever occur in the instrumental lines explains why they usually remain unnoticed by listeners: it is natural to focus on the (non-repetitive) vocal parts and try to understand the text, so that the accompaniment often receives less attention. If our sensory input is divided into repetitive and non-repetitive signals, the brain will always focus on the new, as yet unknown information and allocate less energy and attention to the unchanged, already known sounds.[10]

Repetitive rhythmic patterns play an important part in music therapy. Music can be used to relax and calm people in stressful situations (for example in dentistry, surgery or psychotherapy); in this case patients are exposed to music without having to act in any way themselves. Other types of music therapy require the patient to become musically active, albeit not with the goal of improving musical skills but to establish some kind of non-verbal communication with the therapist.[11] Communication is often established by therapist and patient beginning to agree on a shared rhythmic pattern, based on a regular pulse: "Within the transference, the therapist offers the patient the possibility to come into a kind of pulsing. This is a very magical moment ('moment of synchronicity') ... and can lead to a breakthrough in the therapy."[12] Mourners in a requiem mass are not themselves musically active, thus finding themselves rather in the position of patients in

---

[10]   Even performers can miss these patterns. When my university's choir recently performed Fauré's requiem I asked its members later whether they had noticed them. Most of them had not.

[11]   Leslie Blunt, "Clinical and Therapeutic Uses of Music". *The Social Psychology of Music*. Edited by David J. Hargreaves and Adrian C. North. Oxford, New York and Toronto: Oxford University Press, 1997, 249–67, 250–1.

[12]   Joe De Baker and Tony Wigram, "Analysis of Notated Music Examples Selected from Improvisations of Psychotic Patients". Edited by Thomas Wasch and Tony Wigram. *Microanalysis in Music Therapy. Methods, Techniques and Applications for Clinicians, Researchers, Educators and Students*. Edited by Thomas Wasch and Tony Wigram. London and Philadelphia: Jessica Kingsley, 2007, 120–33.

stressful or painful situations. Yet the use of repetitive rhythmic patterns in this requiem may also fulfil a therapeutic function, and can develop a calming and soothing effect that may even be enhanced by the fact that most recipients will not consciously notice the patterns. By listening to the same music, the mourners attending the mass are individually comforted and also tuned in to the same "wavelength" (quite literally, given the structure of the repetitive patterns), thus also experiencing a "moment of synchronicity". According to Philip Tagg, short, repetitive phrases are one of Western funeral music's regular features, yet they are complemented here by most of his other features too: minor keys, slow tempo, low register (lack of violins!), low tessitura and low volume are all in evidence – all of them much easier to recognise than the rhythmic patterns. Towards the end, however, the composer introduces more positive, openly comforting music: the "In Paradisum" turns to a major key, higher registers and higher tessitura in order to assure the grieving family and friends of the deceased's ascent to paradise.

Fauré wrote his requiem for liturgical use, even though today it is most often performed in a concert situation. Its main function is thus to address the family and close friends of someone who recently died and who are in need of comfort and consolation. The repetitive wave-patterns used extensively in this requiem do exactly that; they have an almost hypnotic effect; I would like to suggest that it helps soothe the emotional pain of the congregation exposed to this music, and thus plays a significant part in the consolation process. The fact that they operate on a quasi-subconscious level makes their impact possibly even bigger.

There is no evidence that Fauré consciously wrote his requiem the way he did in order to soothe and comfort a grieving congregation. Yet whether or not the rhythmic patterns were written with this intention in mind matters less than the effect the music has on its listeners. Fauré's requiem is an example of the use of repetitive elements for reasons of emotional support of a grieving community. If performed during a requiem mass it is unlikely to trigger the cathartic effect as described by Hutcheon and Hutcheon; however, if performed in a concert situation (as is the norm nowadays) the cathartic experience is certainly much more likely. For reasons of space it is not possible to investigate other aspects of Fauré's requiem in greater detail. It is now time to have a closer look at a very different use of repetitive elements in another nineteenth-century requiem.

The Motto of Death in Antonín Dvořák's Requiem

My second example is Antonín Dvořák's Requiem Op. 89, composed in 1890 and premiered at the Birmingham Music Festival 1891. The work is set for full orchestra and with a duration of some 90 minutes, much longer than Fauré's; unlike its French counterpart it is clearly designed for concert performance rather than liturgical use. While Fauré had lost his parents not long before embarking on the composition of his mass, Dvořák had experienced no personal loss but decided to write his requiem purely for aesthetic reasons. As in the case of Fauré, I would like to focus again on just one aspect of this work: its so-called "motto". A motto is a brief musical motif that occurs not just once but is repeated at crucial points of a composition, thus providing a unifying force.

The motto is prominently displayed at the very beginning of Dvořák's requiem.

Example 14.6   Dvořák, *Requiem* Op. 89, "Requiem aeternam", begin first violin[13]

The way this motto is structured and used in this composition lets it stand apart from the rest of the music in several ways. At this point, at the beginning of the work, only the violins and violoncelli are playing, all presenting this motif. It stands alone, unaccompanied by other instruments, and thus without any harmonisation. It is also presented in an instrumental rather than a vocal line, so that no link to a text can decode any possible meaning attached to it. While later in the requiem we can occasionally witness the motto being presented by singers, the vast majority of its occurrences is unaccompanied and instrumental. But the most interesting feature of the motto is its internal structure. As we can see in Example 14.6, it moves at first up from its opening note, then leaps just below it in order to finally return to its starting point. It is as if someone tries to get away from something (the opening pitch), tries it in both possible directions but eventually fails and falls back to where he was before. The attempt is quite weak in the first place as the move only gets a semitone away from the central note in either direction – the semitone being the smallest interval available to a composer in tonal music. The key at this point is B flat minor, but neither a minor nor any major scale contain two semitones in a row, so the pitch of one of the notes needs to be altered in order to allow for the intended movement – in this case it is the third note, which is an E natural instead of the lower E flat that would be part of the B flat minor scale (this E natural is called a "chromatic" note as it "colours" the scale in an unusual way). Furthermore, the motto clearly emphasises the opening and closing note F as its main pitch. Normally one would expect at the beginning of a piece the root of a scale (here B flat) to be emphasised, yet the composer chose to focus on another note, thus initially obscuring what key the piece is set in. Another way of obfuscating a musical parameter is the motto's rhythm. Its third note is set as a syncopation, a note that does not enter on a beat (here the third one of the 4/4 common time metre) but rather starts and finishes it off. The fourth note, a quaver, then compensates for the syncopation, thus preparing the fifth note which, as the phrase's final one, has to enter on the beat. The fact that the third beat of the bar

---

[13]   Antonín Dvořák, *Requiem* Op. 89, full score, Prague: Editio [*sic*] Bärenreiter 2001, 1.

is avoided through the syncopation delays an immediate clear recognition of the metre.

Together, all these features allow for a reading of this motto as representing "otherness" in music. Its key as well as its metre are at least temporarily obscured by its structure; it contains an unusual chromatic note, it appears unharmonised and separated by a rest from what is to follow and thus both vertically and horizontally detached, while its melodic structure looks like a weak attempt to flee from something. I propose to interpret this motto as Dvořák's musical representation of death and dying, something that is as "other" to and detached from life as the motto is from the "normal" music found elsewhere in the requiem. This reading is further supported by the motto's link to the chiasm, a Baroque musical "figure". In Baroque music specific musical "figures" were used to represent well-known emotions and states of mind (most famous is possibly the "sigh motif", a syncopated chromatically descending figure). The chiasm is made of four notes which are put together in such a way that allows for a line drawn from the first to the last one to cross a line connecting the two middle notes. Dvořák's motto fulfils this condition. It is made up of five rather than four notes, but the fourth one is identical with the fifth and is only present to compensate for the syncopation, so it does not really count. The two lines resemble a cross, thus referring to the Greek letter chi (spelled as "X" and reflecting the opening letter of the title "Christ" in Greek) and in its very shape also a cross. In Baroque masses one often finds this figure in relation to Christ, particularly to the crucified and dying Christ. This reference to death – albeit to that of a particular individual – may reinforce my reading of the motto as representing death. The motto features at central points in all movements up to the offertory. It appears at crucial moments (such as the begin of both the "Tuba mirum" and the "Lacrimosa" sections). It is rarely subjected to thematic variation as we usually find in nineteenth-century tonal music and its melodic shape as well as its rhythmic structure are rarely altered, expanded or reduced. With the beginning of the "Sanctus", Dvořák introduces a new motivic idea which is related to yet also completely different from the motto.

Example 14.7   Dvořák, *Requiem*, "Sanctus", solo bass, begin[14]

If we take the first four notes of this melodic line, we find that the first and the last one are identical, while in relation to these framing notes the second one moves down and the third one up. This can again be called a chiasm as the two

---

[14]   Dvořák, *Requiem*, 245.

lines connecting the outer and the inner notes would cross. Yet in every other conceivable way these notes differ from the motto: they do not contain a chromatic note but only notes common to the scale in operation at this point (B flat major). There is no syncopation here (and because of that no need for an additional note to compensate for it; this descendant of the motto thus consists of only four notes). The new motto is neither horizontally nor vertically detached; here and elsewhere it acts as the opening gesture of a longer melodic line. Instead of weak semitone steps away from the framing notes, we have much larger and more forceful leaps. The first leap goes down rather than up, so that the largest leap in the middle of the four notes moves upwards rather than downwards, which gives the motto a far more optimistic touch. Finally, unlike the motto its descendant features the root pitch of its scale (B flat). So while this four-note motif is clearly derived from the motto, Dvořák has removed or changed everything in it that represents its "otherness". One might read this as an attempt to turn death and dying from the alien, ultimate "other" into something that is part of normal musical proceedings or, by extension, of life. In this version we do not have to fear it any more, it does not stand apart and is fully integrated. I propose to call this the "counter motto" of Dvořák's requiem. The "Sanctus" is the most positive text of the requiem mass; it contains no reference to death, fear and last judgement and may therefore provide the best possible opportunity to introduce this positive turn of events. Dvořák sets it in B flat major, a more optimistic key than the B flat minor which opened the piece.

The following two examples show the opening of the next two movements of Dvořák's requiem, the "Pie Jesu" and the "Agnus Dei".

Example 14.8   Dvořák, *Requiem*, "Pie Jesu", first flute, bars 1–8[15]

Example 14.9   Dvořák, *Requiem*, "Agnus Dei", first violin, bars 1–6[16]

15   Ibid., 271.
16   Ibid., 279.

In both cases, the counter motto can be identified again as the opening motif. In the "Pie Jesu" the leap between its third and fourth notes is filled by a number of quavers, but since the four "core" notes of the motto fall onto the strong beats of the bars, they are still dominant and easily recognisable. In the "Agnus Dei", the violins play a three-note motif made of two quavers and a crotchet, so that the counter motto's final note is the first one of that motif's second presentation. Both movements are set in minor keys, which already indicates that the counter motto has no free reign after (and even within) the "Sanctus". The original motto appears at first occasionally, later more often, and challenges its distant cousin. The "Agnus Dei", as this requiem's final movement, then presents a new version of the motto, which is again clearly derived from the original yet simultaneously quite different in character:

Example 14.10   Dvořák, *Requiem*, "Agnus Dei", choir soprano, bars 10–13[17]

Here the central note (again a B flat), after a few repetitions, moves at first up one step, then via the central note to the note below B flat in order, finally, to return to its starting point. The fact that the central note is repeated in the middle – between the upper and the lower neighbour notes – destroys the cruciform *gestalt* of this motif; it no longer is a chiasm. In its stepwise motion and due to the fact that it moves first up and then down it is much closer to the original motto than to the counter motto. There is, however, neither a chromatic note nor a syncopation present, the motif features mainly in the vocal parts, it starts with the main note of the B flat minor scale and is usually harmonised. So it stands in many ways between the two other motti, which is why I propose to call it the "compromise motto". It is introduced on the "Agnus Dei" text, the final plea for mercy in the face of death and judgment. At this point, it is still open as to how the requiem will end – it could, like many other nineteenth-century settings (namely those by Fauré and Verdi), finish on a positive, consoling note, or it could reinforce the fear and power of death. The compromise motto appears to indicate a development away from the original detached death, to a slightly more positive and consoling view of it. However, the compromise motto does not mark the end of developments. The "Agnus Dei" text is followed by the "Lux aeterna", but next there is an unliturgical repeat of the "Agnus Dei", now using the original instead of the compromise motto. Since the "Sanctus", the motto had always been present in the background, but now it suddenly takes centre stage again, dominating proceedings for the final

---

[17]   Ibid., 280.

section of the piece. Both the counter motto and the compromise motto no longer feature at all and the requiem ends with a reinforcement of musical otherness.

If the motto does indeed stand for death and dying and both the counter motto and the compromise motto for some kind of "domestication" of death by way of removing the elements of its otherness and integrating it melodically, harmonically and rhythmically into "normal" musical proceedings, then Dvořák's requiem clearly indicates that this attempt is ultimately unsuccessful. As the dominance of musical otherness is restored at the end of his requiem, any attempt to strip death of its otherness, its general opposition to life, appears fruitless – at least in Antonín Dvořák's view. In his requiem mass repetitive elements – the motto and its counterparts – are used in a very different way than in Fauré's composition: they create an aesthetic dualism, a dialectic discourse between two different concepts of death. Yet the result of this discourse is not a compromise but the re-establishment of the original proposition.

Antonín Dvořák wrote his requiem for the concert hall; his target audience is not a grieving congregation in a church. The requiem is not dedicated to anyone in particular; it does not commemorate a specific individual but rather makes a general point about death. As such, Dvořák's work can serve much better than Fauré's composition as an example of a "cathartic" requiem according to Linda and Michael Hutcheon's hypothesis. Its audience is not let to think of any particular deceased but rather invited to contemplate death as a general phenomenon, as something that we should get used to. However, Dvořák teaches us that death will never become a "normal" part of life, just as the motto ultimately retains its musical otherness. Yet whether or not death can be "domesticated", by defining its boundaries it always forms an important part of our identity.

Conclusion

In the late nineteenth century the requiem as a musical genre was in the process of moving from its earlier function of intercession on behalf of the dead and consoling the bereaved to consolidating its new position in the concert hall where it entered into a discourse with an emotionally more neutral audience. According to Philip Tagg, the different target audiences result in different compositional strategies reflected in the different function of repetitive elements in both works. According to my reading of the scores, Gabriel Fauré's requiem focuses on emotional support for a grieving congregation while Antonín Dvořák's composition presents us with a more intellectual discourse regarding the relation of death to life and human identity. Still, these compositions are not polar opposites since emotion plays an important part in Dvořák's work too (as indeed in any piece of music), with highly dramatic moments for example in the sequence and the "Agnus Dei". The emotional impact of Fauré's piece, on the other hand, is based on a highly intellectual compositional strategy (not just with regard to the repetitive patterns, but through many other parameters too). Music reflects both emotion and intellect to varying degrees, yet never just one or the other alone. Fauré helps us cope with the loss of the loved ones death has taken away from us, while Dvořák makes us contemplate the role of death in relation to our self, our identity. Both approaches are necessary; emotion and identity complement each other.

References

Tagg, Philip. "'Universal' Music and the Case of Death". *Critical Quarterly* 35/2 (1993): 54–98.

Hutcheon, Linda and Michael Hutcheon. *Opera: The Art of Dying*. Cambridge, MA and London: Harvard University Press, 2004.

Fauré, Gabriel. *Requiem* (1893 version), John Rutter (ed.). Oxford and New York: Oxford University Press, 1984.

Blunt, Leslie. "Clinical and Therapeutic Uses of Music". *The Social Psychology of Music*. Edited by David J. Hargreaves and Adrian C. North. Oxford, New York and Toronto: Oxford University Press, 1997.

De Baker, Joe and Tony Wigram. "Analysis of Notated Music Examples Selected from Improvisations of Psychotic Patients". Edited by Thomas Wasch and Tony Wigram. *Microanalysis in Music Therapy. Methods, Techniques and Applications for Clinicians, Researchers, Educators and Students*. Edited by Thomas Wasch and Tony Wigram. London and Philadelphia: Jessica Kingsley, 2007.

Dvořák, Antonín. *Requiem Op. 89*, full score, Prague: Editio [*sic*] Bärenreiter 2001.

Chapter 15

War without Death: America's Ingenious Plan to Defeat Enemies without Bloodshed

John Troyer

Part 1: Bodies in Caskets

In April 2009, Steve Coll, a writer for the *New Yorker* magazine and an author of several books on the American wars in Afghanistan, argued that President Barack Obama's inheritance of the wars in the Middle East came with several choices. One particular choice meant a policy change that directly involved representations of military deaths:

> On April 5th [2009] … television cameras recorded the arrival at Dover Air Force Base of a casket containing the remains of Staff Sergeant Phillip Myers, of Hopewell, Virginia, who was killed in Afghanistan [Figure 15.1]. For the past eighteen years, the military has banned the media from witnessing the arrival home of a soldier killed overseas, even if the soldier's family wished otherwise. No more. These caskets, too, are Obama's inheritance. Gradually, the President is fashioning a turn in national-security policy – by insisting, first of all, on an end to denial.[1]

The deliberate and visible presentation of military dead to both next of kin and members of media organizations is, as Coll rightly points out, a choice by President Obama to deny wartime deaths no longer. Air Force Staff Sergeant Phillip Myers' *post-mortem* repatriation, after his death in a roadside explosion at age 30, marked the end and the beginning of a new visual order for US war dead. As never before, the dead soldiers produced by the wars in Iraq and Afghanistan would no longer be hidden; the United States would be fighting wars in which the deaths of its own would finally be acknowledged. The concept of "war" would no longer avoid death as both a possibility and end result.

The Ban

US Secretary of Defense Robert Gates reversed the 18-year media ban in early 2009 after an internal Department of Defense review and an examination of how

---

[1]   Steve Coll, "No Nukes," *New Yorker*, April 20, 2009: 32.

Figure 15.1   Sgt. Phillip Myers
Source: U.S. Department of Defence

allied countries, such as Canada and the UK, publicized the return of their own dead soldiers.[2] Secretary of Defense Gates began his tenure during President George W. Bush's administration and reversing the media ban was something that Gates had wanted to do during Bush's final year. At that time, however, Gates met internal resistance to the suggested policy change. When Barack Obama was elected President he made it clear that he wanted the ban reversed.

The new US military policy is an amalgam of bureaucratic language but states in summary that:

1. designated next of kin have the right to attend the military service at Dover Air Force in Dover, Delaware where the remains are sent;
2. next of kin can choose whether or not their sons' or daughters' casketed remains are photographed by the media;
3. if the next of kin cannot afford to travel to the ceremony in Dover, then the Department of Defense assists with the expenses.[3]

---

[2]   The public procession of UK ward dead through the town of Wootton Bassett is one key example studied by the U.S. Department of Defense.

[3]   To read the full, official policy see: www.army.mil/usapa/epubs/pdf/ad2009_02.pdf. The long-term policy goal of the United States military is to have each individual soldier decide whether or not he or she approves of the media photographing their *post-mortem* repatriation so that next of kin know in advance.

Yet, reversing the ban meant that a decision had been made, sometime in the past, to actually implement this policy. The questions to ask, then, are twofold: what did the ban on viewing the return of soldiers' remains entail and what was the ban's history?

For the last 18 years, and through both Democratic and Republican Presidential administrations, the photographing or televising of soldiers' dead bodies arriving and exiting Dover Air Force Base was explicitly prohibited. Different Presidents periodically lifted the ban for specific repatriations. In 1983, for example, President Reagan allowed televised coverage of the return of dead marines killed in Beirut, Lebanon. But in March 2003, immediately before the war in Iraq began, the Bush administration imposed an extremely strict ban on all death images at all domestic and foreign military bases, including the main Dover facility. Not even family members of the deceased were allowed to watch the ceremony. What makes Dover Air Force Base so important to this narrative is that it is the headquarters for the US Militaries' Mortuary Affairs unit, which is responsible for the "dignified transfer" of soldiers' bodies. Dignified transfer is the term used to describe the repatriation of solders' remains onto American soil. In the Charles C. Carson Center for Mortuary Affairs at Dover Air Force Base, the bodies of dead soldiers are cleaned, embalmed or cremated, and, regardless of the final disposition method, placed in a dress uniform. The overall goal of the mortuary staff, the largest mortuary of its kind in the world, is the dead bodies' *viewability*. Indeed, roughly 85 percent of those killed in action are at least partially viewable by family members.[4] In the event that the body is too badly damaged, the remains are sealed in bags, covered with a blanket, and a dress uniform is pinned over the top. All remains and personal belongings are placed in the coffin, which is then covered with an American flag.

The dignified transfer and mortuary preparation work is extremely rigorous. An April 2008 *Esquire* magazine article entitled 'The Things That Carried Him' documents the rigors of the preparation process by following a dead soldier's body from Iraq to America. Chris Jones, the article's author, explains:

> Karen Giles [Director of the Carson Center for Mortuary Affairs] tells a story about a young airman, who was polishing the brass on a dead soldier's uniform jacket. He was using a little tool, a kind of buffer, to make sure that every button shined. A visitor complimented him on his attention to detail. "The family will really appreciate what you're doing," the visitor said. But the airman replied, "Oh, no sir, the family won't know about this." The airman told him that the family had requested that their son be cremated, and just a short while later, he was.[5]

---

[4]   Chris Jones, "The Things that Carried Him," *Esquire*, April 17, 2008: 10.

[5]   Chris Jones, "The Things that Carried Him," *Esquire*, April 17, 2008: 11.

The history and politics surrounding whether or not images from Dover Air Force base become public is equally complex. US Military leaders have historically called that part of the transfer, from the plane to the mortuary, the "Dover Test." What the Dover Test refers to is the American public's acceptance of dead soldiers returning home from war. This was an enormous issue during the Vietnam War and the political unease over Dover's visual power encapsulates these 2004 comments from the mother of dead soldier:

> They killed my son and they did not permit me to be there to see the coffin. They said it was for health reasons, and … they did not want the public to see it and they did not want the newspapers there … They don't want any of this being shown because it's reality. A coffin strikes home. If you don't see the coffin you just say: "Oh, there's another one who has died." But when you show the coffin, you show families, you show people and emotions. This is what they are doing; this is what they do not want you to see.[6]

Interestingly, the Bush administration's comprehensive ban was not always in effect. Dignified transfer images were initially available in late 2001 during the opening days of the Afghanistan War. Most conspicuously, the flag-draped coffins of military personnel killed in the Pentagon on September 11, 2001 and handled by the Mortuary Affairs Unit at Dover were widely disseminated. This last point, that the Bush administration relaxed the media ban for the September 11, 2001 military dead, only helped foster a cynical belief that the "ban" was a decision steeped in propaganda; a political choice that explicitly ignored the reality of death in both Iraq and Afghanistan. Indeed, a clear, and rather convincing case, can be made that the decision to ban the images was a purely political one since the majority of families who have now been given a choice on whether or not to open the dignified transfer to the media choose to allow it. In late April 2009, for example, 14 out of 19 families agreed to let the media view the dignified transfers when they were asked.[7]

The Legal Fight

Another problem with the previous policy (particularly during the Bush administration) was that by banning the images from public view, curious individuals simply fought harder to have the pictures released. As a result of these legal battles, images of the dignified transfers began to appear in public. In early 2004, an independent researcher named Russ Kick filed a Freedom of Information Act request with the US Military for any dignified transfer images. The request

---

[6]   Andrew Buncomber, "The Image Turning America Against Bush," *The Independent*, April 24, 2004: 1.

[7]   "Remember That Excuse for Not Showing Coffins Coming Home from War? Turns Out Families OK With It," *Editor and Publisher*, April 27, 2009: 1.

Figure 15.2   Kick Dover photograph

was initially denied but then during the appeals process Kick mysteriously received a CD containing 361 images from Dover. I say "mysteriously" because Kick was not supposed to receive those images, nevertheless someone in the Air Force approved the release. The person who allowed the images to be released has never been named[8] (see Figure 15.2).

As soon as Kick had the CD, he posted the photos on the Internet and the images were in the public domain. What was compelling but not shocking about the images was the total lack of gratuitous imagery. All of the images displayed the respectful, 15-minute long dignified transfer of flag-draped coffins from military planes to the Mortuary Affairs Center. This is contrary to what one Pentagon official at the time, John Molino, Deputy Undersecretary of Defense, stated about why the ban was meant to keep the images hidden: "Quite frankly, we don't want

---

[8]   To see most of the images go to: www.thememoryhole.org/nonwp/war/coffin_photos/dover.

Figure 15.3   Begleiter/NSA Archive image

the remains of our service-members who have made the ultimate sacrifice to be the subject of any kind of attention that is unwarranted or undignified."[9]

The Bush administration's concern, that the Dover images would be used in undignified ways, was simultaneously coupled with other arguments such as that showing the photos would reveal quasi-secret military information. The oddest part about the images released to Kick was that the Department of Defense was photographing and videotaping all of the arrivals for "historical documentation" but then not telling the families about that policy. Many large American news outlets, such as the *New York Times* and *CNN*, expressed surprise at the sheer volume and existence of the images. The Kick images, however, were just the beginning of the legal fights over dignified transfer photographs.

In 2005, the Department of Defense released 700 more images after a court battle with University of Delaware Journalism Professor Ralph Begleiter and the National Security Archive at George Washington University. These images, however, were different from the ones released to Kick. The military personnel in these images were often partially covered by black boxes to prevent (the government suggested) individual identification and/or for "operational security"[10] (see Figure 15.3). This last point, that the rationale for blocking soldiers' faces and portions of their uniforms was for operational security met with intense skepticism. Thomas Blanton, Director of the National Security Archive made the following statement: it is "an outrage and

---

9   "Pentagon Angered by Military Dead Photos," *New York Times*, April 22, 2004: 1.

10   To see these images go to: www2.gwu.edu/~nsarchiv/NSAEBB/NSAEBB152.

an insult that they blacked out those faces of the honor guard, when today on the Pentagon website you can see photos of US soldiers in Iraq. I can only imagine they put those black boxes there to make the photos unusable."[11] Yet, the American public has consistently supported the release of dignified transfer images. In 2004 public support stood at 60 percent and that number had not diminished by 2009.[12]

The crux of the entire situation thus lies in understanding that the Department of Defense's definition of a *dignified* representation of the dead body is a political choice and not simply a policy directive. Both the 2004 and 2005 image releases revealed these representational politics by demonstrating a policy at odds with a public desire. What these legal fights over the dignified transfer photos also made partly visible was the Department of Defense's concern regarding how opponents of the wars in Iraq and/or Afghanistan might use the images. That said, it seems clear that a different kind of rationalization was at play given that the Department of Defense was already taking photographs and then hiding the images for some unstated, future historical reason. What the media ban seemed to engage was a naive hope on the part of elected political officials (many of whom lacked any previous military experience) that somehow American soldiers would not die in a war. Or, that if the dead bodies in the flag-draped caskets were kept out of sight then the public would not notice that death results from warfare.

It is this peculiar rationalization, that war causes death but not American war dead, which I find most disturbing. On the one hand, seeing blatant governmental obfuscation at play when discussing the rationale for the media ban is hardly surprising. On the other hand, it is an entirely different situation to have both elected and appointed officials seeming to believe that individuals entering into combat zones would not risk potential death. When it became clear that US soldiers were dying (let alone the populations of other countries) a choice was made to simply reinforce the media ban and hide that politically uncomfortable truth. This decision then led to the various bureaucratic obstacles put in place to prevent the images of US war dead from ever being shown, which in turn simply fueled the entire movement to reveal the photographs. At the core of this governmental policy was an idea that war could exist without human death. It is the *war without death* concept that I think needs more discussion since the very premise is itself an historiographical fight, one that begins in the late nineteenth century with Prussian General Carl von Clausewitz.

Part 2: War without Death

In the mid-nineteenth century, Carl von Clausewitz authored a "theory of warfare" after fighting in various late eighteenth- and early nineteenth-century European

---

[11]   Ann Scott Tyson, "Hundreds of Photos of Caskets Released," *Washington Post*, April 29, 2005: 1.

[12]   Ann Scott Tyson and Mark Berman, "Pentagon Rethinks Photo Ban on Coffins Bearing War Dead," *Washington Post*, February 17, 2009: 1.

conflicts. His most famous book, *On War*, was written between 1816 and 1818 and then published posthumously in 1832. In his book, Clausewitz offers the following response to the question: What is War?

> Kind-hearted people might of course think there was some ingenious way to disarm or defeat an enemy without too much bloodshed, and might imagine this is the true goal of the art of war. Pleasant as it sounds, it is a fallacy that must be exposed: war is such a dangerous business that the mistakes which come from kindness are the very worst ... This is how the matter must be seen. It would be futile – even wrong – to try and shut one's eyes to what war really is from sheer distress at its brutality.[13]

Yet, this is precisely what seems to have occurred with the dead bodies returning to the United States during the Bush administration's ban. The logic of the ban suggested that if the images were kept hidden from the general public then somehow the very concept of warfare producing dead bodies would be negated. Ironically, it seems as if the greatest propagandistic tool offered by the images (one that would surely inflame American nationalism) was to show all the caskets being carried off all the planes all the time. That kind of policy choice could surely have been used to fuel greater support for the war. The decision would have also met resistance and criticism from the war's opponents but that hardly suggests that the photos would have been defined as anti-war images. Yet, by hiding the photographs, the Bush administration absolutely exposed some of its own large, internal insecurities, about the realities of war producing dead American bodies.

One contemporary thinker that the entire image-banning episode caused me to reappraise was Jean Baudrillard and his book *The Gulf War Did Not Take Place*. The book is a series of essays written both before and during the 1991 Persian Gulf War in order to critique media representations of that war. Baudrillard's key 1991 insight seems even more pertinent today when applied to the dignified transfer ban:

> it is not a question of being for or against the war. It is a question of being for or against *the reality of war*. Analysis must not be sacrificed to the expression of anger. It must be entirely directed against reality, against the evidence; here, against the evidence of this war.[14]

What this suggests is that the fundamental way modern nations such as the United States now fight wars is, publicly, to argue against the actual evidence of that war being fought. In the event that arguing against the evidence is not possible then national authorities simply hide the evidence from public view.

---

[13]   Carl von Clausewitz, *On War*, trans. Michael Howard and Peter Paret (New York: Alfred A. Knopf, 1993), 84.

[14]   Jean Baudrillard, *The Gulf War Did Not Take Place*, trans. Paul Patton (Bloomington: Indiana University Press, 1995), 9.

Figure 15.4   George Bush – Mission Accomplished

As a result of a policy trying explicitly to ignore the reality of war, a 2003 image of President Bush on a US Battleship with the sign "Mission Accomplished" across the back can appear all over the world while photographs of dead soldiers are simultaneously taken and hidden from public view (see Figure 15.4). In short, to acknowledge the dead is to acknowledge that death occurs in wars and that these acknowledgments involve one of the highest forms of human sacrifice. If and when a nation's leader begins to discuss those killed in war then the reasons used to validate the war by that same leader need to be fundamentally sound. By the late spring of 2003, when it became clear that the Bush administration was presenting information about the need to invade Iraq that was wrong, the easiest course of action was to continue to hide the evidence of war, i.e., the coffins with dead bodies. But, by hiding the dead bodies from view, the decision-making process itself came across, in the very least, as juvenile, and it also appeared that the decision-makers just wanted to ignore the reality of the Iraq War. What ignoring that reality creates is a void between what is known and what is said, a discrepancy that then becomes an opportunity for groups to fill that void by drawing explicit attention to the thing being ignored. One group that did just that was the Westboro Baptist Church when it started a campaign of protests outside soldiers' funerals in 2005.

Part 3: The Westboro Baptist Church Protests

The Westboro Baptist Church (WBC) is a denominationally unaffiliated, conservative Christian church based in Topeka, Kansas.[15] Under its leader, Fred Phelps, the WBC has a history of protesting outside funerals in order to draw attention to what its members believe is the current moral decline of the United States. The WBC's most infamous protest slogan is "God Hates Fags" and the group has repeatedly made that statement since 1998 when Phelps and his followers (mostly family members) protested outside Matthew Shepard's funeral. Shepard was a young man from Laramie, Wyoming, who was killed by two other men because he was gay. The WBC's general protest messages are simple enough: God killed a certain person because he or she was gay or lesbian (as in the case of Matthew Shepard); or because the United States now condones homosexuality (according to the WBC) God exerts His disapproval of this social acceptance by causing people to die in the most tragic of ways.

What the wars in Iraq and Afghanistan offered the WBC was an opportunity to transform the military funerals being held for dead soldiers into theological protest sites. At all of the military funeral protests, the Westboro Baptist Church clearly states on large, professionally printed signs that a soldier died because the United States accepts homosexuality. Shirley Phelps-Roper, Fred Phelps' daughter, explained the group's motives this way: "These aren't private funerals; these are patriotic pep rallies. Our goal is to call America an abomination, to help the nation connect the dots. You turn this nation over to the fags and our soldiers come home in body bags"[16] (see Figure 15.5). These protests have caused a great deal of anger for many families resulting in state legislatures across the United States beginning to enact laws that prohibit protests at funerals. These anti-protesting laws open up an entirely different kind of dilemma, since restricting the protests does in fact restrict freedom of speech. One state, Wisconsin, has barred people from displaying signs that convey "fighting words."[17] The state of Illinois enacted the "Let them Rest in Peace Act" which shields families from protests and punishes repeated offenders with three years' prison time and a fine of up to $25,000.[18] One father in the state of Maryland, Albert Snyder, took Phelps to court in 2007 for protesting outside his son's military funeral and he won a multi-million dollar lawsuit. Albert Snyder ultimately lost the court case on appeal and was ordered to pay the WBC's $16,500.00 in court fees. In October 2010, the United States Supreme Court

---

[15]   The official Westboro Baptist Church website: www.godhatesfags.com.

[16]   Karl Lydersen, "5 States Consider Ban on Protests at Funerals," *Washington Post*, January 30, 2006: 1.

[17]   Lizette Alvarez, "Outrage at Funeral Protests Pushes Lawmakers to Act," *New York Times,* April 17, 2006: 1.

[18]   To read a description of this law go to: www.illinois.gov/pressreleases/ ShowPressRelease.cfm?SubjectID=1&RecNum=4891.

Figure 15.5   WBC dead soldier protests

heard both side's arguments about the funeral protests. [19] The case, *Snyder v. Phelps,* made an intriguing addition to the Supreme Court's long history of free speech cases, and in early March 2011 the Court released its decision. In an eight-to-one majority decision, the Supreme Court found that, "The First Amendment shields Westboro from tort liability for its picketing in this case."[20] As of late 2011, the Westboro Baptist Church continued to protest near funerals for deceased US military personnel.

The WBC funeral protests are more often than not met by several different kinds of counter-protest groups and the counter-protesters usually outnumber the WBC members by dozens (see Figure 15.6). One counter-protest group, the Patriot Guard, consists of a few hundred motorcycle riders who surround the families at the funerals and then block the WBC protesters from being seen or heard.[21] A fundamentally important element of the WBC protests, and one that made the protesting such an effective form of social antagonism, was the governmental decision to hide soldiers' remains. The banning of images transformed what

[19]   Robert Barnes, "High Court: Justices to Consider 'Funeral Protests' in Free-Speech Case," *Washington Post*, May 31, 2010.

[20]   *Snyder v. Phelps*. United States Supreme Court. March 2011: 2. To read the full decision go to: http://www.supremecourt.gov/opinions/10pdf/09-751.pdf

[21]   It is worth noting that the United Kingdom's Home Office banned Fred Phelps from entering the UK since it was determined that his behavior and rhetoric inspired hatred. Phelps did not help his situation by stating: "God hates England. Your Queen is a whore. You're going to hell." See Stephen Bates, "Anti-gay American Cleric Banned from UK for Inciting Hatred," *Guardian*, February 19, 2009.

Figure 15.6   Patriot Guard

could and should have been a moment of grief into something shameful for the families. If the return of the military dead had actually been embraced, televised, and made common then at least part of the advantage given the WBC by hiding the dead bodies could have been neutralized. The WBC's claims would still have been outlandish, absurd and derogatory but by showing the coffins coming off the planes, the opportunity to single out a seemingly taboo image would have been greatly decreased.

What is peculiar is that the WBC has not used any of the dignified transfer images released by either Kick or Begleiter for protest signs. Or, at least, I have not been able to locate any uses of the dignified transfer images at protests, which would seem an easy visual source to further antagonize the public. In no uncertain terms, the WBC protestors heightened their social disruption by making the dead soldiers' hidden bodies explicitly visible vis-à-vis a simple reference to the missing bodies. The referencing of the bodies (along with gratuitous language and imagery) forced funeral goers to negotiate the Bush administration's policy decisions about both the war and the dignified transfers. Yet the WBC accomplished these acts without any images of the dead soldiers. The refusal to acknowledge the presence of the dead body by the Bush administration provided the Westboro Baptist Church with more than enough discursive space to enflame human passions.

Fred Phelps and his church members simply stated that a dead soldier's body existed and by making that statement in an inflammatory way, they forced a political confrontation with the Dover policy. It is no small coincidence, I think,

Figure 15.7   Civil War embalming demo
Photo: Scott Magelssen

that the WBC protested for years outside funerals of gay and lesbian activists but not one state passed a law limiting, restricting or outright banning the protests. As soon as military personnel funerals became targets, then the protection of public sensibilities required new state laws. In this way, what the WBC has accomplished by making the dead soldier so visible is both useful and offensive when contemplating the impossibility of war without death.

Part 4: The Civil War Re-Enactments[22]

Another and final way of critiquing the image ban is to contemplate what a war without death would actually resemble. One kind of warfare that results when death is removed is American living-history re-enactments. Here I am thinking explicitly about re-enactments of the American Civil War, a war where roughly 620,000 individuals died and which remains the deadliest conflict in American history. It was also, apropos of this chapter, the first American war to be photographed. When American photographer Mathew Brady exhibited images of the war in 1862 in New York City, the *New York Times* commented:

---

[22]   Scott Magelssen, Associate Professor of Theatre Arts at Bowling Green University, contributed research for this section.

> Mr. Brady has done something to bring home to us the terrible reality and
> earnestness of war. If he has not brought bodies and laid them in our dooryards
> along the streets, he has done something like it. At the door of his gallery hangs
> a little placard, "The Dead of Antietam" [September 17, 1862. 23,000 dead].[23]

Yet for all the unbelievable violence associated with the American Civil War, the
contemporary re-enactments involve men and women coming together to play-
act killing each other without the reality of death. These events are the ultimate
expression of a war without death. In fact, the only things missing from the re-
enactments were fake dead bodies and even that has been remedied.

In June 2007, the Museum of Funeral Customs in Springfield, Illinois
(now closed) began a living history program aimed at increasing the public's
understanding of American funeral practices in explicit ways. The Museum
of Funeral Customs' re-enactments featured play-by-play demonstrations of
nineteenth-century embalming science, including the use of scalpels to make
incisions into arteries, the injection of preservative fluid, and the effects of death
on the body (see Figure 15.7). For the program, costumed re-enactors portray
embalmers and other figures associated with funerary practices from the period.
The demonstration's key innovation was the use of a "dead body," usually played
by hobbyist enactors or members of the audience.

Jon Austin, former Executive Director of the Museum of Funeral Customs,
explained that the first set of re-enactments was experimental. He needed to "feel
out" how much audiences wanted to hear about historical embalming practices and
how much detail they could tolerate. The early re-enactment choices were rather
conservative: "We started doing embalming demonstrations without a corpse,"
Austin stated, but Mark Brown, an event organizer and fellow re-enactor (as well
as a licensed funeral director) advised them to use a body in the demonstrations.
Brown then secured some young battle enactors as volunteers for the job. The
move made sense, according to Austin, by adding "realism" and making the
demonstrations less abstract.[24] For the rest of that summer the enactments used a
"dead body."

The addition of the corpse to the demonstration, Austin stated, created a huge
audience draw. Austin described an event weekend in Jacksonville, Illinois, where
the museum had set up the embalming table and period equipment under a shade
tree but without a body. The occasional passers-by took some interest. When
Austin got a volunteer body on the table later in the day, however, people started
gathering "like crazy." At another re-enactment event a program advertised the
embalming demonstrations ahead of time and drew such a crowd that Austin had
to deliver the demo 360 degrees in the round to include the whole audience.[25] It is

---

[23]   "Brady's Photographs," *New York Times*, October 20, 1862.

[24]   Jon Austin, Personal Interview. Whitehall, IL, April 8, 2008. All quotes and details
about the re-enactments were taken during these interviews.

[25]   Jon Austin, Personal Interview. Whitehall, IL, April 8, 2008.

no surprise that people crowd around the embalming tent for the demonstrations for, up to this point, the representation of death in Civil War living history had been largely absent, with the morbidity of war being something that the Civil War re-enactments worked hard to eclipse, with the soldiers themselves seeming hardly ever to "die" leaving most Civil War re-enactments to fulfill a certain kind of American fantasy where there is warfare but warfare without death. The embalming re-enactments, though but few in number, offer one of the rare performances at these events where death is made explicit, absolutely mandatory, to the proceedings. Along the way, the public hears a narrative about the human corpse that is largely unknown today. The contemporary American funeral, across both theological and secular lines, was greatly shaped by this nineteenth-century mechanical procedure and is, ironically, given the significance of this innovation, absolutely invisible to the contemporary eye. In other words, what the embalming demonstrations indicate is that the embalmed body of 2010 reaches back to the Civil War and its mechanical production of dead bodies without death.

Conclusion

Members of the Bush administration wanted a war without American death, or at least a war where visual evidence of death was made difficult to see. Yet when the inevitable dead bodies produced by warfare began to accumulate, the stockpile of images became too hard to hide and the battle over the reality of war, as Baudrillard suggests, took hold. The overall dilemma caused by this impossible kind of warfare is that the vast majority of the public forgets about the war; individuals remain distracted by other events unless a direct family member and/or someone close has died in combat. And while these seem obvious points they are still problems when thinking through the long-term social effects of sustained military combat.

The war for the general public becomes a war without death and a war without any definition, a kind of real-time Civil War re-enactment being fought in distant lands which creates protest opportunities for extreme right Christian groups. The absurdity of the situation is only compounded by the vastness of the tragedy. When all of these elements are combined, they do nothing but obscure the dead body produced by war. This too, namely, the bringing of death back into the public's understanding of modern warfare, will be an impossible task for President Obama.

References

Alvarez, Lizette. "Outrage at Funeral Protests Pushes Lawmakers to Act," April 17, 2006: 1.

Austin, Jon. Personal Interview. Whitehall, IL, April 8, 2008.

Barnes, Robert Barnes. "High Court: Justices to Consider 'Funeral Protests' in Free-Speech Case," *Washington Post*, May 31, 2010.

Baudrillard, Jean. *The Gulf War Did Not Take Place*, trans. Paul Patton (Bloomington: Indiana University Press, 1995).

Buncomber, Andrew. "The Image Turning America Against Bush," *The Independent*, April 24, 2004: 1.

Coll, Steve. "No Nukes," *New Yorker*, April 20, 2009: 32.

Jones, Chris. "The Things that Carried Him," *Esquire*, April 17, 2008: 10.

Lydersen, Karl. "5 States Consider Ban on Protests at Funerals," *Washington Post*, January 30, 2006: 1.

Tyson, Ann Scott. "Hundreds of Photos of Caskets Released," *Washington Post*, April 29, 2005: 1 and Mark Berman. "Pentagon Rethinks Photo Ban on Coffins Bearing War Dead," *Washington Post*, February 17, 2009: 1.

von Clausewitz, Carl. *On War*, trans. Michael Howard and Peter Paret (New York: Alfred A. Knopf, 1993).

Index